Newcastle City Council

Newcastle Libraries and Information Service

☎ **0845 002 0336**

Due for return	Due for return	Due for return
04/07/08		
28/07/08	23 JUL 2016	
24/08/08		
10/1		
19/8/10		
16/8/12 MH		
19 JUL 201		

Please return this item to any of Newcastle's Libraries by the last
date shown above. If not requested by another customer the loan
can be renewed, you can do this by phone, post or in person.
Charges may be made for late returns.

OUTBACK

For Rick and Rhian

OUTBACK

THE DISCOVERY OF AUSTRALIA'S INTERIOR

DEREK PARKER

SUTTON PUBLISHING

First published in the United Kingdom in 2007 by
Sutton Publishing Limited · Phoenix Mill
Thrupp · Stroud · Gloucestershire · GL5 2BU

British Library Cataloguing in Publication Data
A catalogue record for this book is available from the British Library.

Hardback ISBN 978-0-7509-4297-3
International trade paperback edition ISBN 978-0-7509-4821-0
Paperback ISBN 978-0-7509-4298-0

Typeset in Sabon.
Typesetting and origination by
Sutton Publishing Limited.
Printed and bound in England by
J.H. Haynes & Co. Ltd, Sparkford.

Contents

Acknowledgements

First I must acknowledge the staff of Mosman Public Library, who have been endlessly helpful not only in recovering books from their stacks, but in ordering copies through the inter-library service. Theirs is a model of what a public library should be. I am grateful also to the librarians and staff of the State Libraries of Victoria, South Australia and New South Wales; the J.S. Battye Library of West Australian History; the National Library of Australia, Canberra, and the Mitchell Library, Sydney; and to Rick Pool who kindly read the MS for errors of fact (though any that remain are of course my responsibility); the Speaker of the House of Assembly, South Australia, and his Deputy Clerk, Malcolm Lehman; Jacqueline Korn and Alice Wilson, my past and present agents; Jaqueline Mitchell, commissioning editor at Sutton, who proposed this book, my editor Anne Bennett, typesetter Mary Critchley and as always my wife, whose advice, invariably at first ignored, equally invariably turns out to be invaluable. Toorak and Fille, our fifteen-year-old expatriate wire-haired fox terrier and his half-Australian daughter, show an easy disregard for the perils of the bush which the explorers, with their devotion to their own dogs, would find admirable.

Metric Conversion Table

km	miles	km	miles
1	0.6	55	34.2
2	1.2	60	37.3
3	1.9	65	40.4
4	2.5	70	43.5
5	3.1	75	46.6
6	3.7	80	49.7
7	4.3	85	52.8
8	5.0	90	55.9
9	5.6	95	59.0
10	6.2	100	62.1
15	9.3	200	124.3
20	12.4	300	186.4
25	15.5	400	248.5
30	18.6	500	310.7
35	21.7	750	466.0
40	24.9	1,000	621.4
45	28.0	2,500	1,553.3
50	31.1	5,000	3,106.9

Illustrations

Illustrations

Introduction

The explorers who attempted to open up and map the vast Australian continent are virtually unequalled in their fortitude. Neither Kit Carson tramping across the Sierra Nevada nor Francis Younghusband in the high Himalayas, not William Clark and Meriwether Lewis trudging over 8,000 miles from Missouri to Oregon nor David Livingstone fighting through the African jungle from Lake Mweru to Nyangwe confronted and conquered such adversities as bludgeoned Ernest Giles, who twice crossed the horrifying Gibson Desert on foot, George Grey, who blundered aimlessly along the arid coast of Western Australia, or Robert O'Hara Burke and William John Wills, both of whom ended their lives in the dry dust of Cooper's Creek.

George Leigh Mallory's reply to the journalist who asked why he wanted to climb Everest, 'Because it's there',[1] is one given by many explorers, and certainly some of the men who strode out into the vast unfathomable central spaces of Australia would have identified with it. At the end of the journals of his expeditions, Grey comments that 'an explorer is an explorer from love, and it is nature, not art, that makes him so'.[2] Most explorers would probably also identify with that remark. But the motives of the early Australian explorers were mixed. The Prussian Ludwig Leichhardt conceived the idea of becoming an explorer before he left Europe – indeed, before he had any notion of which land he might explore: Africa? South America? The Far East? The Scot John McDouall Stuart heard of Charles Sturt's intention to search for the Inland Sea which was believed to occupy the centre of the continent, was inspired, and applied to join him. The idealistic army officer George Grey thought of Australia as a place where a new egalitarian society might be established – but again was inspired to explore by the achievement of Sturt. Then there were the 'professionals' like Sturt himself, Oxley and Mitchell, who had more readily identifiable ambitions: to open up the vast new country, and in particular to discover, perhaps on the other side of the great rocky deserts, fine stretches of arable land which could sustain the immigrants pouring into the country from Europe. The heart of such an immense continent simply could not be barren: hope of an Elysian centre, generously watered by bountiful rivers emptying into a great inland sea, persisted until almost the end of the nineteenth century. And indeed good arable land did exist in what by European standards were enormous tracts – but in area were vastly outweighed by immense plains where nothing grew except rough grasses and the terrible spinifex that tore mercilessly at clothes and limbs.

After the initial decades when the country was seen simply as a useful receptacle for the criminals for whom room could not be found in the overcrowded prisons of England, immigrants began to arrive in New South Wales in increasing numbers. Before 1810 only four hundred free settlers had made the decision to emigrate to Australia. At the end of the next decade there were 1,941 people who hoped to be able to live off the land – 665 of them children (mostly the children of convicts, but themselves counted as 'free', and who would grow up and become a generation in need of land to cultivate). The governors of the colony recognised that more land would be needed to sustain all these mouths than the countryside in the immediate vicinity of Sydney, and made the fact clear to their masters in London.

It became important to find a way through the Blue Mountains, a barrier which until 1813 seemed impassable. A way *was* found – and so was rich pastoral land. Government money became available for further exploration – and financial rewards were a possible result of success. Men who had no practical experience of any form of exploration, let alone of the peculiar problems they would face in Australia, arrived with ambitions to open up the continent, not only for their country's good, but for their own.

Introduction

The earliest explorers set out into the unknown with what now seems a near appalling *insouciance*, almost totally ignorant of the difficulties that lay ahead. How could they know that the climate of the continent, whose size they were scarcely able to comprehend, could in one place deluge them with appalling rain (over 4,000mm a year fell on the Queensland coast south of Cairns) or inflict on them the most terrible drought (the annual rainfall in the Simpson, Gibson and great Victoria Deserts is negligible). They had no notion that they could be broiled in intolerable heat (an *average* of over 40°C in the interior of Western Australia, where a temperature of 53.1°C has been recorded) or almost frozen to death at 0°C in the Australian Alps. Consequently, they often set out ill-prepared, inadequately supplied with food and unable to carry the amounts of water needed to sustain them over long treks where they encountered nothing but dry waterholes. Their lack of preparedness was often married to a worrying naïvety: unwilling to load his horses with too much food and water, Leichhardt nevertheless started out with a large oak desk at which to write up his journal. He also took completely useless shoes for his camels, which he believed would protect their feet in the desert, feet that needed no protection. At least he knew something about the climate and the bush itself. George Grey had previously landed in north-western Australia with a party only one of whom had ever *seen* Australia before, and that only from the deck of a schooner. He went ashore with five men, their legs weak from lack of exercise during a long voyage from Cape Town, and with only one water-bottle each. Within hours all their water had gone, the dogs which accompanied them had died of the heat, and they themselves barely escaped with their lives.

What was common to all the explorers was their remarkable persistence, determination and courage – courage that was often almost foolishly optimistic, but which sustained them in circumstances that should have killed them all. No wonder the streets of Sydney, Melbourne, Adelaide and Perth were lined with cheering crowds as the sometimes triumphant but frequently defeated men rode by on their emaciated horses in the tattered remnants of clothing so faded that their original colour could not be discerned. On their way to mayoral and gubernatorial receptions, they were often already planning their next expedition. They may be criticised for their lack of forethought and their almost insane optimism, but no one can fail to admire their spirit and their extraordinary strength of character. Reading their journals, from which astonishing documents I have quoted freely in this book, one wonders time and time again how – and, indeed, occasionally, why – they persisted in their exhausting, tortuous, sometimes fatal treks, on which their horses fell dead beneath them and the sheep or cattle they had taken for food were unable to keep up, had to be slaughtered, and their flesh unappetisingly dried to keep the men alive.

Every explorer encountered Aboriginal people at one time or another, or at the very least was conscious of being watched and carefully observed by them. This is not surprising: there were native Australians in every part of the continent, inhabiting areas as diverse as the tropical lands of the north, the rich lands of the south-east river systems and the great deserts. The Aboriginals[3] certainly found it difficult to understand these strange white men, mounted on animals the like of which they had never seen, who came to share waterholes already insufficient for their own people and who, though starving, refused to eat the good bush tucker which sustained the natives. Unsurprisingly, their astonishment turned to anger when they realised that it was entirely probable that what the white men wanted was their land. Some explorers, Thomas Livingstone Mitchell in particular, have been pilloried as murderous thugs who mowed down the defenceless natives of the country without a second thought. This is some distance from the truth. Mitchell certainly failed to prevent his men from firing on and killing some Aboriginals who attacked them, and he later regretted it, and not simply because an official enquiry criticised him. Other explorers faced similar attacks; some were badly injured and killed. But there was almost always recognition that the Aboriginals were, after all, only defending their homes and their lands, and for the most part the white explorers genuinely regretted having to shoot the men who were attacking them with boomerangs and evilly barbed spears.

The main criticism of the explorers' attitude to the Aboriginal people must surely be not so much that they killed them indiscriminately – most explorers were careful to fire over the heads of their attackers unless and until the spears started to fly, and even then they usually fired to injure rather than kill – but that they failed to understand them. But this too may perhaps be excused: if the interlopers regarded the Aboriginals as little more than animals, it was because the idea of such a people and such a way of life was almost impossible for them to comprehend. Because Aboriginals used only the simplest of tools and had no ambitions to live 'civilised' lives as the explorers understood the term, they were often regarded as leading a hand-to-mouth existence, wandering about in search of largely inedible food. In fact, as the explorers all too rarely discovered, the bush fodder provided the Aboriginal with a standard of sustenance at least as high as that of many Europeans of the time, and starvation and malnutrition were virtually unknown among Aboriginal tribes.

In the end, most explorers came to recognise and acknowledge the Aboriginals' unparalleled knowledge of the country and how to live in it. They saw the great skill they exercised as trackers, the well-established trails over which they moved, and above all came to appreciate their knowledge of where water was to be found, which they generously shared even in times of drought, often saving the lives of the white men. Every expedition was accompanied by Aboriginals, sometimes as beasts of burden, but often as enormously useful and valuable guides.

I have had marvellous material with which to work in preparing this book: all the explorers kept journals, and their accounts of their journeys are remarkable documents, often written under extremely difficult circumstances, but written with persistent diligence and often in the most graphic language. These men continued to scrawl entries in their journals when too weak to do anything else, and the results are by turns exciting, terrifying and moving. That best of Australian writers on the subject, Tim Flannery, has rightly remarked that Giles's account of the death of Gibson[4] is 'one of the most powerful things in our literature'.[5]

Throughout, I have been faced with the problem of trying to make the routes taken by the explorers even moderately clear to readers unfamiliar with the map of Australia. The difficulty often applies even to those who know the lie of the country quite well, including Australians themselves. The explorers often tramped through areas of the continent still almost completely devoid of place-names on all but the most detailed localised maps. There is the additional problem that the names the explorers gave to mountains, waterholes and other features of the landscape have sometimes been changed; sometimes the places themselves have vanished, and their names are all we have of them. It has been an unequal struggle, which in the end has largely defeated me. I provide some maps which indicate roughly the areas of Australia through which my subjects travelled, and in some cases maps which show in rather more detail the often tortuous routes they followed. But in the end, the accounts must be read for the adventures they chronicle rather than in any way as a guide to the country.

Neither is this book a series of brief biographies. While I trust that the characters of the explorers emerge in the course of their adventures, it is the adventures themselves that matter.

ONE

In the Beginning
1688–1834

The Dutch discovered Australia in the first years of the seventeenth century, but by the 1650s had decided that they could make nothing of such a barren continent. The first Englishman to set foot on Australian soil was William Dampier, the son of a Somerset farmer and a pirate in the tradition of Drake and Ralegh. Commissioned by the Lord High Admiral of England, the Earl of Oxford, to lead a voyage of discovery to New Holland (as Australia was then called) he landed at King Sound, on the north-western coast of Western Australia, in January 1688, and explored a very small strip of land just north of the present tourist town of Broome.

Why the Earl of Oxford wanted to know more about the continent than he had already heard from the Dutch is a mystery, but he was a patron not only of the buccaneering Dampier but of the notorious pirate Captain Kidd and we can safely assume that the idea of profit, whether in terms of gold, slaves or simply good land for emigrant settlers, was not far from his mind.

Dampier found, he reported, 'a very large tract of land. It is not yet determined whether it is an island or a main continent; but I am certain that it joins neither to Asia, Africa nor America.' His description of the coast is recognisable today: 'The Land is of a dry, sandy soil, destitute of Water, except you make Wells; yet producing divers sorts of trees; but the woods are not thick, nor the trees very big. Most of the Trees that we saw are Dragon trees as we supposed. . . . The other sorts of trees were not known by any of us. There was pretty long Grass growing under the Trees; but it was very thin. We saw no Trees that bore Fruit or Berries.'

1

Dampier's exploration of the coast was extremely limited. He noted some tracks 'of a beast as big as a great mastiff dog' and observed the natives, of whose way of life he had the low opinion which was to be shared by most of the first Europeans to encounter them: they were, he thought, 'the miserablest People in the world . . . they differ little from Brutes. They are tall, straight-bodied and thin, with small, long limbs. They have great Heads, round foreheads and great brows. Their eyelids are always half closed to keep the Flies out of their eyes; they being so Troublesome here that no fanning will keep them from coming to one's face and, without the assistance of both hands to keep them off, they will creep into one's Nostrils and mouth too, if the lips are not shut very close.'[1]

He careened his boat and cleaned her bottom, then sailed on to Christmas Island and Sumatra. He returned in 1699 on an official British Admiralty expedition, and at Roebuck Bay, near Broome, found himself forced to shoot one of a group of Aboriginals which had attacked him. Unlike some later explorers, he was 'very sorry for what had happened'. For the first time, he observed typical Aboriginal markings on the body of a man he thought the chief of a tribe:

> He was painted . . . with a white Circle of white Paste or pigment (a sort of Lime, as we thought) about his eyes, and a white strip down his Nose from his Forehead to the tip of it. And his Breast and some parts of his Arms were also made white with the same paint; not for Beauty or Ornament, one would think, but as some wild Indian warriors are said to do, he seemed thereby to design the looking more terrible; this his Painting adding very much to his natural Deformity; for they all of them, have the most unpleasant Looks and the worst Features of any people that ever I saw, though I have seen great variety of Savages.[2]

Failing to find any fresh water, he stayed in the area very briefly, then sailed on. For another seventy years no other Englishman came within sight of Australia, or New Holland as it had been named by the Dutch traders of the East Indian Islands, who had landed on the west coast of the continent without understanding what they had found. Then James Cook, sailing for the east coast of Van Diemen's Land (later renamed Tasmania) unexpectedly sighted land, which turned out to be the coast of what is now New South Wales. He sailed northward, looking for a place to go ashore, and fixed on what seemed a promising harbour, which he at first called Stingray Harbour because of the large number of stingrays he sighted there, but then renamed Botany Bay.

Cook was no more an explorer of the continent than Dampier; but he did investigate the immediate surroundings of the bay, finding areas of cultivable soil before sadly ignoring the entrance to Port Jackson, and thus failing to discover one of the finest harbours in the world, then sailing on up the east coast surveying it as he went and claiming it for Britain as New South Wales (the Union Jack was meticulously hoisted every time he or his men went ashore). Points on the shore still bear the names he gave them: Port Stephens, Cape Byron, Smoky Cape. But exploration was restricted to a careful survey of the coast. When the *Endeavour* crashed on to Endeavour Reef and had to be repaired, the pause in his progress up the coast allowed Joseph Banks to become the first in a long line of botanists who drew, painted and collected Australian plant species (he was not only the first but the greatest of them all, cataloguing over 3,600 plant species and bringing over 30,000 back to England, nearly one-third of them previously unknown).

The first real explorers of inland Australia were from among the soldiers, convicts and administrators who were carried from England in the years after 1787 and established Port Jackson, to become known as Sydney.[3] The first governor, Arthur Phillip, sent parties out to find good, well-watered land which could be profitably farmed. With a small party, Phillip then followed a river from Port Jackson to its head, where he founded the settlement he named Rose Hill (now Parramatta). They then moved on towards the Blue Mountains, naming Mount Carmarthen and the Landsdowne Hills after his masters in London.

It was important to explore the river system around Port Jackson. Phillip traced the Hawkesbury river until rocky falls stopped their progress; its full length was not to be surveyed for many years (it flows over 470km from the Great Dividing Range north and east to the Tasman Sea). Meanwhile Watkin Tench, a marine captain, and his friend Lieutenant Dawes, led a party west from Parramatta to the banks of a river as broad as the Thames – a section of the Hawkesbury, later named the Nepean. They were accompanied by the two earliest recorded Aboriginal explorers, or at least the first of the many Aboriginals who were persuaded or forced to accompany the long line of later explorers. These two were called Colbee and Boladaree. Tench, who was one of the few Englishmen to find the Aboriginals fascinating and to make a real attempt to understand them, found the pair delightful:

> They walked stoutly, appeared but little fatigued, and maintained their spirits admirably, laughing to excess when any of us either tripped or stumbled, misfortunes which much seldomer fell to their lot than to ours. . . . They imitated the leaping of the kanguroo [sic]; sang; danced; poized the spear and met in mock encounter. But their principal source of merriment was again derived from our misfortunes, in tumbling amidst nettles, and sliding down precipices, which they mimicked with inimitable drollery.[4]

The earliest explorers lacked the horses, and later camels, to carry their equipment. Tench described how one party set out: 'Every man (the governor excepted) carried his own knapsack, which contained provisions for ten days: if to this he added a gun, a blanket, and a canteen the weight will fall nothing short of forty pounds. Slung to the knapsack, are the cooking kettle and the hatchet with which the wood to kindle the nightly fire and build the nightly hut, is to be cut down.'[5]

But despite these early expeditions the extent of the river system around Sydney remained obscure, and Phillip's attempts to map the area, though amazingly successful considering the difficulties he experienced, finally failed – it was Tench and Dawes who solved the puzzle in 1791, confirming their suspicion that the Hawkesbury and Nepean rivers were in fact one. The result of their effort was psychologically important: a real step had been taken in mapping and understanding a larger part of the country around Port Jackson than had hitherto been known. They had, incidentally, to devise their own way of mapping the land. Being mariners, they steered by the compass, and tediously counted the number of paces they took from one recognisable point to another: 2,200 paces, they reckoned, represented 1 mile. Occasionally they noted major landmarks, but very often the land they recorded was so featureless that they might as well have been at sea, and if they had not been seamen would have been irretrievably lost.

Settlers longed to cross the beautiful but forbidding Blue Mountains, which hemmed them in from north to south, and see what lay beyond. They found it almost impossible. The traveller was impeded by a succession of ravines so impassable that all efforts with scaling-irons, hooks and ropes failed – Henry Hackings's 1794 expedition managed to cover only 24km in five days, while George Bass, trying to find a way through in 1797, concluded that it was 'impossible to find a passage even for a person on foot'.[6] Attempts to use the rivers failed: waterfalls and rapids proved impassable.[7]

The most ambitious and determined of the early explorers, Francis Louis Barrallier, made his attempt on the Blue Mountains in 1802, and surveyed the Hunter river before ending up on the summit of a mountain all of whose sides seemed so perpendicular that he could not quite fathom how he had managed to scale it. There seems to have been some idea at this time that the mountains were ruled by a powerful Aboriginal tribe, for Governor Philip Gidley King writes of sending Barrallier on 'an embassy to the King of the Mountains',[8] but His Majesty could not be found. Eventually, Barrallier's supplies became so depleted that he had to kill snakes for food before he and his men almost fell down the cliffs prior to staggering back to Sydney to report to the governor that in his view the Blue Mountains formed an insurmountable barrier. King in turn reported to London that, regrettably, he had reached the conclusion that this was indeed the case, and that the idea that it might be possible to reach good agricultural land on the other side of the Blue Mountains must be abandoned.

But the idea was too good to be abandoned. Europeans had now attempted to settle the land around Sydney for twenty-five years, and through year after scorching year had found it so parched and difficult to cultivate that it seemed vital to everyone that better grazing must be discovered if any settlement was to survive. In May 1813 Gregory Blaxland and William Charles Wentworth, two young squatters, and their friend Lieutenant William Lawson, an army officer, decided to make another attempt on the Blue Mountains. With four convict servants and four horses, they cut their way through thick brushwood to reach one impassable precipice after another. Finally defeated by an unscalable 120-metre cliff, they retraced their steps and though short of supplies and all suffering from malnutrition, took another direction, following natural ridges and gradually climbing up and up, past what are now the popular tourist resorts of Leura and Katoomba, to reach Mount York, from which they saw what appeared to be a plain covered with rich grass – grassland sufficient, they calculated, to support all their stock for at least thirty years. They had marked out a road by which future travellers could easily pass through the mountains, and the tourists who now flock to Leura and Katoomba follow the same route. Lawson went on to head the military at Bathurst, when that town was founded, while Wentworth (only 22 when he made the epic journey) became an admired statesman and orator, and founder of Sydney University.

As soon as he heard the welcome news that the Blue Mountains had been crossed, Governor Lachlan Macquarie, the best and most popular of the early governors of the colony, commissioned G.W. Evans, a former shopkeeper dismissed for fraud who had taught himself surveying and was now Deputy-Surveyor of Lands, to lead a second expedition across the Blue Mountains. Evans was no sluggard: in pouring rain he took a mere fortnight to gain the furthest point reached by the previous three explorers – to find that they had only half solved the problem – the mountains that lay ahead were almost as impassable as those behind had seemed. Nevertheless he found a way through, and reached the site of Bathurst, in the middle of a rich plain. Once back on the other side of the mountains he told the governor that he calculated that a road could be built through them in three months.

Delighted, Macquarie appointed a landowner, William Cox, to supervise the building of such a road, and offered free pardons to any convict who would volunteer his labour to build it. In six months, between July 1814 and the following January, an astonishingly short time, thirty convicts built the Great Western Highway – 161km long, with over a dozen bridges, following the route marked out by Blaxland. The convicts all got their pardons. Evans went on to discover another river, which he again named after the governor – the Lachlan. This seemed to flow determinedly dead north, and must surely empty into some inland lake or sea.

The Blue Mountains conquered, it should be possible to settle on the land beyond them some of the Europeans who wanted to make a new life for themselves in New South Wales. Before 1810 only four hundred people had come as free immigrants; by 1820 the figure had risen to 943 men, 333 women and 665 children, all of whom hoped to acquire land and in one way or another make a living from it. There was simply not enough land for them on the Sydney side of the Blue Mountains, and Macquarie decided that they must concentrate on opening up the area beyond. In 1817 he instructed his surveyor-general, John Oxley, to follow up Evans's route and see what he could find.

TWO

The Great Inland Sea
John Oxley, 1817–18

John Joseph William Molesworth Oxley was a Yorkshireman, born in the shadow of Kirkham Abbey in 1783. His navy service took him to Australia in 1802, where ten years later he was appointed Surveyor-General. On good terms with the governor, he was an obvious choice to lead an expedition into the unknown interior on the far side of the Blue Mountains. His first expedition surveyed 1,100km of New South Wales; his second discovered the fertile Liverpool Plains.

Almost everyone in the colony now believed that somewhere in the centre of Australia there must lie a vast inland sea, and John Oxley was perfectly convinced of its existence. Such an enormous space could not, he thought, simply be empty. And since the Macquarie river, which joined the recently discovered Lachlan, was only one of several that appeared to flow north and somewhat west and never to reach the sea, it seemed clear that they must empty themselves into a large lake somewhere inland.

Governor Macquarie penned a careful set of instructions. Oxley was charged with three particular tasks: 'First, to ascertain the real course or general direction of the Lachlan river, and its final termination, and whether it falls into the sea, or into some inland lake. Secondly, if the river falls into the sea, to ascertain the exact place of its embouchure, and whether such place would answer as a good and safe port for shipping; and thirdly, the general face of the country, nature of the soil, woods, and animal and natural productions of the country . . . and descriptions of such natives or aborigines of the country as you may happen to see.'[1]

G.W. Evans was to accompany Oxley as second in command and the party included Alan Cunningham, a botanist from Kew Gardens, sent to Australia especially to gather plants and seeds for the King's gardens. Carrying enough portable boats to convey the whole group of thirteen men, Oxley's first expedition set out on 6 April 1817 with five months' provisions drawn by thirteen packhorses. The explorers first made their way through Bathurst, a growing town 200km east of Sydney, and over rain-sodden ground towards the WEST Lachlan river. By then the weather had become more pleasant though colder; on the night of 21 April the temperature dropped to 26°F, and they woke to frost. The scenery was delightful – and promising. From Mount Molle, Oxley looked down over 40 miles of 'gentle hills, thinly timbered, with rich intervening valleys, through which flow small streams of water . . . excellent land, well watered'.[2]

On 25 April they reached the steep banks of the Lachlan, set up a depot there and encountered their first Aboriginals, who were friendly, knew some English phrases and had clearly been in touch with European settlers. Oxley took the opportunity to learn and record some Aboriginal words: *Nh-air* (eyebrows), *narra* (fingers), *Mem-àa* (a native man). Then the explorers launched their boats and took to the water, floating gently upstream for a little of the river's 1,500km length, marvelling at the excellent supply of fish (one day they caught a 31-kilo cod). Eventually the river dissipated into small, unnavigable rivulets trailing through swampland and, on 4 May, Oxley found that the largest boat had had its bottom stove in by a submerged tree. Two days later they came to rapids and the explorers had to take to the riverbank again. The nature of the land had changed considerably: 'It is impossible to fancy a worse country than the one we were now travelling over,' wrote Oxley; 'intersected by swamps and small lagoons in every direction; the soil a poor clay, and covered with stunted, useless timber. It was excessively fatiguing to the horses which travelled along the banks of the river, as the rubus and bromus were so thickly intermingled that they could scarcely force a passage.'[3]

A few days later they found themselves in the middle of a swamp, in which the horses frequently became bogged down; the animals became exhausted, sometimes losing their loads as a consequence – one threw Oxley's instruments to the ground, breaking his barometer. One day the expedition had to stop four times to unload and reload them. From a hilltop there was nothing to be seen for the 25 or 30 miles between them and the next high land but marshes and swamps. On 14 May he decided to change direction and head towards the south-west, where he hoped to find another river draining the marshes.

The going was now much easier; however, after an excess of water, the explorers now lacked it – within a week they were parched but could find only pools of muddy water which was unfit even for the horses and dogs to drink. Again the horses began to fall under their loads, and only the occasional small waterhole enabled them to survive until 1 June, when after thirty-six hours without a drop to drink they were led to a more generous supply – but by then one horse was so 'knocked up' that Oxley had to shoot it.

Things got no better; Oxley and his company trailed through flat, birdless desert, with no animals and no sign of human life. 'Nothing can be more melancholy and irksome than travelling over wilds, which nature seems to have condemned to perpetual loneliness and desolation,' he wrote. The country, he concluded, could never be settled: it was 'useless for all the purposes of civilised man'.[4] On the King's birthday, 4 June, he planted some acorns, peach and apricot stones and quince seeds 'with the hope rather than the expectation that they would grow and serve to commemorate the day and situation, should these desolate plains be ever again visited by civilised man, of which, however, I think there is very little probability'.[5]

They were now making only very slow progress, the horses at times going without water for more than forty-eight hours. Sometimes he had to send them miles out of their way in a desperate attempt to water them – he doubted whether they could endure such a miserable existence for much longer. The men were no better off, lack of water making it almost impossible for them to swallow the salt pork which was their main diet, rations that were very occasionally varied by kangaroo or wild dog. As for the landscape, it was so bare and barren that they might have been the only living creatures on the face of the planet. For a whole week they saw no Aboriginals, no birds, no animals except a single wild dog. By 21 June Oxley was reluctantly compelled to regard the expedition as useless as far as discovering any cultivable land was concerned:

> The farther we proceed north-westerly, the more convinced I am that, for all the practical purposes of civilized man, the interior of this country westward of a certain meridian is uninhabitable, deprived as it is of wood, water, and grass. With respect to water, it is quite impossible that any can be retained on such a soil . . . for, like a sponge, it absorbs all the rain that falls. The wandering native with his little family may find a precarious subsistence in the ruts with which the country abounds; but even he, with all the local knowledge which such a life must give him, is obliged to dig with immense labour little wells at the bottom of the hills to procure and preserve a necessity of life. . . .[6]

On 23 June they reached the Lachlan river and, weakened by dysentery, followed it downstream through unpleasant swamps, the stench of rotting vegetation in their nostrils. On 9 June, their horses having been deprived of drinking water for forty-eight hours, Oxley decided to turn back. Before he turned the expedition around he cut the words 'Dig Under' into the bark of a tree, burying beneath it a wine bottle containing an account of their journey, and expressed his feelings in 'Lines on quitting the Lachlan swamps':

> From sickly marshes, and unhealthy plains
> Where Lachlan's turbid waters spread
> From silence death, and desolation dread
> While hope our guide, sweet soother of our pains
> Springs in each breast and lightens every fear
> The path to happier times, in light hope tread
> To where old ocean spreads its bosom bare
> And breaths and smiles to dissipate our cares.[7]

The party then made its disconsolate but happily uneventful way back to Sydney, its journey of almost 12,000km having increased the colonists' knowledge of New South Wales, but revealed (as Oxley reported to Macquarie) that 'the interior of this vast country is a marsh, and uninhabitable'. Oxley had also found no sign of the Inland Sea.

Five months later, in May 1818, and again encouraged by Macquarie, Oxley set out once more, this time to explore the Macquarie river, in the hope that around one of its many bends the expected Inland Sea would appear.

Two substantial boats were launched, and the journey northward proved continually interesting – the channel was sometimes broad, sometimes so narrow that only the depth of the water prevented the current from being too fast for safety. At one stage, at a point where the Macquarie was 230m wide and deep enough, he considered, to float a 74-gun battleship, he really believed he was on the point of finding what he sought: 'I was sanguine', he wrote in his journal, 'in my expectations of soon entering the long sought for Australian Sea. . . .' But the Macquarie 'eluded our further search by spreading on every point amongst the ocean of reeds that surrounded us . . . there was no channel whatever among these reeds . . .'.[8] Having spent four days lost in a measureless swamp, once again he had to admit defeat and sadly concluded that even if the river did eventually lead into an inland sea, the boggy nature of the terrain was such that it could be of no use to settlers. He decided to turn eastwards, traversing more unknown country – the vastness of the Australian continent was becoming clear to him. Like most explorers, he knew in theory that the land was huge – seventeen years earlier Matthew Flinders had sailed right around it – but only when faced with the problems of crossing it did its size become real to him.

Things, however, were to become more interesting, for on 18 July his deputy, George Evans, a good surveyor and an excellent artist, returned from a foray to report that he had found another substantial river, which he had named the Castlereagh after the

British statesman and Secretary for the Colonies. Its current was flowing north – another sign, surely, that like the other rivers it must be disgorging into a large inland body of water. The fading vision of the great Inland Sea was revived. But spirits were only temporarily lifted, for now the expedition again became bogged down in marshes. On 21 July, Oxley complained of the alternate brush and marsh through which they struggled: 'Whatever obstacles the former opposed to the progress of the horses, were nothing to the distress occasioned by the latter, in which they sank up to their knees at every step.'[9] Dismounted, up to their waists in water, the men struggled to emerge at last on to upland, eventually on 26 April reaching a hill from which they saw fertile plains stretching into the distance – fine pastoral land, beautiful grazing country. Oxley named it the Liverpool Plains (not after the English city, but the English Prime Minister). Through the plains flowed the Peel river (Robert Peel had been another prime minister). 'It would be impossible,' Oxley thought, 'to find a finer or more luxuriant country than it waters. . . . The grass was most luxuriant; the timber good and not thick: in short, no place in the world can afford more advantages to the industrious settler.'[10]

On 11 September they paused at the Apsley Falls, which 'so far surpassed any thing which we had previously conceived even to be possible that we were lost in astonishment at the sight of this wonderful natural sublimity, which perhaps is scarcely to be exceeded in any part of the eastern world'.[11] Eventually, after passing through countryside which seemed Arcadian, on 23 September they reached the summit of a mountain and saw sea ahead – not the Inland Sea, but the Tasman Sea. Their final peril was the descent, the following day, to a river below, which seemed to lead to the sea.

'How the horses descended I scarcely knew,' wrote Oxley; 'and the bare recollection of the imminent dangers which they escaped makes me tremble. At one period of the descent I would willingly have compromised for a loss of one third of them to ensure the safety of the remainder. It is to the exertions and steadiness of the men, under Providence, that their safety must be ascribed. The thick

Oxley and his companions found Apsley Falls (now part of Apsley Gorge National Park) a site of 'wonderful natural sublimity'. *(Drawn by George Evans)*

tufts of grass and the loose soil also gave them a surer footing, of which the men skilfully availed themselves.'[12]

Travelling down the Hastings river (as Oxley named it) to the coast, they found a natural harbour which seemed an excellent place for a settlement. They called it Port Macquarie and by 1821 a penal colony had been established there. Later, after the convicts had left, it became a major export port for wheat, corn and cedar wood.

The journey back to Sydney was fairly easy as far as the nature of the country was concerned, but they did have a serious brush with Aboriginals, who speared one of the men in the back and in the buttocks.[13] There was another attack on several men while they were bathing, but they escaped – though without their clothes.

At Government House a small gathering was held in honour of the returned explorers, but their reception was otherwise muted – the public either knew nothing about their journey, or at least showed no interest in it, unlike the thousands who would crowd the streets to welcome later expeditions home. Though Oxley had found some excellent country for settlers and made a record of the previously unknown terrain he had traversed, he had failed to find the Great Inland Sea. But he, and most people, still believed it must exist.

In 1818 James Meehan, a convict condemned for his part in the Irish uprising of 1798, discovered Lake Bathurst and the Goulburn Plains. In 1824–5 Hamilton Hume and his friend William Hilton Hovell were the first white men to lay eyes on the Australian Alps – the Snowy Mountains, glittering unexpectedly before them in a desert which everyone had thought was parched and sunbaked from coast to coast. They went on to pioneer a route from Sydney to Port Phillip Bay, where Melbourne was to be founded. Major Edward Lockyer, a Devonshire man, undertook the first extensive exploration of Western Australia in 1826; he only covered 64km, but was successful in discovering fine farming land; the following year Captain James Sterling set out with equal enthusiasm; and on 2 May 1829 Captain Charles Fremantle hoisted the Union Jack on the spot where the town bearing his name now stands.

In 1827 Allan Cunningham forced his way from Sydney right up to Queensland. Edmund Lockyer, the discoverer of Queensland's Lockyer and Stanley rivers, led the first extensive expedition to Western Australia, and with twenty soldiers and twenty-four convicts raised the Union Jack at the site of Albany on Christmas Day 1826, claiming the whole of Australia for the King.

But apart from the named and recognised explorers, anonymous squatters and travellers regularly explored uncharted territory and put down roots, and while the feats of the great explorers will always be celebrated, the opening-out of Australia was also the result of the less extraordinary but no less useful and brave discoveries of a host of men whose names are lost in the procession of immigrants that, between 1788 and the beginning of the twentieth century, filled in the previously vacant map of this extraordinary continent.

THREE

Mapping the Rivers
Charles Sturt, 1827–30

John Oxley had failed to find the Great Inland Sea, but nine years later everyone still believed in its existence, and Charles Sturt was the next explorer to try to unravel the mystery of the river system in New South Wales. Sturt, born in Bengal while his father was a judge for the West India Company, was sent back to England to be educated and at Harrow learned the manners of an English gentleman, manners which set him apart from most of the men he would later meet in Australia but which, far from marking him out as an expatriate snob, were to endear him to almost everyone who knew him. Joining the army, he fought under Wellington, the Iron Duke, and at the end of 1825 his regiment was ordered to escort two convict ships to New South Wales and remain there on police duty. He sailed without enthusiasm from Cork on the Mariner *on 14 January 1827, arriving in Sydney on 23 May. Though he disliked the idea of being so far from Europe – it seemed more like exile than service – sailing through the Heads, the perpendicular cliffs which frame the entrance to the harbour, he could not but be impressed by the prospect before him:*

I am free to confess, that I did not anticipate any thing equal to the scene which presented itself both to my sight and judgement, as we sailed up the noble and extensive basin we had entered, towards the seat of government. A single glance was sufficient to tell me that the hills upon the southern shore of the port, the outlines of which were broken by houses and spires, must once have been covered with the same dense and

16

gloomy wood which abounded every where else. . . . The labour and patience required, and the difficulties which the first settlers encountered in effecting these improvements, must have been incalculable. But their success has been complete: it is the very triumph of human skill and industry over Nature herself. The cornfield and the orchard have supplanted the wild grass and the brush; a flourishing town stands over the ruins of the forest; the lowing of herds has succeeded the wild whoop of the savage; and the stillness of that once desert shore is now broken by the sound of the bugle and the busy hum of commerce.[1]

Sturt felt that life was passing him by. At the age of 32, he had accomplished nothing of note. He now saw a chance of advancement, and contrived to be appointed private and military secretary and brigade major to the Governor, Major-General, later Sir, Ralph Darling. A speedy promotion, it was probably the result of his extremely agreeable and appealing personality: he was open-hearted, transparently honest and took others at their face value unless circumstances dictated otherwise. He was also a naturally religious man, who took no decision without praying about it; but he had no superior or patronising airs, and Darling soon came to regard him as extremely dependable and trustworthy.

His tasks as military secretary were far from taxing: there was a certain amount of secretarial work, but his day-to-day activities seemed chiefly to consist of accompanying Darling to such events as the annual gathering of the Female School of Industry and the inaugural meeting of the Australian Racing Club.[2]

There is no evidence to explain why, in September 1828, Darling commissioned Sturt (as the Governor put it in orders) 'to endeavour to determine the fate of the Macquarie river, by tracing it as far as possible beyond the point to which Mr Oxley went, and by pushing westward . . . to ascertain if there be any high lands in that direction, or if the country be, as it is supposed, an unbroken level and under water'. There is, however, evidence of the Governor's motives in mounting the expedition. The years 1826, 1827 and 1828 were ones of extreme drought, when even weeds stopped growing in the sparse and sunbaked earth. Oxley had found much of the ground over which he had travelled very wet and marshy, which perhaps suggested an area where drought conditions were immaterial. For some time Darling had also wanted to send out an expedition of exploration for more general reasons, and hearing of this Sturt probably seized his opportunity and put his name forward. On 10 November 1827 he wrote to a friend, Isaac Wood: 'In February I take an expedition into the interior to ascertain the level of the inland plain and to determine the supposed existence of an inland sea. This will not be unattended with danger; however, it is a most important trust, and if I succeed, as I anticipate, I shall earn some credit.'[3]

Apart from the search for the Great Inland Sea, about which there had been so much speculation over the previous fifty years, Sturt was also ordered to make records of the aspect of the country he traversed, its climate, flora and fauna, and of its people – 'the nature of their amusements, their diseases and remedies, their objects of worship, religious ceremonies, and a vocabulary of their language'.[4]

The expedition set out on 10 September and comprised six convicts and Sturt's body-servant Joseph (or 'John') Harris, a fellow Dorset man who had been his batman in Ireland and had come out to Australia with him. These, the horses and some bullocks were laden with the usual accoutrements explorers thought necessary to carry with them, including such conveniences as shaving brushes, telescope, knives, forks and spoons, frying pans and a teakettle, and a portable boat complete with sails and oars and set on a four-wheeled carriage drawn by two bullocks.

With an agreeable and experienced assistant, Hamilton Hume, and two soldiers for protection (Hopkinson and Fraser,[5] the latter a pleasantly eccentric fellow much given to drink) Sturt and his expedition made their way first along the route which Oxley and other explorers had laid down, across the Blue Mountains and on to Wellington, north-west of Sydney, and then along the east bank of the Macquarie river. On the way Sturt, riding a little ahead of the rest of the party, made his first contact with a family of Aboriginals, who 'were much terrified, and finding that they could not escape, called vehemently to some of their companions, who were in the distance. By the time Mr Hume came up, they had in some measure recovered their presence of mind, but availed themselves of the first favourable moment to leave us.' Characteristically, Sturt made no attempt to detain them or show any dislike or impatience with them, 'in consequence of which they afterwards mustered sufficient resolution to visit us in our camp'.[6]

At Mount Harris, Sturt established a base camp. Nearby, he and Hume found the traces of Oxley's earlier expedition, with the fire-places at which he and his men had warmed themselves and the remains of one of the two boats which Oxley had been forced to abandon. This prompted Sturt to consider his own position:

A reflection naturally arose to my mind on examining these decaying vestiges of a former expedition, whether I should be more fortunate than the leader of it, and how far I should be enabled to penetrate beyond the point which had conquered his perseverance. Only a week before I left Sydney I had followed Mr Oxley to the tomb. A man of uncommon quickness, and of great ability, the task of following up his discoveries was not less enviable than arduous; but, arrived at that point at which his journey may be said to have terminated and mine only to commence, I knew not how soon I should be obliged, like him, to retreat from the marshes and exhalations of so depressed a country. . . .[7]

No one could blame Sturt for wondering at this stage how his expedition would turn out. The heat was beginning to tell on the members of the party: a temperature of 149°F in the sun made for arduous trekking. Two of the men, Reilly and Spencer, suffered badly from the heat and their eyes especially from the dust and the sweat which continually ran into them. Another had a bad attack of dysentery. Nevertheless, things had gone well up to this point, and Sturt felt able to send the two men whose eyes were troublesome back to Sydney with a situation report for the Governor. Then he and the rest pressed on, forcing their way through thick reeds in the middle of which they were forced to camp, in a place which it would have been impossible to reach were it not for the drought which had dried the marshes in which Oxley had become bogged down.

Sturt now decided he must try to discover the extent of the marshes which surrounded them. To this end he sent Hume off to the north, while he took to the boat to explore the tributary of the Macquarie river which watered the area. His excursion was a failure: the channel was tortuous, the reeds so high that the surrounding country could not be seen; the boat had frequently to be lifted over tree-trunks which impeded the way, and when the men got into the water to do so, their legs were covered with leeches. Myriads of mosquitoes tortured them. The boat hit a submerged log, was holed and had to be patched up with the use of a tin plate. Finally, the stream whose course they were following suddenly dried up. They turned round and returned to the camp.

There, Hume reported that he had found a small, clear lake to the north, which he believed was fed by the Macquarie. The whole party moved off in that direction, again with great difficulty; eventually they got bogged down and nothing was to be done but abandon any attempt to move further north. Sturt was at a loss, but finally decided to split the party: he and two men to explore to the north-west, Hume with the other two to follow the marsh's eastern side.

Not long after setting out on his journey, Sturt experienced a disconcerting incident. First, he and his party were almost surrounded by flames and they had no idea how this fire had started; fortunately there was little material to feed the fire, and skirting its perimeter they came to an Aboriginal camp:

A young girl sitting by the fire was the first to observe us as we were slowly approaching her. She was so excessively alarmed, that she had not the power to run away; but threw herself on the ground and screamed violently. We now observed a number of huts, out of which the natives issued, little dreaming of the spectacle they were to behold. But the moment they saw us, they started back; their huts were in a moment in flames, and each with a fire-brand ran to and fro with hideous yells, thrusting them into every bush they passed. I walked my horse quietly towards an old man who stood more forward than the rest, as if he intended to devote himself for the preservation of his tribe. I had intended speaking to him, but on a nearer approach I remarked that he trembled so violently that it was impossible to expect that I could obtain any information from him, and as I had not time for explanations, I left him to form his own conjectures as to what we were, and continued to move towards a thick brush, into which they did not venture to follow us.[8]

Panic was usually the understandable reaction of the Aboriginals, whose first sight this was of white men – or indeed of horsemen; initially they supposed man and horse to be one animal, like mythical centaurs, and their terror only intensified when the men dismounted. Rather than mistaking their panic for antagonism, Sturt was time and again able to allay their fears and to an extent befriend them.

When they met again Sturt and Hume, comparing notes, came to the conclusion that the marshes were more limited in extent than they had at first thought, that the land in the area was largely flat, although with some minor hills, and that much of the soil appeared to be rich enough to yield good crops if cultivated. 'Yet', Sturt concluded, 'upon the whole the space I traversed is unlikely to become the haunt of civilized man, or will only become so in isolated spots, as a chain of connection to a more fertile country; if such a country exist to the westward.'[9]

As to the Great Inland Sea, there was still no sign of it. Indeed, for much of the time they found no water of any kind, although at one point a pigeon led one of the men to a tiny puddle, which just served to alleviate their thirst. Sometimes they were reduced to hanging up their handkerchiefs full of mud and drinking the drops which percolated through the cloth.

Dimly, between the reeds or brush, they occasionally discerned dark figures; but the Aboriginals mostly kept well away, until:

As we were travelling through a forest we surprised a hunting party of natives. Mr Hume and I were considerably in front of our party at the time, and he only had his gun with him. We had been moving along so quietly that we were not for some time observed by them. Three were seated on the ground, under a tree, and two others were busily employed on one of the lower branches cutting out honey. As soon as they saw us, four of them ran away; but the fifth, who wore a cap of emu feathers, stood for a moment looking at us, and then very deliberately dropped out of the tree to the ground. I then advanced towards him, but before I got round a bush that intervened, he had darted away. I was fearful that he was gone to collect his tribe, and, under this impression, rode quickly back for my gun to support Mr Hume. On my arrival I found the native was before me. He stood about twenty paces from Mr Hume, who was endeavouring to explain what he was; but seeing me approach he immediately poised his spear at him, as being the nearest. Mr Hume then unslung his carbine, and presented it; but, as it was evident my appearance had startled the savage, I pulled up; and he immediately lowered his weapon. His coolness and courage surprised me, and increased my desire to communicate with him. He had evidently taken both man and horse for one animal, and as long as Mr Hume kept his seat, the native remained upon his guard; but when he saw him dismount, after the first astonishment had subsided, he stuck his spear into the ground, and walked fearlessly up to him. We made him comprehend that we were in search of water; when he pointed to the west, as indicating that we should supply our wants there. He gave his information in a frank and manly way, without the least embarrassment, and when the party passed, he stepped back to avoid the animals, without the smallest confusion. I am sure he was a very brave man; and I left him with the most favourable impressions. . . .[10]

Sturt's attitude, as has been pointed out,[11] was that of an educated English gentleman who had learned to treat other men, whatever their rank or kind, as he himself would wish to be treated. It paid off, time and again, and saved not only trouble for himself and his companions, but the lives of those Aboriginals who, when they came across other explorers, were treated inconsiderately and often, with little excuse other than panic, killed.

At the end of January, moving down the banks of a stream they called New Year's Creek, they were viciously attacked by swarms of kangaroo flies, which rose from the ground in their thousands; the men put handkerchiefs over their faces and stockings over their hands, but were bitten through everything. The animals too were bitten, and went almost mad trying to escape. 'I never experienced such a day of torment,' wrote Sturt, 'and only when the sun set did these little creatures cease from their attacks.'[12]

Shortage of water was now a severe problem. The creek and any small waterholes were drying up, and often the water they did find was so polluted that when they boiled it, half of it was left as sediment. Then, on 2 February, they suddenly found themselves on the bank of a fine broad river, a river whose presence had been hidden from them until the moment they came upon it. The channel was 75m wide (approximately 80yd), the water clearly deep; there were waterfowl in abundance. 'Our surprise and delight', wrote Sturt, 'may better be imagined than described. Our difficulties seemed to be at an end, for here was a river that promised to reward all our exertions . . .'.

The men immediately rushed down the bank to drink – only to find that the water was salt. Neither man nor beast could slake their thirst; the cattle contented themselves with standing in the river to cool off, only their noses exposed. Fortunately the water of a small stream nearby proved potable, and despite his disappointment Sturt was pleased, for he felt sure that such a huge body of salt water must disgorge itself into the Great Inland Sea – which Sturt referred to as 'the Mediterranean'. He pressed on excitedly downriver for 40 miles before concluding, reluctantly, that the greatest discovery of all must wait for another occasion. In the meantime, he named the newly discovered river the Darling. What else?

Wearily the men began to retrace their steps, only to fall into what might have developed into a real conflict with the Aboriginals. Three or four of these, surprised by the expedition, called out and were joined by a dozen more. One of them, the oldest and apparently the most influential, began to make the most threatening gestures, but when Sturt and the rest of the party refused to be terrified, the group (some of whom had painted themselves in readiness for a fight) fell quiet and within the shortest time the whole party had become docile and began to demonstrate the use of the seine (net) they had laid for fishing. Sturt's calm and gentlemanly attitude to the Aboriginals had borne fruit once again.[13] 'The great point', he wrote, 'is not to alarm their natural timidity: to exercise patience in your intercourse with them; to treat them kindly; and to watch them with suspicion, especially at night.'[14] As a consequence he was able to observe them much more closely than those explorers who contemptuously drove them away. He was able to see and note the way in which they marked their bodies, both with scars and with paint of some kind, and to examine the cloaks of kangaroo skin which they occasionally wore over their otherwise naked bodies. He attempted to make notes of their language, but in the end gave up – it was simply too difficult. The men, he thought, were 'much better looking than the women', but despite his courteous treatment of both Stuart was forced to conclude that 'they are a people, at present, at the very bottom of the scale of humanity'.[15]

On 22 February, the party reached Mount Harris and rested there for a fortnight, recovering their strength with the help of plentiful supplies of food and water, including the meat of a buffalo Sturt had slaughtered.

There was still work to be done. The party followed the course of the Castlereagh river, discovered ten years earlier, and to Sturt's pleasure found that it eventually combined forces with the Darling. Finally, they turned north to plot the confluence of the Macquarie with the Darling, in the heart of dismal, drought-reduced country where they could ride for a whole day without seeing a blade of grass or a drop of water: no natives, no wildlife, not even a bird. Sturt left a bitter picture of it:

In the creeks, weeds had grown and withered, and grown again; and young saplings were now rising in their beds, nourished by the moisture that still remained; but the largest forest trees were drooping, and many were dead. The emus, with outstretched necks, gasping for breath, searched the channels of the river for water, in vain; and the native dog, so thin that it could hardly walk, seemed to implore some merciful hand to despatch it.[16]

Enough was enough. By the end of March 1829 they had returned to Sydney and Sturt had submitted his report to the Governor. His discovery of the Darling river alone had rendered the expedition worthwhile, together with his investigation of the Macquarie marshes and the streams which ran in and around them. It is no wonder that Governor Darling reported to the Secretary of State in London that his protégé had carried out his task with 'patience and zeal which do him infinite credit'.

Darling was now excited by the idea that 'his river might, if the Murrumbidgee joined it and both proved navigable, be a wonderful channel for the supply of settlers in a whole new area of Australia', and was eager to discover more. Meanwhile, Sturt had rejoined his regiment, but within eight months was commissioned by the Governor to explore the Murrumbidgee as far as a possible junction with the Darling. Thus it was that at 5 a.m. on the morning of 10 November 1829 he was off again, this time carrying a specially commissioned 8ft collapsible whaleboat, and a still through which he could filter the salt water of the Darling. Since Hume was unable to accompany him on this second expedition, Sturt took George MacLeay, the son of the Colonial Secretary.

My servant Harris, who had shared my wanderings and had continued in my service for eighteen years, led the advance, with his companion Hopkinson. Nearly abreast of them the eccentric Fraser stalked along wholly lost in thought. The two former had laid aside their military habits, and had substituted the broad brimmed hat and the bushman's dress in their place, but it was impossible to guess how Fraser intended to protect himself from the heat or the damp, so little were his habiliments suited for the occasion. He had his gun over his shoulder, and his double shot belt as full as it could be of shot, although there was not a chance of his expending a grain during the day. Some dogs . . . followed close at his heels, as if they were aware that they were about to exchange their late confinement for the freedom of the woods. The whole of these formed a kind of advanced guard. At some distance in the rear the drays moved slowly along . . . and behind followed the pack animals.[17]

The company passed, and sometimes stopped at, a number of farms and properties on their march through Liverpool and across the Goulburn Plains to the Murrumbidgee. They had some difficulty in crossing the river, making a sort of ferry from their collapsible boat on which they hauled their goods across. The horses and cattle presented more of a problem; finally two of the men managed to drive them across through water so fast-flowing that they were almost carried away. In the end, the only casualty was a convict, William Mulholland,[18] who stripped himself for the work, but came to regret it when he was swept into a bed of vicious stinging nettles.

Once again, Sturt was impressed by what seemed the natural friendliness of the Aboriginals with whom, from time to time, the explorers came into contact; sometimes families of two or three, but on one occasion a whole tribe of almost fifty. 'Their manners', he recorded,

were those of a quiet and inoffensive people, and their appearance in some measure prepossessing. The old men had lofty foreheads, and stood exceedingly erect. The young men were cleaner in their persons, and were better featured than any we had seen, some of them having smooth hair and an almost Asiatic cast of countenance. On the other hand, the women and children were disgusting objects. The latter were much subject to diseases, and were dreadfully emaciated. It is evident that a number of them die in infancy for want of care and nourishment. We remarked none at the age of incipient puberty, but the most of them under six. . . .

While there seemed some small differences between these people and those of other areas,

the sunken eye and overhanging eyebrow, the high cheekbone and thick lip, distended nostrils, the nose either short or aquiline, together with a stout bust and slender extremities, and both curled and smooth hair, marked the natives of the Morumbidgee [*sic*] as well as those of the Darling.[19]

Sturt was now in unexplored country. Still obsessed with the idea of his 'Mediterranean' he pressed on, sometimes over land so arid, hard, stony and dry that nothing could grow; sometimes over marshy terrain in which the wagons sank up to their axles and the horses to their knees.

It occurred to him that it would be less unpleasant to continue the expedition by water. The collapsible 8ft whaleboat which they carried with them would not hold both men and stores, so he set his carpenter, Joseph Clayton,[20] to find and fell a suitable tree and build a second, smaller vessel. Within a week, Clayton had assembled the whaleboat, built a second, half her size, painted them both and put up a makeshift wharf from which they could be loaded. Sturt then chose six men to accompany him downriver while the others were to wait a week after which, if Sturt had not returned, they were to make their way back to Goulburn Plains carrying a report to the Governor.

On 7 January, at a little after six in the morning, Sturt embarked on what was at first a comfortable voyage; only two oars were needed to guide the ships' progress, and most of the party could lie back and enjoy a pleasant rest. However, on the second day and just after they had encountered some Aboriginals and given them presents, disaster struck. The smaller boat hit a submerged log and sank in 12ft of water together with several casks of meat and the still intended to provide potable water.

They managed to haul the skiff ashore, but the head of the still and most of the carpenter's tools had been thrown out of it. With no little ingenuity Sturt's men contrived to locate the submerged objects in the muddy water. Though none of them could swim well, they lowered themselves down to the riverbed by holding on to an oar stuck into the mud and so recovered most of the lost articles, but not the head of the still. Exhausted, the party slept so soundly that Aboriginals were able to creep into the camp and steal their only frying pan, some cutlasses and tomahawks.

Next morning the still head too was recovered and the party pressed on, making good progress downriver. The current increased as they went, and after between 30 and 35km they struck turbulent and perilous waters:

> The channel . . . suddenly contracted, and became almost blocked up with huge trees, that must have found their way into it down the creeks or junctions we had lately passed. The rapidity of the current increasing at the same time, rendered the navigation perplexing and dangerous.

As dusk fell

> the men's eye-sight failed them . . . and they mistook shadows for objects under water, and *vice-versa*, and the channel had become so narrow that, although the banks were not of increased height, we were involved in comparative darkness, under a close arch of trees, and a danger was hardly seen ere we were hurried past it. . . .[21]

They stopped for the night, and next day found progress even more difficult: huge trees sometimes lay across the river, their jagged branches ready to hole any boat that struck them, while the current became tumultuous, sweeping them along so fast they found it impossible to control the boats. Then, suddenly, they shot out into 'a broad and noble river' some 180m (200yd) wide.

Sturt was uncertain which river he had now joined. If anything, it seemed to be increasing in volume and breadth. Could it be the Darling? At all events there were few difficulties in navigating it. But now a new problem arose. For some time shadowy figures had been glimpsed moving about on the riverbanks, and sometimes

Aboriginals had emerged into the sunlight, either just watching rather sullenly as the boats passed, or, with their bodies heavily painted, dancing, shouting and shaking their spears in what seemed a decidedly unfriendly manner. On 16 January, when a number of them appeared, Sturt beckoned to them, and one or two swam across to the camp and spent the night by the fire; next morning about eighty men and women swam around the boats trying to catch hold of the oars. On the following evening, a number of the men came to the camp, and Fraser and Harris talked and laughed with them – and, perhaps when some drink had been taken, decided to demonstrate the use of the razor by shaving the most prominent of the visitors, who was both amused and delighted.

Three days later, their encounters with the natives took a more serious turn. A great crowd of Aboriginals was seen assembled under some trees – 'a vast concourse', Sturt recorded – painted, armed and threatening. When the explorers tried to land, the natives made it clear that that would not be welcome:

> We approached so near that they held their spears quivering in their grasp ready to hurl. They were painted in various ways. Some who had marked their ribs, and thighs, and faces with a white pigment, looked like skeletons, others were daubed over with red and yellow ochre, and their bodies shone with the grease with which they had besmeared themselves. A dead silence prevailed among the front ranks, but those in the back ground, as well as the women, who carried supplies of darts, and who appeared to have had a bucket of whitewash emptied over their heads, were extremely clamorous.[22]

Sturt guided the boats on downstream in mid-channel, the Aboriginals following along the bank, occasionally throwing their spears towards the explorers. At length, the boats came to a large sandbank on which a crowd of natives had gathered. Though Sturt was extremely reluctant to fire on them, he suspected that that might be inevitable. He distributed arms, and told the men that they should all fire one volley, after which the boats would be defended by bayonets, his gun and those of the two soldiers, whose aim would be better. He himself took aim at an Aboriginal man who stood in front of the crowd and appeared to be its leader.

Then an extraordinary thing happened. Four men appeared on the riverbank, racing towards the water. Their leader threw himself into the river, waded to the sandbank and confronted the leader of the mob.

Seizing him by the throat, he pushed him backwards, and forcing all who were in the water upon the bank, he trod its margin with a vehemence and an agitation that were exceedingly striking. At one moment pointing to the boat, at another shaking his clenched hand in the faces of the most forward, and stamping with passion on the sand; his voice, that was at first distinct and clear, was lost in hoarse murmurs. . . .[23]

It was the man whom Harris had shaved a night or two earlier. So astonished were the explorers that they allowed their boats to drift

Attacked by a 'vast concourse' of highly hostile Aboriginals, Sturt prepared, reluctantly, to fire on them. *(Sturt's* Journal*)*

on to a shoal. Striking away from it, Sturt decided to land on the riverbank, among a smaller crowd of about seventy natives (he estimated the crowd on the sandbank to be nearer six hundred). To his relief, curiosity rather than anger appeared now to be their chief emotion: within a quarter of an hour all antagonism seemed to have evaporated and many of the men on the sandbank swam over, including their influential friend, to whom Sturt made a grateful present.

Next morning, Sturt realised that they were sailing along yet another river, this one lined with richly grassy banks and handsome trees – the men said the scene was exactly like an English landscape. On landing, Sturt named the new river the Murray, raised the Union Jack and, as the men gave three cheers,

> The eye of every native [was] fixed on that noble flag, at all times a beautiful object, as it waved over us in the heart of a desert. They had, until that moment, been particular loquacious, but the sight of that flag and the sound of our voices hushed the tumult, and while they were still lost in astonishment, the boat's head was speedily turned, the sail was sheeted home, both wind and current were in our favour, and we vanished from them with a rapidity that surprised even ourselves, and which precluded every hope of the most adventurous among them to keep up with us.[24]

Sturt thought that he had achieved almost everything he had been asked to do. But while there was new country to be surveyed and new discoveries to be made, while stores were sufficient and the men fresh enough to venture further, he was not minded to turn back. So on he went, breaking up the smaller of the boats, the skiff, of which he believed he would have no more need. On 4 February he was surprised to see seagulls overhead. Could this mean that the coast was near? The lushness of the country through which they had travelled now gave way once more to flat and level wastes. He continued his meticulous record, laying down every bend of the river by compass, so that a chart could be made which would provide the most complete possible record of the Murray's course.

The number of Aboriginals they saw on the bank seemed to increase and at the same time they looked less healthy. Many, even most of them, suffered from either leprosy or syphilis, which made it difficult to put up with their continual desire to grope at the limbs and faces of the explorers when they went ashore, and Sturt was certainly not inclined to humour her when a hideous old woman attempted to embrace him: 'all were in a complete state of nudity', he recorded, 'and really the loathsome condition and hideous countenances of the women would, I should imagine, have been a complete antidote to the sexual passion.'[25] Not entirely, it seems, for he noticed that Fraser 'was no wise particular as to the object of his attention'.

As they approached the mouth of the Murray, the natives they saw appeared more healthy, but also more aggressive and less interested in Sturt's attempts to befriend them. The explorers came at last not to the sea, but to a lake, which Sturt called the Alexandrina after the princess who would later become Queen Victoria. He was impressed by the sight, but at the same time disappointed not to find the river flowing directly into the sea and, moreover, could ascertain no way in which that might be possible.

On 9 February they camped by the lake, hoping to find the sea the following day. Sturt was impressed by the prospect before him: 'It was now near sunset; and one of the most lovely evenings I had ever seen. The sun's radiance was yet upon the mountains, but all lower objects were in shade. The banks of the channel, with the trees and the rocks, were reflected in the tranquil waters, whose surface was unruffled save by the thousands of wild fowl that rose before us, and made a noise as of a multitude clapping hands, in their clumsy efforts to rise from the waters.'[26]

His determination to reach the sea won out despite the exhaustion of his men, who were simply no longer capable of hauling their boat over the mud shoals that lay in the direction in which the ocean might lie. Sturt had been worried about the men for some time. Their diet had become increasingly poor: the salt beef had gone rotten and was fit only for the dogs; the men would not eat fish; and there had been no wildfowl to shoot, so they lived more or less on flour. Flour, tea and some sugar were indeed all they had left and even these were beginning to run short. Movingly, as Sturt records, the men refused to touch the sugar: 'They said that, divided, it would benefit nobody; that they hoped MacLeay and I would use it, that it would last us for some time, and that they were better able to submit to privations than we were.'[27] Many of the party had suffered from the harsh sun and had trouble with their eyes – Sturt himself had increasing difficulty in seeing clearly.

On 12 February Sturt left camp at 3 a.m. with MacLeay and Fraser and tramped for 11km until they finally staggered on to a beach. He called the place Encounter Bay, and immediately turned back to the camp and invited the men to go to the sea. 'They accordingly went and bathed, and returned not only highly delighted at this little act of good nature on my part, but loaded with cockles, a bed of which they had managed to find among the sand. Clayton [the carpenter] had tied one end of his apron up, and brought a bag full, and amused himself with boiling cockles all night long.'[28]

It now became vital to turn about and head back to the depot where Harris would be waiting with supplies. So they retired across the lake to the mouth of the Murray and began to row upstream. They plied the oars, Sturt and MacLeay taking their turn, from first light until sunset, except when some of the men had to climb out of the boat in order to drag it over shoals and mudflats, after which they sat shivering in their wet clothes, waiting for the sun to dry them. Once they hit a log and had to unload the boat and drag it ashore so that Clayton could repair the damage, then reload and launch it again. On 4 May they reached the confluence with the Darling, and on the 16th the Murrumbidgee.

The Aboriginals, when they caught sight of them, seemed uniformly hostile, made threatening gestures and then attempted to entice the men ashore where, Sturt assumed, probably correctly, they would have been attacked. On one occasion, the native women came down to the riverbank, perfectly naked (as they always were) and 'gave us the most pressing invitation to land . . . trying for some time to allure us by the most unequivocal manifestations of love'.[29] Meanwhile, the spears of the men could be seen in the nearby reeds. Fortunately, even Fraser was wise enough not to fall for the trick.

The party was almost defeated by rapids: they attempted to pull the boat up by ropes, but had not the strength. Then, as if by magic, the Aboriginal whose intervention earlier in their venture had saved them from attack reappeared and persuaded some of his friends to help them. Another tribe which they met a few days later was not so friendly; at night a number of them sneaked up on the camp and were clearly up to no good. Harris, on sentry duty and a crack shot, spotted two of them close to the camp and roused Sturt – 'the blacks' were within a few yards of him. Sturt told him to fire. Harris did so. 'Well, did you kill your man?' Sturt asked. 'No, Sir,' replied Harris, 'I thought you would repent it, so I fired between the two.'[30] It was an excellent illustration of how the leader's attitude to 'the natives' had rubbed off on his men.

A few days later they reached the depot, only to find it deserted. The men were disappointed – they had been looking forward to a rest and some food. For a while they pressed on, but were in such an exhausted state that Sturt decided to send Hopkinson and Mulholland to find Harris and the rest of the party and bring back assistance. Six days passed, and the last of the flour had been eaten, when the two men were seen returning. 'They were both of them in a state that beggars description. Their knees and ancles [*sic*] were dreadfully swollen, and their limbs so painful, that as soon as they arrived in the camp they sank under their efforts, but they met us with smiling countenances, and expressed their satisfaction at having arrived so seasonably to our relief.'[31]

They had walked, in their exhausted state, a distance of over 144km in three days, found Robert Harris and on the way back managed to carry with them some food for their friends. At first their stomachs could not tolerate the meat, but after resting and recovering their strength they were able to march back to Sydney, which they reached on 25 May 1830.

As a human being, Sturt is perhaps the most admirable of all the well-known Australian explorers: good-looking and well-mannered, he was able to charm everyone he met – not by spurious toadying or sanctimoniousness but rather by dint of his unaffected good nature and an inability to believe ill of anyone. An intensely religious man, prayer was to him as natural as breathing, and sustained him through every difficulty: he treated God as a friend and adviser, and consulted the Bible as he would a map or a treatise on navigation. In Sydney, he was celebrated as the most successful explorer of Australia to date: he had drawn a new, thorough map of the south-east of the country, detailing for the first time the complex interconnected river system. As the Governor had hoped, it was not long before squatters made their way to the area and began to develop it.

FOUR

Australian Morning
Thomas Livingstone Mitchell, 1831, 1835, 1845

It might be said that the irascible, determined Thomas Livingstone Mitchell was a failure as an explorer. His expeditions never achieved their objectives and his reputation was (in some ways unfairly) besmirched by various episodes that resulted in the injury and death of Aboriginals. His triumph was in discovering Australia Felix, *some of the richest and most handsome land in New South Wales.*

Little is known of Mitchell's early life. Born in Stirlingshire, Scotland, on 15 June 1792, his father died when his son was still in his teens. Mitchell joined the army, and between 1811 and 1854 rose from the rank of second lieutenant to that of major, but cutbacks after Waterloo resulted in his being put on half pay and subsequently applying for a civil service post. He was duly appointed Deputy Surveyor-General in New South Wales and principal assistant to John Oxley, the explorer, who was then Surveyor-General.

On 23 September 1827 Mitchell arrived in Australia on the convict ship *Prince Regent*, having travelled in rather greater comfort than the convicts battened down below decks – he and his family took the ship's Great Cabin for £200. Two months after he entered the service, Oxley, his superior, who had been ill for some time, died, and Mitchell found himself Surveyor-General.

With enormous vigour, he immediately set about devising a way of accurately mapping New South Wales.[1] When he arrived, he found chaos among the free settlers for they applied for land and took possession before it had been surveyed, a state of affairs that led to endless arguments about boundaries. Mitchell proposed that the territory should be divided into sixteen counties, and each county into sixty-four parishes. To enable this to be done, a trigonometrical survey of the whole colony must be undertaken.

The Governor, Lieutenant-General Sir Ralph Darling, was extremely impressed at the speed with which Mitchell commanded the details of his position, and at first their relationship was placid enough. But the two men were equally intransigent in their views, and sooner or later there was bound to be trouble. Because of his cold personality and almost inhuman insistence on total obedience to the letter of the law, Darling had made himself the most hated man in the colony; while Mitchell was hot-tempered and ready to see a conspiracy against him at every turn. A year after his arrival, Mitchell was writing privately to Hay, a friendly senior civil servant in London, complaining that he was 'persuaded that you can never hear of anything creditable done by me under Governor Darling, whose jealous relatives I may almost charge with a conspiracy against the little fame and credit I have earned by a life of persevering industry'.[2]

It was true that Darling had wanted the position of Surveyor-General for his brother-in-law, and doubtless there was some jealousy, but there is no evidence that he impeded Mitchell's career. It is also the case that Mitchell was himself jealous of Sturt, who had arrived in Sydney four months before him and whose expeditions Darling approved – Sturt was a man, Mitchell said disparagingly, 'who had never travelled anywhere' and it was ridiculous that he should be supported when Mitchell was not. Meanwhile, the Governor was writing to Hay complaining that Mitchell was 'a hardworking, rude, ill-tempered fellow who quarrelled with everyone, and who, I may add, is still as much detested as ever by those who have any business to transact with him. Anxious to get the business of Government done, I was willing to make any sacrifice, and he was allowed to snarl and growl unheeded, until at last his insolence became intolerable.'[3] He followed this up with a letter to the Secretary of State for the Commonwealth demanding Mitchell's dismissal from the civil service.

Happily for Mitchell, even as Darling was writing that letter, the latter was himself dismissed. He left Sydney on 22 October 1831 and soon afterwards Mitchell was able to tell Hay that the acting governor, Col Patrick Lindesay, had 'indulged me with permission to explore our northern interior'.[4]

The expedition was prompted by a rather unusual incident. As Mitchell later told the story,

> A runaway convict, named George Clarke, alias 'the Barber', had, for a length of time, escaped the vigilance of the police, by disguising himself as an aboriginal native. He had even accustomed himself to the wretched life of that unfortunate race of men; he was deeply scarified like them, and naked and painted black, he went about with a tribe, being usually attended by two aboriginal females, and having acquired some knowledge of their language and customs. . . .
>
> After this man was taken into custody, he gave a circumstantial detail of his travels to the north-west, along the bank of a large river, named, as he said, the *Kindur*; by following which in a south-west direction, he had twice reached the sea shore.[5]

Clarke also asserted that he had crossed immense plains to the north, and found that the known rivers all emptied themselves into a larger river which flowed in a north-westerly direction. He called it the Nammoy.

The latter account deeply interested the acting governor. If it was true that a substantial river rose in the mountain ranges and flowed north-west to empty itself into the sea at or near the Gulf of Carpentaria, it would be extremely important as a thoroughfare. Lindesay lost little time in instructing Mitchell to look for it. Apart from his interest in the possible river, it was also true that as more and more free settlers came to Australia, and increasing numbers of convicts eventually served out their sentences or were pardoned, there was a steadily growing demand for good grazing land, and any news of useful areas of such land would be welcome. (The discovery of good pastoral land was a preoccupation of every nineteenth-century Australian explorer.)

The expedition was approved before a new governor had been appointed who might countermand Lindesay's instructions, and Mitchell hurriedly got a party together, hoping that if he set off immediately he could avoid any problem which might arise should the new governor prove less amenable to the plan.

His expedition consisted of an assistant leader, Heneage Finch, two surveyors and fifteen convicts, several of whom proved so reliable that they also accompanied him on his second and third expeditions; one, his personal servant Anthony Brown, took part in all four.

There were two carpenters: Burnett, an inveterate poacher; and Whiting, who had been a Guardsman; four sailors; three bullock drivers; a blacksmith and a groom. James Souter was described as 'medical assistant' and styled himself 'doctor'. Henry Dawkins was servant to one of the surveyors. There were two carts, three drays and a number of packhorses. Apart from the necessary supplies, the party was equipped with eight muskets and six pistols, plus materials from which to construct canvas boats if they needed them – and they did.

Mitchell sent the main party off in advance while he collected sextants, a theodolite and other instruments. He spent a night at Elizabeth Farm, Parramatta, the home of John Macarthur, where he was shown the first olive tree planted in Australia.[6] Meeting up with the others, he embarked on the expedition proper on 24 November 1831. On 8 December he managed to acquire an Aboriginal guide, whom he hoped would be of use in the unknown country which they were approaching. Jemmy, however, didn't like the idea of entering the territory of another tribe and deserted. Mitchell found another guide, 'Mister Brown', who proved more faithful.

The party crossed the Hunter river and came upon what might be described as a road but was more of an unmapped track, which led eventually to a pass across the Liverpool Range. The track ran to a farm established by a Scottish free settler who was waiting for his family to join him. Mitchell was distressed at the condition of many of the Aboriginals he encountered as he started the climb to the Range for they seemed to be suffering from smallpox (it may have been venereal disease). The 'doctor' did what he could for them, leaving them some medicine.

Mitchell was eager to make an accurate record of the country over which they were trekking, but found it difficult because the terrain was singularly flat and uninteresting and he was using the system of triangulation, which depends on the presence of major landscape features; there were few. Reaching the Namoi river at the end of December, he decided to construct the boats and set some men to cutting down pine trees while others were put to work painting the inside of the canvas; then blue gum (eucalyptus) wood was felled and sawn into ribs and thwarts (seats), and pine adzed into thin planks to line the bottoms of the boats. Within three days the first boat was launched, and within another three, the second.

Meanwhile, Mitchell had come across a stockyard set up by George Clarke, who had evidently been living there and working as a bush-ranger. By then Mitchell had received a message informing him that Clarke had managed to escape from prison in Bathurst and might well be on his way back to the Namoi to cause trouble for the explorers.

The boats were successfully launched, but one was almost immediately holed; it was repaired only to be holed again, at which Mitchell gave up any idea of travelling by water, deciding instead to proceed along the riverbank, then turning north into the Nandewar Mountains. In due course, he was able to convince himself that no such river as the Kindur existed: he found another river, but it was the Gwydir, which had been discovered in 1827 by the botanist Alan Cunningham.

Mitchell turned the expedition around – not before time, for scurvy had attacked several of the men. The Aboriginals escaped this scourge by eating the natural fruits of the area, including a sort of cucumber which Mitchell tried, after peppering it, but could not tolerate.

When he returned to Sydney Mitchell had nothing of great importance to report, but was at least able to assure the governor that Clarke's description of the river system was nonsensical. If his expedition had achieved little except some additional mapping of the river systems, Mitchell had proved one thing, namely that any large river flowing to the north-west must be far further north than any white man had previously travelled. All the rivers south of latitude 29° flowed, as far as could be discovered, into the Darling. The convict Clarke had by this time been recaptured, and by cross-questioning him Mitchell was able to assure himself that the man had never in fact gone anywhere near the territory where he claimed the Kindur was to be found.

Mitchell's description of the land he had explored encouraged settlers to make their way in that direction, and soon sheep and cattle stations sprang up around what is now Tamworth (and the commercial centre of a prosperous farming area). He had also learned some practical lessons about the bush: the importance of taking the right amount of supplies, and how vital it was to carry sufficient water. (There had also been less predictable problems – for instance, leaving his rifle unattended for some time he returned to find that bees had filled the barrel with wax and honey.)

Mitchell, too, had his first encounter with the Aboriginal tribes native to the country he passed through. Communication with them was difficult: he addressed them in what he thought was their language, while they spoke to him in what they thought was his. Neither got very far. The attempts by the white explorers to converse were pitiful: 'What for you jerran budgerry whitefellow? Whitefellow brother belongit to blackfellow' might have meant something had the natives had any knowledge at all of English, but as things were the explorers might as well have tried using Esperanto.

Once back in Sydney, Mitchell settled down again, if grudgingly, to his work as Surveyor-General. Then, in 1831, he was instructed by Sir Richard Bourke, the new Governor, to lead an expedition to the junction of the Darling and Murray rivers, following the Darling upstream for two or three degrees of latitude. Sturt had discovered and named the Darling while concentrating on the Murrumbidgee, and had only explored the former for a very short distance.

The pressure of Mitchell's office work was such that it was not in fact until 1835 that he was able to set out again, with an assistant surveyor, the botanist Richard Cunningham (Allan Cunningham's younger brother) and twenty-one men. This time he devised two light whaleboats, one fitting inside the other, and more substantial than the unsatisfactory canvas ones put together during his previous expedition. He also took, this time, two 'mountain barometers' to calculate altitude by measuring barometric pressures, carried by two men, and borrowed an excellent chronometer with which to compare local time from the observatory at Parramatta.

Between March and May the second expedition made its way from Sydney to Bourke, which was to become the gateway to the Outback and the centre of a pastoral district that produces more wool than anywhere else in New South Wales. Mitchell used the Victoria Pass (which he named after the future Queen) to cross the mountains, and climbed the highest peak between the Blue Mountains and the Indian Ocean, Mount Canobolas (1,397m/ 4,583ft above sea level), the two men trailing behind with a barometer, a sextant and a theodolite, enabling him to take bearings to use in his triangulation survey of the area.

Mitchell was enjoying himself, as his diary reveals:

The sense of gratification and repose is intense and cannot be known to him whose life is counted out in a monotonous succession of hours of eating and sleeping within a house; whose food is adulterated by spices and sauces intolerable to real hunger – and whose drink, instead of the sweet refreshing distillation from the heavens, consists of vile artificial extracts, loathed by the really thirsty man, with whom the pure element resumes its true value, and establishes its real superiority over every artificial beverage.

The natives whom we met here were fine looking men enjoying contentment and happiness within the precincts of their native woods. Their enjoyment seemed derived so directly from nature that it almost excited a feeling of regret that civilised men, enervated by luxury and all its concomitant diseases, should ever disturb the haunts of these rude but happy beings.[7]

It was, as he was to realise sooner rather than later, too romantic a view but at least it goes some way to show that Mitchell was by no means instinctively antagonistic to the Aboriginals, as some of his detractors have asserted.

Richard Cunningham, the 42-year-old botanist, had been enjoying himself quite as much as Mitchell, but had developed the unfortunate habit of wandering off from the main expedition from time to time, unaccompanied, in search of specimens. This he did on 17 April, and though Mitchell sounded a bugle and fired several shots in an attempt to guide him back, he did not return. Mitchell organised searches: Cunningham had no food or water and the situation was clearly serious. On the evening of 28 April, a search party returned having found his horse dead; they brought back his saddle and bridle, his whip and one glove. Two days later a line of footprints was discovered, made by someone wearing shoes and leading to a fresh-water pond – but there were also footprints of naked feet, apparently tracking the botanist.

Nothing more was found by the expedition, and it was not until December that Lieutenant Zouch, an officer of the mounted police, came across a knife, a glove and part of a cigar-case in the baggage of three Aboriginals of the Myall tribe, on the banks of Lake Bogan. Wongadgery, Boreeboomalie and Bureemal confessed to murdering Cunningham for no special reason – they had simply clubbed him to death – and led the policeman to a place called Currindine, where he found a coat, a hat and some bones, which he interred. Only Bureemal was ever tried for the murder; the other two escaped from a careless trooper who was supposed to be guarding them.

Having given up all hope of finding Cunningham, Mitchell led the main expedition on along the line of the Bogan river to the Darling, finding several traces of Sturt's earlier expedition. The water of the Darling proved fresh – contrary to Sturt's experience – and Mitchell made camp on its banks, setting up a stockade and calling the place Fort Bourke, after the Governor. He then launched his two boats, but there were so many submerged logs and other obstructions that surveying the river's course by water proved impracticable and they were forced to return to Fort Bourke and continue along the banks.

They came across a gum tree in whose bark Hamilton Hume, Sturt's assistant, had carved his name in 1828. Mitchell admitted to himself in his diary that he entertained some hopes of finding 'a sea' – the myth of the Great Inland Sea died hard.

From time to time he made contact with a number of Aboriginal tribes, the relationship between them and the invading white men varying between curiosity and a sort of friendship – one Aboriginal fisherman, passing by on what looked like a raft, threw Mitchell a fish with a friendly wave. They were welcomed at one Aboriginal village and conversed (as far as was possible since neither party spoke the other's language) for some time with the chief, to whom Mitchell gave a greyhound puppy – one of the dogs which accompanied every expedition into the Outback – and a hatchet, which he had to show the chief how to use.

On 11 July, just at the moment when Mitchell had decided that the expedition should be completed, there was real trouble. He heard shots and after a while one of his men staggered into the camp, wounded and bleeding. Joseph Jones had been sent to the river for water, carrying a large teakettle. The leader of the local Aboriginal tribe had seized the kettle, at the same time clubbing Jones and knocking him out. A sailor who had accompanied Jones fired, wounding the Aboriginal in the groin. Threatened by members of the tribe, the sailor fired into the crowd, wounding a woman carrying a child.

The infuriated tribe made to attack some of the men who were trying to rescue a bullock bogged down in nearby mud. Spears were thrown, but no one was wounded. Meanwhile, the injured woman died. That evening, the sounds of mourning natives could be heard and Mitchell 'regretted most bitterly the inconsiderate conduct of some of the men'. Even so, he could not bring himself to deem the Aboriginals worthy of a great deal of consideration. 'It seemed impossible, in any manner, to conciliate these people, when united in a body,' he wrote. 'We wanted nothing, asked for nothing; on the contrary, we gave them presents of articles the most desirable to them; and yet they beset us as keenly and with as little remorse as wild beasts seek their prey.'[8] It did not occur to him nor, it must be said, to some other explorers of the period, that the Aboriginals might not consider the gift of a few tomahawks and gee-gaws as proper recompense for the disturbance to their age-old way of life or the confiscation of their lands. In his worst mood, Mitchell thought of them as being below the beasts, though he acknowledged their natural intelligence and quickness of wit, and the speed with which they understood the use of some of the appliances they had never before seen.

He turned for home. There was, he believed, nothing more to be achieved and moreover at least two men were seriously ill, one with scurvy and one with dysentery. From Fort Bourke they dragged their way home rather disconsolately, with more men falling victim to scurvy – one of the two invalids had to be carried and lost all his teeth. The return journey was at least without incident. Looked at dispassionately, the expedition had not achieved a great deal. Mitchell had discovered the series of lakes which he called Laidley's Ponds, now the Menindee Reservoirs and part of the Kinchega National Park, but he had certainly not succeeded in travelling down the Darling river as far as the sea, and although he had followed its course for 500km, had added little to previous knowledge of the area.

Mitchell's description of the ranges to the west of the Darling interested the Governor sufficiently to persuade him to send Mitchell out again, to survey the countryside between the left bank of the Murray and Murrumbidgee rivers and the Snowy Range. So in mid-March 1836 Mitchell set out on his third expedition, this time to confirm definitely that the Darling joined the Murray at the point where Sturt had originally supposed. If by any chance it did not, he was to follow the Darling to the sea, wherever its estuary might be. This third expedition was to be his major achievement.

While much of the equipment Mitchell took on his third expedition was left over from the previous one – the boats and boat-carriage, for instance – this time Mitchell fitted out the twenty-three convicts who would accompany him with elegant 'uniforms' consisting of grey trousers with white braces and red woollen shirts. His party included a butcher, a cook, a 'medical attendant' (also responsible for carrying the barometer), a blacksmith, two 'collectors' (one to collect birds, the other plants), a groom who was also the expedition's official trumpeter, and a shoemaker. There was, too, one 'civilised' Aboriginal, John Piper, who, Mitchell was assured, would be too afraid of 'the savage natives' of the interior to desert. All the men except Piper were armed with rifles, pistols, muskets, carbines[9] and bayonets. Eleven of them had been with Mitchell on one of his earlier explorations, and he had persuaded the governor to pardon them at the end of a successful expedition.

The third expedition reached the Lachlan river, which had been known to Oxley – indeed Mitchell found a tree on which Oxley had carved his name nineteen years earlier. The river was completely dry, but Mitchell decided to follow its course. By this time he had concluded that the man whom he had appointed his second in command, one William Darke (a draughtsman who worked for him), was – not to put too fine a point on it – a fool, and had sent him packing back to Sydney having dispatched a message to one of his assistant surveyors, Granville Chetwynd Stapylton, asking him to join the party as quickly as possible. Stapylton duly arrived on 11 April, having raced from Sydney at top speed, and was immediately put to work surveying Lake Cargelligo. In the meantime Piper picked up a woman, or *gin*, as the Aboriginal women were called, acquiring her as 'wife' with the help of presents of an opossum skin cloak and various trinkets. She proved useful for fetching and carrying, as did another woman, a widow called Turandurey, who joined the party with her daughter Ballandella. Mitchell also acquired two intelligent Aboriginal boys, both of whom were called Tommy: Mitchell christened them 'Tommy Came-first' and 'Tommy Came-last'; they were adept at hunting, and remained with the expedition until the end. The Aboriginals on the expedition were also helpful in pointing out which non-poisonous wild plants could be used to supplement the explorers' diet.

The course of the Lachlan was confusing – was it possible that it was in fact the river which Sturt had mistaken for the Darling? Drought meant that the party faced the usual problem of water shortage, and when water was available it was not always welcome: at one point a dead body was found floating in a waterhole; diving at another waterhole to spear fish, Piper brought up instead a human leg.

On 5 May, Mitchell reached Booligal, the furthest point to which Oxley had travelled, and a place which had also been visited by Sturt. A week later he suddenly saw water ahead, and found himself on the banks of the Murrumbidgee, a 'magnificent stream'. 'I was delighted', Mitchell wrote, 'to find that this corner of Australia could supply at least one river worthy of the name. After thirsting so long amongst the muddy holes of the Lachlan, I witnessed, with no slight degree of satisfaction, the faded cattle drinking at this full and flowing stream, resembling a thing of life, in its deep and rippling waters.'[10] He wrote as though it was he who had discovered the river: Sturt, of course, had passed along this very route, but (it must be said) Mitchell was always keener to record his own achievements than to recall those of either Sturt or Oxley.

He followed the Murrumbidgee to Balranald, then, leaving Stapylton, his second in command, established with some of the men at a depot near Weinby, went on to the Murray and followed the river to a point near Tapalin. This part of the expedition was not without incident: on 16 May one of the horses fell into the river and drowned while trying to drink; then a week later Mitchell's own horse was kicked by a mare and its thigh broken, so that it had to be shot. But worse was to come. On 24 May, they reached a beautiful lake, Lake Benanee, 25km in circumference, near which there was a large Aboriginal encampment. Among them were the three children, two girls and a boy, of the woman who had been killed by the previous expedition. Mitchell was particularly struck by one girl, who 'was the handsomest female I had ever seen among the natives. She was so far from black, that the red colour was very apparent in her cheeks. She sat before me in a corner of the group . . . unconscious that she was naked. As I looked upon her for a moment, while deeply regretting the fate of her mother, the chief who stood by . . . begged me to accept of her in exchange for a tomahawk!'[11]

Other men were less inclined to be friendly, and Mitchell thought that trouble was brewing. That night, all the women disappeared from the area of the camp, fires were seen blazing in a circle round the explorers' camp, and Piper came to Mitchell saying that his *gin* had overheard some of the men plotting an attack. On the morning of 27 May the party started out, but then heard the voices of a large number of Aboriginals raised in what Mitchell supposed to be war cries. He sent Burnett, his overseer, with Piper and a few men to make contact with the natives and discover whether indeed they were preparing an attack. Alerted by a barking dog, the crowd halted and drew back their spears menacingly. One of the white men, panicking, raised his carbine and shot. Mitchell described the ensuing incident in his book about the expedition:

The firing had no sooner commenced, than I perceived from the top of the hill, which I ascended, some of the blacks, who appeared to be a very numerous tribe, swimming across the Murray. . . . By the time I got down, the whole party lined the river bank. . . . Most of the natives were then near the other side, and getting out, while others were swimming down the stream. The sound of so much firing must have been terrible to them, and it was not without effect, if we may credit the information of Piper, who was afterwards informed that seven had been shot in crossing the river, and among them a fellow in a cloak . . . who appeared to be the chief.

Mitchell excused his men's actions, believing the result to be 'the permanent deliverance of the party from imminent danger . . . I was indeed satisfied, that this collision had been brought about in the most providential manner; for it was probable, that, from my regard for the Aboriginals, I might otherwise have postponed giving orders to fire, longer than might have been consistent with the safety of my men.'[12]

The first shot may have been either an accident or the result of panic; and perhaps Mitchell had had no means of preventing the subsequent killing of men who had not actually attacked his party and who, after the initial shot was fired, were already swimming away from the guns, or scrambling off up the bank. It is also understandable that loyalty impelled him to defend his men. But the bloodshed did Mitchell's reputation considerable harm.

After the incident he led the expedition on further upstream, probably to a point not more than 32km north of the junction of the Darling and the Murray, conscious from time to time of the presence of Aboriginals not far away. The Darling was disappointing, appearing little more than a chain of ponds. On 3 January 1838, he buried a bottle in which he placed a paper explaining that, surrounded by hostile Aboriginals and anxious for the safety of his party, he was turning back to the depot where he had left Stapylton. Then he carved the words DIG UNDER on a tree over the place where he had buried it. Should the party be slaughtered, at least there was a chance that someone would discover the circumstances.[13]

Back at the depot, all was well; Stapylton had seen no Aboriginals at all, not even friendly ones. The whole party now moved on, following the course of the Murray upstream to the point at which it joined the Murrumbidgee, and crossing it (with the loss of one bullock, which drowned). On 20 June they came to the junction of the Murray and Little Murray rivers, where grew reeds so thickly colonised by wild fowl that he called the place Swan Hill.[14]

On 21 June there was another fatal encounter, with the Aboriginals near Lake Boga. Piper, out near the shore of the lake with some other men, met an old Aboriginal and asked him the lake's name. The Aboriginal replied that he wouldn't tell him – 'there was too much ask' about him, and he blamed him for bringing 'whitefellows' there. He then called up some other members of his tribe and told them to kill Piper. Two spears were thrown at him, upon which Piper fired and wounded a man in the jaw. The rest fled. Piper reloaded his gun and killed the wounded man. Commenting on the event in his journal, Mitchell 'blamed [Piper] very much for firing' and 'regretted exceedingly the result of his interview'.[15]

Faced with thirty or forty Aboriginals performing what he took to be a hostile dance and brandishing boomerangs and spears, Mitchell fired his pistols in the air, temporarily dispersing the crowd. *(Mitchell's* Journals*)*

He continued, when they proved amenable to contact, to study the Aboriginals and their way of life. Mitchell was particularly impressed by the fact that on the coldest night, when the white men felt that their limbs were freezing, the natives 'stript off all their clothes, previous to lying down to sleep in the open air, their bodies being doubled up around a few burning reeds. We could not understand how they could lay thus naked, when the earth was white with hoar frost; and they were equally at a loss to know, how we could sleep in our tents without a bit of fire to keep our bodies warm.' He was also impressed by the fact that the Aboriginals were uninhibited about going unclothed in summer, their bodies free to enjoy the refreshing breezes and the cool of a bath in any convenient pool. 'It is not improbable,' he remarked, 'that the obstructions of drapery would constitute the greatest of [the Aboriginal's] objections, in such a climate, to the permanent adoption of a civilised life'.[16]

The land through which the explorers were now passing, the western district of Victoria, was rich and lush and splendidly able,

Mitchell realised, to sustain men and beasts: he spoke of it as *Australia Felix*:

> There was no miasmatic savannah, nor any dense forest to be cleared; the genial southern breeze played over these reedy flats, which may one day be converted into clover-fields. For cattle stations, the land possessed every requisite, affording excellent winter grass, back among the scrubs to which cattle usually resort at certain seasons; while at others they could fatten on the rich grass of the plains, or during the summer heat enjoy the reeds amid abundance of water. . . . The fine open country afforded extensive views, and to the eastward and south-east, we saw hills with grassy sides, and crowned with callitris.[17]

At Pyramid Hill, he stood and wondered at the view of 'a land so inviting, and still without inhabitants!'

'As I stood, the first European intruder on the sublime solitude of these verdant plains, as yet untouched by flocks or herds,' he wrote, 'I felt conscious of being the harbinger of mighty changes; and that our steps would soon be followed by the men and the animals for which it seemed to have been prepared.'[18] He returned to the theme again and again, celebrating 'a country ready for the immediate reception of civilized man; and destined perhaps to become eventually a portion of a great empire. Unencumbered by too much wood, it yet possessed enough for all purposes; its soil was exuberant, and its climate temperate; it was . . . traversed by mighty rivers, and watered by streams innumerable. Of this Eden I was the first European to explore.'[19]

Though he seems something of a stolid, unimaginative character, Mitchell was keenly susceptible to natural beauty and relished the experience of waking and sleeping in the quiet of the remote bush:

> An Australian morning is always charming – amid these scenes of primæval nature it seemed exquisitely so. [The notes of] a small bird, resembling the softest breathings of a flute, were the only sounds that met the ear. What the stillness of even adds to such

sounds in other climes, is felt more intensely in the stillness of morning in this. . . . The perfume of the shrubs, of those even that have recently been burnt, and the tints and tones of the landscape, accord with the soft sounds. The light red tints of the *Anthistiria*, the brilliant green of the *Mimosa*, the white stems of the *Eucalyptus*, and the deep grey shadows of early morning, still slumbering about the woods, are blended and contrasted in the most pleasing harmony. The forms in the soft landscape are equally fine, from the wild fantastic tufting of the Eucalyptus, and its delicate willow-like ever-drooping leaf, to the prostrate ruins of the vegetable world. Instead of autumnal tints, there is a perpetual blending of the richest hues of autumn with the most brilliant verdure of spring; while the sun's welcome rays in a winter morning, and the cool breath of the woods in a summer morning, are equally grateful concomitants of such scenes.[20]

The return journey to Sydney was not without hardship, heavy rain in August making the going difficult. But the landscape was fascinating, especially that of the Grampians (a mountain range south-west of the Great Dividing Range, which he named after the Scottish Grampians); here precipitous gorges and strangely shaped sandstone formations were covered by an astonishing range of wild flowers. Mitchell as usual explored thoroughly, climbing Mount William, for instance, and spending two nights in mid-July near its peak in freezing temperatures, taking observations which could be used accurately to map the area. Stapylton wondered at his leader's constitution, which 'must be as hard as iron to stand three days without food wet thro the whole time a bitter wind from the Southward on the summit chilling the frame violently heated with perspiration from the fatigue of the ascent . . . but he appears not at all the worse for it at present but positively in better health'.[21]

A little over a week later he stood on a hill which he named Mount Arapiles, looked out over a lunar landscape and counted twenty-seven circular lakes below him.

Still travelling south-west, he discovered the Glenelg river, and followed it downstream almost to the sea at Discovery Bay – a sandbar prevented him from actually reaching the ocean. Mitchell gave his men a bottle of whiskey with which to celebrate the occasion. Then he turned east, crossed the Fitzroy river, and on 29 August came to Portland Bay, about 250km west of the then still tiny settlement of Melbourne. There, Tommy Came-last, who was a good tracker, reported to Mitchell that in what they assumed was this uninhabited area he had found fresh tracks of cattle and 'the shoe marks of a white man'. Mitchell thought the tracks must be those of a whaling party which had perhaps put ashore there, but was then amazed when they came upon a small settlement with some soundly built dwellings with well-stocked gardens (the potatoes and turnips 'surpassed in magnitude and quality any I had ever seen elsewhere').[22] A ship lay at anchor nearby, in the bay.

The houses belonged to the Henty brothers, the sons of a Sussex farmer who had emigrated with his wife and seven sons, settling first near Perth, but then deciding to move to Van Diemen's Land. One of the brothers, Edward, had peeled away from the family, and in 1834 set up at Portland Bay, chartering a vessel to bring him, his livestock and some labourers from Launceston. He was later joined by three of his brothers at what was the first real settlement in Victoria. Mitchell admired the fortitude and success of the men, and left them on good terms, his own men laden with as many vegetables as they could carry, wading across the Fitzroy river with the parcels on their heads.

Mitchell continued to survey as he went. Three times he climbed Mount Napier, an extinct volcano, to make sure his observations were correct. There was another break in the journey, to carry out triangulation at Mount Abrupt; Mitchell noted that the view from the summit was perhaps the most impressive of the whole expedition. In the meantime, there was tedious plodding through soft, muddy ground, the cattle and horses tired out by their efforts. The party split in two, Stapylton taking charge of the smaller group, which was to camp for a fortnight to rest the cattle, and then to follow Mitchell and his party.

With astonishing energy considering that for some time there had been a serious shortage of food, Mitchell pressed on, climbing

Mount Alexander (which reminded him of the Pyrenees) and riding up Mount Macedon. He crossed the Goulburn river, 50m wide, and named the Campaspe river after a mistress of Alexander the Great, a classical education being a considerable help in naming geographical features, once one had run out of the names of influential patrons and those of one's friends and colleagues.

Further on, past the Ovens river, they reached the Murray again, and crossed it. By this time there was a real problem with shortage of supplies, which was resolved in the short term by shooting one of the horses. At no point during this third expedition did Mitchell seriously fear starvation; but there were plenty of times when food and water were scarce – occasionally, the men went without water for as long as two days. Their provisions ran out again at the end of October, but with explorers' luck, they chanced upon a small shack and an old man who was able to let them have two days' supply of food and water.

By then, they were relieved to find themselves back on a road; a proper *road*, noted Mitchell, underlining the word. He had not seen a path with a reasonable surface for the entire seven months, a period during which he and his party had travelled over 4,000km. At Sydney, he was happy to report not only his successful survey of a large tract of previously unknown land, but also his discovery of *Australia Felix* – a happy country whose fertile soil looked likely to support settlers with every chance of success and prosperity.

The Governor was impressed by the geographical element of the report, but unimpressed by the accounts of skirmishes with the Aboriginals and at Mitchell's failure to keep his men out of such trouble. Such was his disquiet that he set up an Enquiry by an Executive Council consisting of himself, the Bishop of Australia and the Colonial Secretary. They summoned witnesses and concluded that they 'would not too severely blame a want of coolness and presence of mind which is the lot of few men to possess' (words that would not have delighted Mitchell), and that while they did not wish to mar 'the credit of so useful an enterprise', they 'were distressed that Mitchell should have exhibited a spirit more of exultation than regret' when speaking of it.[23]

Mitchell went back to England with his wife and eight children, on eighteen months' leave at half pay. He prolonged his visit, actually remaining in England for two years, writing an account of his expeditions, which was published in 1838 in two volumes. The book was a success in every way except financially. The erstwhile explorer busied himself trying for a knighthood, but found this uphill work;[24] he was, however, made an honorary doctor of civil law by the University of Oxford, where his books were enthusiastically received. He greatly enjoyed praise, and would have liked to enjoy it longer, but finally had to return to work or lose his position. Thus he was seated back at his desk, if a little late, on 4 February 1841.

Governor Bourke had left Australia in December 1837 to be replaced by Sir George Gipps, who admired Mitchell even less than had Darling – Gipps had written to London asserting that Mitchell had made 'no discoveries which could be turned to profit, with the exception perhaps of the fertile land of Australia Felix, which would surely have been reached by the ordinary advance of our graziers, even though he had never visited it'.[25]

There were several causes of controversy between them, mainly to do with administration. In 1843, a plan was afoot to investigate the possibility of laying down a road from Sydney via Bathurst and Fort Bourke either to Port Essington[26] or to the head of the Gulf of Carpentaria. The advantage of such a road lay in the fact that an overland route from Sydney to the Indian Ocean would greatly shorten the time it took for supplies and produce to make their way from New South Wales to Britain, and would also allow traffic to avoid the dangers of navigating the Torres Straits. Mitchell, though now 54 years old, was eager to lead an expedition; he discussed the possibility with the German naturalist Friedrich Leichhardt, who was also interested at the prospect.

There was some delay before Gibb gave Mitchell the go-ahead – the British government was worried about the expense. Then in August

1844 Leichhardt set off with an expedition from Moreton to Port Essington, which covered some of Mitchell's proposed route. Final approval was not given to Mitchell until November 1845, by which time not only Leichhardt[27] but Sturt too had almost completed their expeditions, covering much of the area Mitchell had hoped to be the first to explore.

Mitchell finally set off on his fourth expedition on 8 December 1845, intent on chaining his whole route.[28] His party included his servant Brown, described as a 'tent-keeper', Edmund Kennedy, assistant surveyor and second in command, W. Stephenson, surgeon and natural history collector, eight bullock-drivers, two carpenters, a shoemaker, a blacksmith, a barometer-carrier, twenty-three convicts (two of them 'chainmen') and the ubiquitous Piper. There were seventeen horses, three carts, eight drays, 112 bullocks and 250 sheep (the former carrying supplies and pulling the carts and drays, the latter for food). There were provisions, Mitchell calculated, for a year. There were also two boats made, this time, of iron. When not afloat, they did duty as cattle troughs.

On his fourth expedition Mitchell's two iron boats came in handy as drinking troughs. *(Mitchell's* Journals*)*

At first, Mitchell travelled over country with which he was already familiar, from Boree to Fort Bourke, past the scene of Cunningham's murder. The temperature was intolerable – up to 130°F in the shade – and almost immediately there was a shortage of water, three dogs died from the heat, and the eyes of several of the men, including Mitchell, suffered from the dryness of the atmosphere. One morning Mitchell woke to find himself almost completely blind. He sent a convict and an Aboriginal guide, Yuranigh, to collect leeches from a pond and applied fourteen to his eyes: by evening he was so recovered that he could observe the stars keenly enough to note his latitude.

Now there was trouble with Piper (surely Mitchell might have foreseen this?). The 'civilised' Aboriginal had received a great deal of publicity as a result of the previous expeditions, and had got above himself. Though a truly dreadful shot, he had insisted on carrying a double-barrelled gun (of which everyone was terrified), had grown lazy, and stole the rations of the two other Aboriginals who had joined the expedition. He had also sneaked off and visited some nearby *gins*. Mitchell decided he could do without such irritating diversions and dispatched him, under escort, to the nearest police station. It meant losing two men, but it was well worth it to be rid of such a troublesome character.

Reaching the junction of the Murray and Darling rivers, Mitchell received a dispatch from his second son Roderick (an engineer now a Commissioner of Crown Lands in New South Wales), who had recently journeyed down the Darling. He was able to pass on some useful information about the rivers to the north of his father's position. These included the Narran and Balonne, the junction of which Mitchell reached on 1 April. Ten days later he reached a fine lake, which he named Lake Parachute, and on whose bank he established a depot. Within a week, as he was setting off once more to the north, he received a discouraging dispatch announcing Leichhardt's triumphant return to Sydney from Port Essington: his own hopes of being the first to reach the Indian Ocean by land were dashed.

The party had encountered few Aboriginals during their expedition, but on 2 May heard some near their camp, and the following morning three men approached the explorers:

Intense curiosity in these men had evidently overcome all their fears of such strangers. They were entirely naked, and without any kind of ornament or weapon, offensive or defensive. With steady fixed looks, eyes wide open, and serious intelligent countenances, what passed in their minds was not disguised, as is usual with savages. On the contrary, there was a manly openness of countenance, and a look of good sense about them, which would have gained my full confidence, could we but have understood each other. . . . There must be an original vein of mind in these aboriginal men of the land. They had never before seen white men, and behaved as properly as it was possible for men in their situation to do. At length we set out on our journey . . . my horse seemed very much to astonish them.[29]

On the road, Mitchell indulged his passion for hill-climbing as he went (he named Mounts Redcap, Abundance, Bindango and Bindyego – the two latter Aboriginal names; he was always eager to use these when he could discover them from local tribesmen). On 8 May he came to another splendid tract of country, 'a champaign region' he called it, where a fine landscape stretched as far as the eye could see, well watered by rivers and supporting excellent woodland. He named the area FitzRoy Downs. On 17 May he reached the Maranoa river, from there deciding to travel due north, confident that he would find, if not the Great Inland Sea, at least a great river flowing to the Gulf of Carpentaria.

After a month spent exploring the peaks of the Great Dividing Range, on 21 July Mitchell believed he had at last found the head of a river that flowed north, or at least north-west. But as had happened earlier, it soon petered out into a chain of ponds. He gave up the search and turned south again, once more crossing land which seemed to him wonderfully fertile. When he veered westward, however, still looking for the fabled river, he struck rough country. A scrub of matted vines hung down in front of the explorers and, if they weren't seen in time, pulled the men off their horses. Then dense forest almost completely impeded their progress, and many hours were spent forcing their way through scrubs. Next day they pushed through a malga scrub, 'the "malga" being a tree having hard spiky dry branches which project like fixed bayonets, to receive the charge of ourselves, horses, and flour-bags'.[30]

In mid-August Mitchell arrived at a river which he thought really must run into the Gulf of Carpentaria; but it changed direction and petered out. On 15 September, however, he believed he had triumphed. He rode out to a gap in a rocky ridge, climbed on to one of the highest rocks, and saw 'a line of trees [which] marked the course of a river traceable to the remotest verge of the horizon. There I found then, at last, the realization of my long cherished hopes, an interior river falling to the N.W. in the heart of an open country extending also in that direction. Ulloa's[31] delight at the first view of the Pacific could not have surpassed him on this occasion, nor could the fervour with which he was impressed at the moment have exceeded my sense of gratitude, for being allowed to make such a discovery.'[32]

He rode on over more splendid pastoral country and reached the banks of the river, as broad as the Murray and 'the Eldorado of Australia', as Mitchell believed; a river that in essence led to India. He turned east, making for Sydney, and arrived home on 29 September with the news of his find. A new governor, Sir Charles FitzRoy, was delighted and awarded gratuities to the men who had accompanied Mitchell, and promised to recommend a pardon for those convicts who had taken part.

Alas, Mitchell's great discovery was an illusion. The river he had found and named the Victoria was actually the Barcoo, which changed course not far from where he had come upon it, and flowed south-west to join Cooper's Creek and thence into Lake Eyre. But though the main purpose of his last expedition had not been achieved, he had discovered some of the richest arable land yet found in Australia. He was also an exceptionally gifted surveyor and, as his published journals show, no mean author. His reputation was perhaps unfairly sullied by the fatal clashes his men had with the Aboriginals; he alone among the great explorers is still regarded with suspicion for that reason, yet others were just as culpable.

It is worth remembering, too, that if Mitchell treated the Aboriginals with sadly typical condescension, he did not stint his praise of such of their qualities as he admired, and was generous to those who had assisted him on his expeditions, in particular to Yuranigh, who had accompanied him throughout the whole of the last expedition, and whom he regarded as his 'guide, companion, counsellor and friend' whose 'intelligence and judgement rendered him so necessary to me that he was ever at my elbow'. So sympathetically did Mitchell describe the man in his book about the expedition that a reader was moved to send a guinea, to be forwarded to Yuranigh. Unfortunately, the Aboriginal died before the present reached him. Mitchell had a stone placed over his grave:

> To Native Courage Honesty and Fidelity
> YURANIGH
> who accompanied the Expedition of Discovery
> Into Tropical Australia in 1846 lies buried here
> According to the Rites of his Countrymen.

Mitchell himself went back to England for a while, then returned to his work in Sydney. In 1851 he fought the last duel ever to take place in Australia, the result of a dispute between him and a Mr Donaldson, during an election campaign. The two men exchanged three shots, the last of which passed through Donaldson's hat. Mitchell died on 5 October 1855, leaving the Surveyor's Office in a severe state of disarray, his duties (an official minute alleged) 'very much neglected and very imperfectly performed'.[33] He was nevertheless buried with full military honours.

Between 1831 and 1837 discoveries continued to be made piecemeal. In 1831 Governor Darling dispatched Captain Collet Barker, of the 39th Regiment, to explore the country to the west of Lake Alexandrina. Barker discovered a fine site for a port at the mouth of the River Torrens. In a sense he thus became the founder of Adelaide, though it was Surveyor-General Col William Light who, in 1836, approved the place as a site for the city. Barker mysteriously vanished near the mouth of the Murray river. However, there was no mystery surrounding the deaths of two Hobart men, Joseph Tice Gellibrand and George Brooks Hesse, who went out into unknown country near what is now the Carlisle State Park, in Victoria. They were killed by Aboriginals, protecting their territory, and their bodies thrown into Lake Colac. They enjoyed posthumous fame, however, for in searching for their remains other men found excellent pastoral land.

The quest for good grazing land drove the explorers who uncovered the riches of Victoria – John Batman, for instance, the son of a convict who, together with a government surveyor, John Helder Wedge, first found fine pastoral land in 1835 in the area of what is now the Plenty river, 35km from Melbourne, and 'bought' 245,000 hectares of land from the local Aboriginal chiefs in exchange for a motley collection of knives, beads, scissors, mirrors and flour. They went on to discover the Yarra river and, following it towards the sea, found a delightful waterfall, and thought the spot would make a pleasant place for a village. Within three years, Melbourne had been founded there and grew large enough to be declared a city.

FIVE

The Heroic Heart
Edward John Eyre, 1839–41

*Eyre was the first explorer to make substantial efforts to find
land in South Australia good enough to graze livestock and be
farmed by the new generation of free settlers who began to
flood into the country in the late 1830s. As was the case with
almost all the great Australian explorers, he was born far from
the scorching wastes which almost claimed his life – at
Whipsnade, in Bedfordshire, on 5 August 1815, the third son of
a local curate. When he left school his father gave him £400
and bought him a passage to Sydney on the barque* Ellen. *The
16-year-old sailed on 13 October 1832, landing in Australia on
28 March the following year.*

Unlike most of the other early explorers, Eyre actually had good
experience of the bush country. After a very short time in
Australia he realised that his only chance of making some kind of
life for himself was to get out of the town, which he did after only a
month as the result of a lucky encounter with a fellow passenger on
the *Ellen*. Captain Edward Dumaresq was the brother-in-law of
Ralph Darling, the Governor of New South Wales, and younger
brother of Henry Dumaresq, an extremely wealthy farmer. When
Eyre was introduced to Henry Dumaresq, the latter kindly invited
him to visit him on his station, St Heliers, on the Hunter river,
150km or so north of Sydney. His sensible advice to the boy was
that he get some practical experience of farming, and he gave him an
introduction to William Bell, a settler with a property 40km away,
at Cheshunt Park. There, as a sort of paying apprentice, Eyre was
shown the business of rearing sheep and cattle. He learned quickly

and within a month had invested in 400 lambs, which cost him over half his dwindling capital. By the end of the year he not only felt sufficiently confident to buy eight rams and two ewes, but also to purchase his own property, 500km away at Molonglo Plains, near what is now Canberra.

He bought the land sight unseen, but fortunately found it to be a reasonably good investment, and within two months had built himself a thatched homestead with two main rooms and a couple of lean-to bedrooms. He called it Woodlands. As a landowner he was able to apply for convict labour, and was assigned six convicts, one of whom, John Baxter, he appointed overseer; he also employed two servants, one of them an excellent drover. Within a very short time he had established himself as a settler.

So far Eyre's good sense had paid off, but his luck did not hold. At Woodlands he was visited by John Morphy, another fellow passenger on the *Ellen*. Morphy talked him into taking a share in a flock of 5,000 sheep which were to be collected from the Liverpool Plains, near Tamworth, almost 700km away. The plan was that Eyre would keep them for three years, then sell them. However, when he and Morphy arrived at the farm at Page's river, they were appalled to find that the sheep were diseased – the scab caused them to lose their wool, and made it illegal to sell them for meat or to move them across country.

Eyre and Morphy wasted nine months treating the sheep, a tedious and unpleasant business during which they lived in a tarpaulin tent. When his animals were cured, Eyre had to drive them to Woodlands over the trackless Great Dividing Range, a task that at least taught him much about the unrelenting nature of the country in which he had settled and of his capacity to put up with hardship, for the two men spent many days in harsh weather without sleep or shelter of any kind.

There was not in the end a great deal of profit from the deal, or from Eyre's partnership with Morphy (which he soon dissolved). Having proved himself capable of putting up with any hardship with which overland travel might tax him, Eyre decided in January 1837 to sell Woodlands, give up farming and instead make money by overlanding stock to Port Phillip, the area of which the central town, still only a collection of a dozen or so wattle-and-daub huts and many tents, was named after the British Prime Minister, Lord Melbourne. A Robert Campbell commissioned him to drive some of his stock to Port Phillip, and Campbell's son Charles advanced him £500 against expenses. In Sydney to gather together supplies for the journey, Eyre met the explorer Charles Sturt, with whom he became firm friends and who advised him on the nature of the land that lay between Sydney and Port Phillip. On 1 April 1837, Eyre set out – late because all his men had got drunk the night before and needed several hours to recover.

He had divided his party into two. An English couple, a shepherd and a watchman, herded 414 sheep; Baxter led 78 head of cattle, with eight men and a young man described as a 'gentleman', who it seems went along for the excursion (this occasionally happened; it was the case with the unfortunate young artist who accompanied Grey on his West Australian expedition).[1]

It was a hard but successful enterprise. Crossing the Murrumbidgee river presented some difficulties, but on 15 July Eyre arrived at Fawkner's Hotel, Melbourne's first public house, together with two young Aboriginal boys he had come across on the way. He became devoted to Cootachah (whom he nicknamed Yarry) and Joshuing, who were good trackers and useful interpreters, and nearer his own age – he was now 22 – than his other companions. By 2 August the whole party had reached the town, having accomplished the 756km journey in thirteen weeks with the loss of only 14 sheep, though 86 lambs had been born on the way.

It had been an effective and profitable trip, and Eyre now made his way back to Sydney via Hobart (there was no direct sea-route between Sydney and the inconsiderable town of Melbourne) with Baxter, two dogs and the two Aboriginal boys. At Launceston Baxter decided to walk to Hobart with the two dogs (presumably to save money) while Eyre and the boys went on by mail coach. While waiting for a passage, Eyre was glad of some relaxation, and took the opportunity to take Yarry and Joshuing to the theatre, where they were the centre of attention, given sweets by the ladies in the audience. The boys thought less of the actors than they did of the troops they saw parading later in the town, where again their presence excited much interest and they were surrounded by the curious people of Hobart. (There was practically no contact between the townspeople and the local Aboriginals of the Nuenonne tribe, whom only seven years earlier the Governor had described as 'a horde of savages whose prowess is not equal to their revengeful feelings', and actually offered £5 for every adult and £2 for every child delivered alive to the Hobart police station.[2])

On 4 October the *Marion Watson* left Hobart, arriving a week later at Sydney. (Here the latest news was of the death of the king and the succession of a young queen, Victoria.) Eyre was eager to repeat his success, and now decided to be the first to drive stock overland to Adelaide. It would be a much longer journey, over unknown country, and there were stories of dangerous, antagonistic native tribes. This did not deter Eyre, who consulted Sturt on how to use a sextant and artificial horizon to determine latitude,[3] and on 8 November was off again to Campbell's farm at Limestone Plains, where 300 head of cattle were rounded up. With these plus a few sheep to slaughter for food on the way, he left for Adelaide on 21 December, accompanied by Baxter, six other men, Yarry, Joshuing and a third Aboriginal boy, Unmallie.

The route which he had chosen, on advice from Sturt and based partly on information gathered by Mitchell, proved to be hard going. Tramping over many miles of scrubland without grass or water disheartened him and his men, some of whom deserted (they had run out of tobacco, they said, and wanted to go to Melbourne rather than on to Adelaide).[4] To compound his difficulties, Mitchell's maps proved inaccurate. Eyre decided on another route, near the Murray river. He had had time, on the way, to look about him:

Of birds we saw many varieties I had never seen before, particularly the parrot tribe, besides those were beautiful birds the rose cockatoo and the crested pigeon of the marsh – both of whom were numerous. The cliffs which enclose the valley of the

Murray are of singular and interesting formation, consisting principally of cream-coloured limestone, and rising to a height of three or four hundred feet. In these fossils are plentifully embedded and very handsome, and I doubt not valuable specimens might be procured by anyone who had time to give his attention to the subject.

He was also sanguine about the future of the area:

Though the line of road between this colony and New South Wales is far from being favourable for the immigration of sheep, yet I consider it by no means an impractical one, and think that if they are brought in small flocks and a favourable season be selected, the experiment may be safely and successfully attempted, and the colonists of this flourishing settlement have the pleasure of seeing an additional source of wealth and prosperity introduced to them at a much lower rate than can be attained by water.[5]

Eyre again made an excellent profit, returning to Sydney by sea and wasting no time in organising another trip, leaving for Limestone Plains again within twelve days. He now became the first man to herd sheep from New South Wales to Adelaide – a thousand of them, together with six hundred head of cattle. This time the journey was as trouble-free as could be, apart from the fact that the young Aboriginal Unmallie had a fight with one of the men and ran off; to replace him Eyre recruited another Aboriginal boy, Neramberein, whom he nicknamed Joey. The party reached Adelaide on 12 March 1839, having taken only twenty-one weeks to tramp 1,540km. An advertisement appeared in the newspapers offering '1,000 aged wethers fit for immediate slaughter. These superior sheep have never had any disease and having been all selected large and strong for travelling, present to the butcher an opportunity rarely to be met with of obtaining meat of the very best description.'[6]

Eyre, who had got £2 a head for sheep he had bought for 10 shillings each, presented a joint to the Governor, who thought it 'could not be surpassed in appearance by any in a London butcher's shop at Christmas'.[7] Eyre made a profit of £4,000, although half of it went to Campbell.

Eyre had become so gripped by the challenge of finding his way through unmapped country, and his interest so roused by his talks with Sturt, that having a tidy sum of money at his command he decided to set up his own expedition of exploration to the country north of Adelaide. His preparations made, on 1 May 1839 he started out on a three-months' expedition into the unknown, accompanied by Baxter, Cootachah and Neramberein, ten horses, three dogs and eight sheep (for food).

Passing the last sign of human habitation, a settlement on the Gawler river, he forded the Broughton (which he named after his acquaintance the Bishop of Sydney) and another river which he called Crystal Brook, because of the clarity of its water. He crossed a range of hills which he named after his partner Campbell, then came to the arid Flinders Ranges. Here all seemed desolate wasteland. From Mount Arden he discerned in the distance what looked like a glittering white sea – his first sight of Lake Torrens. Yet a tramp on foot of over 56km, during which he almost died of thirst, revealed only more sandy desolation. His supplies almost exhausted, Eyre decided to turn back to Adelaide, where he wrote up his report of the expedition while Baxter got drunk.

Eyre's first expedition was not very profitable as far as important discoveries were concerned. He rested for a mere month, then was off again, this time to explore what is now known as the Eyre Peninsula,[8] and to discover whether it might be possible to find a line of communication with the far west.

He sailed from Adelaide on 8 July 1839 and landed 650km along the coast at Port Lincoln, at the southernmost tip of the Eyre Peninsula (it was later to be considered as a site for the capital of South Australia). From there he set out on 5 August 1839, his twenty-fourth birthday. The usual difficulty of finding drinkable water (he came across only three springs during the whole 1,000km journey) drove him on through barren, melancholy country – although he was the first to see one of the most beautiful of all desert flowers, the desert pea:[9] 'quite new to me and very beautiful;

the leaf was like that of a vetch, but larger, the flower bright scarlet, with a rich purple centre, shaped like a half globe with the convex side outwards . . . something like a sweet pea in shape . . . altogether one of the prettiest and richest looking flowers I have seen in Australia'.[10] It was also on this trip that he confirmed that the shining salt sea he had seen earlier was indeed a lake, and named it Lake Torrens.

Eyre concluded that the most profitable area for exploration was probably the land to the north. He wrote an article for the *South Australian Register* in which he theorised about the possibility of finding a route between Adelaide and Western Australia, and not only offered to lead an expedition, but to find one-third of the necessary horses and pay one-third of the expenses. The offer was enthusiastically accepted by the governor and notables of the town, who believed that any possible route from Adelaide to Perth would be well worth developing. The citizens of Perth were less sanguine. Western Australia was a free colony, and the idea that convicts might make their way there was a constant fear. The *Perth Gazette* was much against the proposal to open out any kind of path between West and South Australia: 'The steady course of the country should not be disturbed by such wild adventures. What is South Australia to us? . . . They have revelled in moonshine long enough, and we ought not to be such fools as to be caught by a mere puffing proposal. If we wish to see them, we can soon find our way, and we require no puffing advertisement from the neighbouring colony of high-minded pretensions.'[11]

Eyre, undaunted, began to build his team. Baxter, a serious drunkard who had nevertheless proved a knowledgeable and shrewd overseer, would accompany him, together with the two Aboriginal boys, Neramberein and Yarry. He invited along a young friend, Edward Bate Scott, and also commissioned Corporal Coles, the soldier who had accompanied Grey on the north-west coast, and was now personal servant to the surveyor-general, who kindly loaned him to Eyre.[12] John Houston and Robert McRobert were to drive the drays; there were thirteen horses and forty sheep (for food) and sufficient stores to last the expedition three months.

The enthusiastic ladies and gentlemen of Adelaide rode out with Eyre and his companions as they set off on their 1840 expedition, making the occasion resemble a chaotic fashionable rout. *(Eyre's* Journals*)*

By 18 June 1840 Eyre was ready to leave. There was a great farewell breakfast at Government House, at which Sturt presented Eyre with a silken Union Jack sewn by the ladies of Adelaide, which (Sturt said in his address) Eyre was to carry 'to the centre of a mighty continent, there to leave it as a sign to the savage that the footstep of civilized man has penetrated so far'.[13]

The party rode off, surrounded by a large number of men on horseback and ladies in carriages. A contemporary illustration of the occasion looks more like the record of a society fox-hunt than the start of a serious expedition. 'We had moved off at a gentle canter,' wrote Eyre, 'but were scarcely outside the gates before the cheering of the people, the waving of hats, and the rush of so many horses, produced an emulation in the noble steeds that almost took us from the control of their pace as we dashed over the bridge and up the hill in North Adelaide – it was a heart-stirring and inspiriting scene.'[14]

They made good progress through the rich country north of the Gawler, and on 3 July arrived at a base Eyre had established earlier at Mount Arden. He left the main party there and rode on with only one of the Aboriginal boys to Lake Torrens, where he found 'the dry bed of the lake coated completely over with a crust of salt, forming one unbroken sheet of pure white, and glittering brilliantly in the sun. On stepping on this I found that it yielded to the foot, and that below the surface the bed of the lake consisted of a soft mud, and the further we advanced to the westward the more boggy it got, so that at last it became quite impossible to proceed . . .'[15]

There was no way of crossing the lake and to follow its shore was impossible for there was neither water nor grass for the horses; if rain fell, the water in any pool quickly became saline. A disturbing mirage made it impossible to guess at the real size of the lake: he named a nearby hill, where he had hoped to find water, Mount Deception. Now very short of water, he decided to make for the Flinders Range (as he had called the range of hills north-east of Mount Arden). To the north-west he eventually found a rocky gully with a deep pool of water: he called the place Depôt Pool, and moved the main party there. When camp was established, he left for another exploration with one of his men and the second Aboriginal boy.[16] They drove a dray loaded with water for 80km, at which point they buried a 250-litre (65gal) can of water before riding on for another 80km and finding another lake, now called Lake Eyre South, but situated in completely barren country. They returned to the buried water and then, on 24 August, to Depôt Pool, having covered 160km of desert. There they prepared for a longer trek, distributing rations and then burying what stores remained, 'to await our return, if ever it should be our lot to reach the place again'.[17]

The whole area around Depôt Pool was clearly not the kind of country which could sustain settlers: there were no rivers to water the Strzelecki Desert (as it is now called), and no land suitable for farming. Eyre had had enough of exploring inland, and decided to turn west and explore the country between Spencer Gulf and King George Sound. The decision weighed on his mind, though no more so than other decisions he had had to make. As he wrote in his journal, in words which every Australian explorer would have approved,

Little indeed are the public aware of the difficulties and responsibilities attached to the command of an expedition of exploration – the incessant toil, the sleepless hours, the anxious thoughts that necessarily fall to the share of the leader of a party under circumstances of difficulty or danger, are but imperfectly appreciated by the world at large. Accustomed to judge of undertakings only by their results, they are frequently as unjust in their censure as they are excessive in their approval. The traveller who discovers a rich and well watered district, encounters but few of the hardships, and still fewer of the anxieties, that fall to the lot of the explorer in desert regions, yet is the former lauded with praise, whilst the later is condemned to obloquy; although the success perhaps of the one, or the failure of the other, may have arisen from circumstances over which individually neither had any control.[18]

At the Baxter Range he divided his party, sending Baxter and two men with one of the Aboriginal boys, seven horses and some sheep west towards Streaky Bay,[19] 420km away, while he, Scott, one man and the other boy made their way to Port Lincoln for additional supplies. They would then join Baxter's group.

On 21 September Eyre set off to the south-west, and on the first evening one of the Aboriginal boys spotted an excellent series of waterholes, which was a good omen. Less good was a brush with a local Aboriginal tribe, some of whose members stole Eyre's horizon glass, a spade, a hoe and various other items unwisely left outside the tents. It was the first serious trouble he had had with the natives, whom he treated with respect and who mostly returned the compliment. He was genuinely interested in them, an interest no doubt sharpened by his close relationship with the two native boys.

Eyre reached Port Lincoln on 4 October, where he set up camp just outside the town and wrote and dispatched a report to the Exploration Committee in Adelaide in which he warmly recommended the route he had followed from Baxter Range to Port Lincoln as a highway for the movement of cattle. On the other hand he could not recommend the countryside itself; it was barren and unlikely to be able to support settlers.[20]

During the three weeks Eyre spent at Port Lincoln, there was an incident which led him to seriously reconsider his friendly attitude towards the Aboriginal tribes of Australia. A 12-year-old white boy, the son of a settler, was speared by natives at a station a short way from Eyre's tent. He had been alone in his father's station when it was surrounded by Aboriginals asking for food. He gave them what bread and rice he had, and when they showed signs of wanting to enter the house, locked the door and faced them with a sword and a gun. Two spears, 7ft long, then struck him in the chest, and the natives ran away. The boy tried to pull the spears out of his flesh and, when he could not, sat down by the fire and attempted to burn them off. He was found late that evening by his brother and taken to the local hospital. The Aboriginal who threw the spear was never found.

Eyre was concerned by the story. He could, he said, have understood it if the Aboriginals had never seen a white child before; sheer fright might have provoked them – besides which, how would white people react if frightening strangers appeared, apparently intent on occupying land which was sacred to them? Thankfully, the incident was almost without precedent: 'I shall be borne out, I think, by facts when I state that the Aboriginals of this country have seldom been guilty of wanton or unprovoked outrages, or committed acts of rapine or bloodshed, without some strongly exciting cause, or under the influence of feelings that would have weighed in the same degree with Europeans in similar circumstances.'

He then went on to list, in a passage that caused some outrage among right-wing readers of his *Journals*, several points of which those white people 'occupying' the country might take note. First, the Aboriginals considered the very presence of white men in their country an act of 'intrusion and aggression'. Second, they could not think why the white man had come at all if not to take their land – which was indeed the motive. Moreover, the land taken by the white men was on the whole the *best* land, rich for cultivation and plentifully supplied with water. Finally, white men had laws which *they* considered important, and they should consider that Aboriginal laws might be equally important to the natives.

These pages are an extraordinarily liberal document, unique among the writings of the Australian explorers. The Aboriginal who protested and even took violent action against the white settlers was, Eyre concluded, 'doing what men in a more civilised state would have done under the same circumstances, what they daily do under the sanction of the law of nations – a law that provides not for the safety, privileges, and protection of the Aboriginals, and owners of the soil, but which merely lays down rules for the direction of the privileged robber in the distribution of the booty of any newly discovered country'.[21]

Three cheers, one might say, for Eyre.

When he had replenished his stores, dismissed one man and taken on another, Eyre set out again on 31 October 1840 towards King George Sound. He arrived at Streaky Bay on 3 November, where he found Baxter in good heart, enjoying the large quantities of excellent oysters available on the mud banks. His companions were looking particularly healthy on this diet, and they certainly needed their health and strength to cut their way for 27km through the most intractable bush. Men and horses were completely exhausted by the time they arrived at Fowler's Bay, where the colonial cutter *Waterwitch* carried, as arranged, some fresh water for them, though not as much as Eyre expected.

At Denial Bay, further on and where he established a depot, Eyre was able to recruit an Aboriginal guide from among a group of friendly natives. Wilguddy, 'an intelligent, cheerful old man',[22] was persuaded to mount a horse – a sensational sight for his friends, who followed the expedition for some time on foot, hunting as they went and presenting the explorers with gifts of snakes, lizards, guanas, bandicoots and rats as a contribution to their stores. A particular delicacy was the eggs of the wild pheasant.

Eyre and Neramberein explored the area, alone, for water but found none, their horses suffering so much from dehydration that they had to tie one up and leave him, hoping to return with water to succour him (which they eventually did). Eyre was always particularly sympathetic to the sufferings of his horses: 'It is painful in the extreme to be obliged to subject them to such hardships,' he wrote, 'but alas, in such a country, what else can be done?'[23]

On 28 November Eyre set out again, with Neramberein, on another attempt to find a way through the trackless desert. Although they took 265 litres (70gal) of water with them, transported on a dray driven by John Houston, it proved completely insufficient for their needs. The explorers' own energy was almost entirely expended in the driving necessary to find water, by the unfortunately useless digging of wells in the desert sand, and in trekking hopefully in various directions, none of which proved fruitful. The horses were driven for four days and nights without drinking, and the Aboriginal tribesmen they met warned them not to go on – there was no hope of finding water in the direction they were taking. Eyre hoped to reach the Great Bight, where the Nullarbor Plain ends in a wall of weather-beaten cliff exposed to the Southern Ocean, one of the longest unbroken lines of cliff in the world, 1,000km long and 100m high. Once or twice he thought he glimpsed the sea but eventually realised that he must retrace his steps to the bay where the *Waterwitch* was waiting.

To lighten the horses' loads he decided to bury what supplies of food and water he had, together with the harnesses and pack-saddles, but could not do so while the Aboriginals were watching, for he knew that the moment he was out of sight they would dig the goods up. So he and the others sat for an infuriating day in the heat waiting for the natives to move on, which they were reluctant to do. Eventually they collected their spears and left; Eyre buried his supplies, and made his tedious way back over 40km of desert, to the cutter.

Not yet beaten, Eyre decided to send Houston and Corporal Coles back to Adelaide on the *Waterwitch* while he made one more attempt to conquer the desert and locate the head of the Bight. He must have known what a hazardous ambition this was. Up to now he had been able to rely on the cutter in an extremity; but as he marched westwards the coast would grow more treacherous, and there would be no safe place for the ship to shelter. Writing to the Governor, he said that after waiting for five or six weeks to rest the remaining horses (four of them had died from their exertions and lack of food and water) he was determined to round the Bight and then strike north to explore the interior.

While he waited for the *Waterwitch* to make the trip to Adelaide and return with more necessary stores, between 30 December and mid-January 1841 he made another short, fruitless attempt to reach the Bight, but was again forced back by lack of water. So far, he had ridden over 1,000km and accomplished little; he could not resist venting his frustration in his journal: 'None but a person who has been similarly circumstanced, can at all conceive the incessant toil and harassing anxiety of the explorer; when baffled and defeated, he has to traverse over and over again the same dreary wastes, gaining but a few miles of ground at each fresh attempt, whilst each renewal of the effort but exhausts still more the strength and condition of his animals, or the energy and spirits of his men.'[24]

The arrival of a cutter, the *Hero*,[25] was welcome not only because it brought fresh supplies, letters and a dog sent to him as a present by Sturt, but because it also carried an Aboriginal called Wylie, a man from King George Sound in West Australia, who could speak the language of the local natives and had wide experience of desert conditions. The ship also brought a letter from the Governor advising Eyre to give up a project which had clearly become quite mad. But Eyre was determined to make one last do-or-die attempt to round the Bight, heartened that he would have such an experienced guide as Wylie. Apart from the Aboriginal, he was determined to take with him as few men as possible: he would ask Baxter to be the only white man to accompany him, and take only him, Wylie, Neramberein and Cootachah. The others would return to Adelaide on the *Hero*.

He was frank with Baxter: the journey he now contemplated would not be of less than 1,300km. Baxter knew as well as he the difficulties of finding water in the desert (though Eyre hoped the expertise of Wylie and the other Aboriginal boys would help, for instance by recovering water from the roots of certain bushes). Eyre could offer nothing but 'unceasing toil, privation, anxiety . . . and more than ordinary risk and danger'. But he was determined 'either to accomplish the object [he] had in view, or to perish in the attempt'.[26] Baxter reluctantly agreed to go with him.

Such reluctance was understandable. Apart from the dangers, what could such a journey hope to achieve? What use could it possibly be? The coastline along which Eyre intended to travel had already been well surveyed by sea, and nothing could be added to what was already known from the marine surveys. It is difficult not to believe that Eyre's sole objective was to become the first white man to cross the desert between West and South Australia. No wonder Baxter was an unwilling partner in so foolish an enterprise.

Eyre and Baxter, with the three Aboriginals, set off again on 25 February 1841 with nine horses, one pony, one foal recently born, and six sheep. Well rested, the horses were in excellent condition – indeed, they were too frisky, for when one was startled, perhaps by a snake, he set off at a gallop and, pursued by the others, raced over the desert for 5 miles, during which they shed all their loads; Eyre and Wylie chased after them, retrieving all the baggage as they went. By the time they caught and reloaded them it was dark, and they had to camp within a few miles of their depot.

On 2 March they reached the head of the Bight, but the journey had started as though to prove Eyre's pessimistic forecast true: it was indeed to require every ounce of fortitude the explorers could muster. The land over which they were travelling was pure desert, and the sand was a curse: 'It floated on the surface of the water, penetrated into our clothes, hair, eyes and ears, our provisions were covered over with it, and our blankets half buried when we lay down at night – it was a perpetual and never-ceasing torment, and as if to increase our miseries we were again afflicted with swarms of large horse-flies, which bit us dreadfully.'[27]

Occasionally, as they tramped along the shore, they came across the wreckage of a ship that had been driven on to the treacherous coast. Progress was so slow that Eyre decided to press on with the youngest Aboriginal and the sheep, leaving Baxter and the others to follow his tracks with the packhorses. After three days of this, the two horses he had taken with him were so dehydrated that they could no longer eat. Eyre was walking in his sleep, jolted awake only when he stumbled or received a blow in the face from the bough of a tree. At three in the morning he and the boy fell to the ground with exhaustion, and slept where they fell.

They were now trudging along the top of high cliffs, 180km from the last waterhole they had managed to find. The sheep were completely exhausted so they made a stockade and left them behind: Baxter ought to find them, if he was successfully tracking them. Eventually the pair came across some waterholes dug by the Aboriginals, and were able to water the horses (the animals had been without water for four days) and drink their fill.

Knowing that Baxter was no doubt also suffering from lack of water, Eyre and one of the boys dug additional waterholes 5ft deep for use when the overseer arrived with the other animals. This was an even more arduous task than one might think for the only tools they could use for digging were some shells left behind by the natives. The following morning (12 March) Eyre and one of the boys rode back to meet Baxter and recover the sheep, which had broken out of their compound; they had to be rounded up and were so dehydrated (they had been six days without water) they could scarcely walk. Eventually, the whole party was reunited and rested for six days (though in heat so terrible they could not possibly have travelled).

On 18 March they set off once more, Eyre, Baxter and Wylie walking, the two Aboriginals riding. The cliffs of the desert coast had now given way to kilometre after kilometre of featureless beach; the process of traversing these exhausted the party psychologically as well as physically. Once again they found no water. The boys occasionally came across a shrub the roots of which would yield a little moisture, but the business of digging them up from a depth of 20 or 30ft was so arduous that the meagre result was too dearly bought.

After two days the horses were so done in they could not carry even the wasted bodies of the boys. Eyre and Baxter discarded every piece of clothing or equipment which was not absolutely necessary, leaving on the beach pack-saddles, horseshoes, buckets, the kegs for holding water, most of their firearms and ammunition, and Eyre's much-prized copy of Sturt's book about his expeditions, given him by the author. Though their loads were now as light as they could be, the horses were in dreadful condition; sometimes they would simply lie down, and time and energy had to be spent getting them to their feet. On 28 March the pony collapsed, could go no further and had to be left to die. Eyre was characteristically grieved and paid a powerful and moving tribute to the horses:

It was a heart-rending scene to behold the noble animals which had served us so long and so faithfully, suffering the extremity of thirst and hunger, without having it in our power to relieve them. Five days of misery had passed over their heads since the last water had been left, and one hundred and twelve miles of country had been traversed without the possibility of procuring food for them, other than the dry and sapless remains of last year's grass, and this but rarely to be met with. No rains had fallen to refresh them, and they were reduced to a most pitiable condition, still they travelled onwards, with a spirit and endurance truly surprising. Whenever we halted, they followed us about like dogs wherever we went, appearing to look to us only for aid . . .[28]

During the day they suffered from extreme heat; during the night from cold – and they had thrown away their blankets. Eyre's favourite mare fell and they had to abandon her, forcing her six-month-old foal to leave her. A few miles further on, another horse dropped in its tracks. By 29 March every drop of water had been used and they had to rely on collecting dew with a sponge. The following day they came to some dunes where the Aboriginals thought there might be water. They dug and, 6ft down, found a fresh spring. Eyre recalled Isaiah 43:19: 'I will even make a way in the wilderness, and rivers in the desert.' For the first time for many days they made tea, thereafter attending to the horses; they dared not allow them to drink freely but each drank almost 4 gallons. A few days later, however, one dropped and Eyre had it killed for food – both Eyre and Baxter subsequently suffered from dysentery.

On 5 April Baxter and one of the boys volunteered to walk the 80km back to the place where the last supplies had been left. They were gone for ten days; two of their horses became so sick that they could not carry anything at all, and the supplies with which they had been loaded were lost.

Baxter was seriously disheartened, and Eyre could scarcely blame him. They were some 1,000km from King George Sound and another 1,000 from Fowler's Bay, stranded in completely unknown country, with provisions which might perhaps last a week, if they were careful. Their horses could scarcely crawl. If Eyre now made the wrong decision, they were lost. He decided that they must not abandon the horses, which even in their weakened state could carry more supplies than the two men possibly could. It would be impossible for them to retrace their steps across the fearful country behind them; surely the land ahead could not be as bad as that. Indeed, he hoped the going might get better and easier. Baxter did not agree: the country was likely, he thought, to become even more fearful, and if they pushed on they would most probably die of thirst. He remembered the large quantity of supplies that awaited them back at Fowler's Bay. But he was obliged to follow any plan his leader put forward – what else could he do? Baxter could not go off on his own. But he was seriously worried. So were the two young Aboriginals.

Food was now almost as short as water. On 16 April, Eyre killed the weakest and most emaciated of the horses; he could not bring himself to eat any of the flesh, but Baxter and the Aboriginals tucked in heartily. On 22 April, while the party was camping for a few days, Neramberein and, surprisingly, Wylie deserted: three days later they returned, having found it impossible to fend for themselves. They all set off again on 27 April.

Two nights later, at half-past ten, Eyre was seeing to the horses a little way from the camp when he was startled by a flash and the report of a gun. He thought it possible that Baxter had wakened and, seeing that he was absent, fired a shot to guide him back to camp. But as Eyre made his way back, he met a hysterical Wylie, who cried incoherently, 'Oh Massa, Oh Massa, come here!' Reaching the camp a few minutes later, he found Baxter lying in a welter of blood, in his death-agony. He had been shot through the left side of the chest and died in Eyre's arms. There was no sign of the other two Aboriginal boys and, apart from a terrified, gibbering Wylie and two murderous boys somewhere in the dark, Eyre was now alone in the desert.

He discovered soon enough that the boys had taken with them most of the food – bread, mutton, tea and sugar – Baxter's pipes and tobacco, and all the water. His double-barrelled shotgun was also missing, as was Baxter's. His handgun was faulty and useless. The first thing he did, before it was light, was search for the horses, which had wandered off. He eventually found them and he and Wylie stayed with them until it was light, for they were restless and might well have run off. It was bitterly cold, and with only a shirt and trousers the traumatised Eyre suffered acutely.

In the morning he discovered that 4 gallons of water remained at the camp, with 40lb of flour and a little tea and sugar; he also managed to clean and repair his gun, almost shooting himself in the process. Before they broke camp he and Wylie wrapped Baxter's body in a blanket but the ground was too rocky for them to dig a grave.[29] Eyre must have wondered who of the two would be left to dispose of the body of the other, for there was no sign of water for three days and a march of 240km. As they walked, they saw in the distance, following behind them, the figures of the two murderous boys. Eyre was determined to confront them, afraid that when their food and water ran out, they might decide to attack him. But as he walked towards them, they retreated.

He shouted to them, but they shouted back: 'Oh, Massa, we don't want you, we want Wylie.'[30] But Wylie was afraid to go anywhere near them. As the explorer moved off, the boys continued to follow, crying plaintively to Wylie to join them. Gradually they fell behind and after about 20km disappeared below the horizon.[31] As usual, water again became a problem: there were many holes in the limestone rock where the natives had collected water but they were all now completely dry. By 3 May the horses, with no water and no grass, were in a pitiful condition; Eyre was surprised they were still alive. As for the humans, 'we were both getting very weak and worn out, as well as lame, and it was with the greatest difficulty I could get Wylie to move, if he once sat down. I had myself the same kind of apathetic feeling, and would gladly have lain down and slept for ever.'[32] In the evening of that day, they found a native track leading down to the beach and there, among the sand-drifts, they found a place where natives had dug for water. And there was water.

The following morning Eyre turned the horses loose to drink as much as they liked; unfortunately there was still no grass for them. Nor was there any sign of Neramberein and Yarry during the three days they spent resting by the waterhole; he knew from experience that they were greedy when it came to food and water and unlikely to ration what they had, and he feared they had met, or would meet, 'a dreadful and lingering death, aggravated in all its horrors by the consciousness that they had brought it entirely upon themselves'.[33] Typically, he was still able to pity and make excuses for them – the younger had, after all, been with him for four years, the elder for two and a half. Exhausted, hungry, thirsty and frightened, it was not surprising they had wanted to leave him and he believed it had only been the fact that they had disturbed Baxter, and then panicked, which had resulted in them committing murder.

The state of the horses slowed their progress when they moved off again on the 6th. Reluctantly, on the 8th, Eyre shot the weakest of the horses, Wylie built an oven and they had roast meat to eat; they hung strips of the meat on the trees to dry, ready to take with them when they moved. The native ate so much that he became ill yet when Eyre woke during the night, Wylie was always sitting in the light of the fire, gnawing on a piece of meat. He carried on eating, almost every hour, until they left their campsite on the 10th when, after a few kilometres, they found a little dry grass for the remaining horses. They tramped on over the tiring sand of the beaches for two days, when both Eyre and Wylie became sick, and had to make camp. Despite (more probably because of) the horse meat which they now had in plenty, they felt themselves growing weaker and weaker.

They moved on more and more slowly. Eyre was making for Lucky Bay (which had been named by Flinders); from there they would still have 500km to walk to King George Sound. Who except Eyre would have thought the feat possible? But on he tramped, urging the exhausted Wylie forward all the way. Sometimes they managed to shoot a kangaroo, pick up some crabs or catch a possum for meat, but they found no water. Day after unremitting day they plodded on, sometimes under burning sun, sometimes through pelting rain, burning hot by day, shivering with cold at night.

On 2 June they arrived at a little bay which Eyre called Thistle Cove and, as they looked for a place to descend from the cliffs to the beach, Eyre thought he saw a sail. When they reached the beach, there was no sign of it – but then not one but two whalers appeared. The two men quickly built a fire, fired shots, waved their handkerchiefs – but there was no response. Then, hoving into view above a sand dune, they caught sight of the masts of a large vessel. Eyre rode along the beach and eventually managed to attract the crew's attention, and was soon being greeted by Captain Rossiter, the English commander of the French whaler *Mississippi*.

Rossiter invited them on board, fed them and assured them that they could stay on the ship as long as they wished. She was early for the whaling season, which did not begin until the end of June or beginning of July, so was in no hurry to go anywhere. Eyre was astonished to be taken ashore by Captain Rossiter and shown a garden he had made, with peas and potatoes growing well; then, on a small island, he saw pens of pigs and sheep, which Rossiter had bought in Madagascar and brought with him.

Eyre was glad to relax, read some old English newspapers and watch Wylie entertaining the crew with the number of ship's biscuits he was able to eat at one sitting. They stayed on board until 15 June, when they insisted on being put on shore, now provided with such generous supplies of food, including a Dutch cheese, 5lb of butter and two bottles of brandy, that the horses were fully laden, and the two men had to walk.

The rest of the journey was monotonous and without incident, but by no means easy. On 18 June, Eyre celebrated the anniversary of the day he had left Adelaide on his Northern Expedition. A few days later, on 22 June, Wylie somehow frightened one of the horses, and they all took off, scattering their loads over the desert. Everything had to be collected, the horses caught and reloaded. One night a spark from their fire set a tarpaulin alight, and some of their stores were lost. Then it began to rain, and soon the whole of Australia seemed to be one huge puddle. They could have bent down at any moment and collected a pint pot of water. Hour after hour they trudged on, soaked through.

At last, on 6 July, they reached the outskirts of the settlement at St George's Sound. Still in pouring rain – their clothes had been wet for three whole days – they left the horses to graze, forded the King's river breast-high in water, Eyre holding his maps and journals above his head, and walked into Albany. There Wylie was recognised by a local native and in a few minutes 'the streets which had appeared so shortly before gloomy and untenanted, were now alive with natives – men, women and children, old and young, rushing rapidly up the hill, to welcome the wanderer on his return, and to receive their lost one almost from the grave'.[34] Eyre found himself weeping.

Eyre went straight to the house of a friend, a Mr Sherrat, and very soon was toasting before a fire in some clean, borrowed clothes, a hot brandy and water in his hand and a procession of welcoming and congratulatory citizens queueing up to greet him. He discovered that a ship would shortly be leaving and booked a passage. Wylie remained at the Sound. He was awarded £2 and a medal, and for the rest of his life received a generous weekly supply of provisions from the government.

Eyre arrived back in Adelaide on 26 July 1841, one year and twenty-six days after leaving it. He wrote his report to the governor, among other things confirming that there was no sign of an Inland Sea (that old canard still preoccupied the stay-at-homes in Adelaide and Sydney), and asserting that as far as he could see the land between Adelaide and Albany consisted entirely of desert alternating with salt lakes or swamps.

He spent much of the rest of his time in Australia (until the end of 1844) trying to build bridges between the settlers of the Murray river and the Aboriginals he had come to respect and like. Of all the explorers, he is the one with most sympathy for the original people of the continent, and when he returned to England and wrote and published his *Journals*, he included a fascinating and highly sympathetic account of 'the Manners and Customs of the

Aboriginals'. He received the gold medal of the Royal Geographical Society, and later served in New Zealand, St Vincent and Antigua.

What had Eyre's great journey achieved? The answer must be, very little. He himself admitted that he had 'no important rivers to enumerate, no fertile regions to point out for the future spread of colonization and civilisation, no noble rangers to describe . . . on the contrary, all has been arid and barren in the extreme'.[35] But who could fail to recognise his astonishing physical and psychological achievements? As much as any other Australian explorer, and more than many, he surely had a heroic heart; Eyre brings to mind Tennyson's lines from *Ulysses*: '. . . strong in will To strive, to seek, to find, and not to yield.'

Between 1834 and 1842 the area of the so-called Australian Alps was opened up. In January 1834, a Czech botanist, Johann Lhotsky, set off with four servants and a single horse and trap towards the Monaro Plains and the Murrumbidgee river. He climbed to Cooma, now a busy tourist town and gateway to the Snowy Mountains resorts, and was the first white man to behold the Snowy river. The furthest point his expedition reached was near today's Thredbo, by which time it was so cold that he hesitated to travel any further – though seeing what seemed to be a fine plain ahead, he made a brave attempt to cross the Snowy. At the nearest point, however, the river was over 60m wide, and Lhotsky's heart failed him. Exhausted, he returned to Sydney.

The year after Lhotsky's attempt, George Mackillop managed to cross the Snowy, near today's border between New South Wales and Victoria, reached the plain his predecessor had seen, and there requisitioned 60,000 acres of excellent grazing land. Four years later, a Scot, Angus McMillan, the manager of a cattle station on the Monaro Plains, set out to look for new grazing land, established a station on the Tambo river and in 1840 discovered and named Lake Victoria and no fewer than six rivers, which he called after his friends – the Thomson, Avon, Mitchell, Macalister, Nicholson and Perry.

It was also in 1840 that Paul Edmund de Strzelecki, a Polish geologist, and his friend James Macarthur climbed Mount Townsend, believing it to be the highest peak of the Alps, only to see a higher peak nearby. Strzelecki climbed this alone – the peak is 2,227m above sea level – on 15 March 1840. He named the area through which he struggled back to civilisation Gippsland. On the return journey, he and his fellow explorers almost died of hunger, forced to fight their way through dense scrub to reach Melbourne on 28 May and prompting a rush of settlers towards the newly discovered land, while over a century later, enormous hydro-electric and irrigation schemes were centred in the Snowy Mountains.

SIX

'What for do you walk?'
George Grey, 1837, 1839

George Grey, completely ignorant of the topography and climate of Australia and unprepared to battle its rigours, faced physical hardships of legendary horror with heroic and eventually triumphant courage – but his exertions were devoid of any useful result.

M rs George Grey was on the balcony of a hotel in Lisbon in the spring of 1812 when she overheard two officers talking about the recent battle against the French at Badajoz. Among the dead, they said, was her husband, Lieutenant-Colonel George Grey of the 30th Foot Regiment. Her shock at the news brought on the premature birth of their son, later also christened George.

The boy grew up with tales of his father's bravery, and after a somewhat desultory education (he disliked school and ran away from it) he attended the Royal Military College at Sandhurst, and entered the army, serving for six years in Ireland. The spectacle of the extreme poverty of the Irish disgusted him, and he conceived radical ideas which did not endear him to his superiors. He flirted with the concept of democracy on the American model, and began to believe that a society could be created, perhaps in distant Australia, which would be more idealistic and fair than that of the Old World. In 1836 he applied to the Secretary of State for the Colonies, suggesting that he and a friend, Lieutenant Franklin Lushington, might explore the country north of Perth, in Western Australia, hoping to discover a river system similar to that of the Murray, which would make it possible for settlers to develop the area. Glenelg approved, the Royal Geographical Society supported the idea and the government agreed to finance the expedition.

Grey set out from Plymouth in June 1837 aboard Darwin's famous barque, the *Beagle*, with Lushington, a surgeon and naturalist, and three soldiers. According to a note of instructions sent by Glenelg to Grey, the expedition was to travel to that part of the Australian coast where Dampier had landed, and from there to trudge down to the Swan river and Perth, 'to gain information as to the real state of North-Western Australia, its resources, and the course and direction of its rivers and mountain ranges; to familiarize the natives with the British name and character; to search for and record all information regarding the natural productions of the country, and all details that might bear upon its capabilities for colonization or the reverse; and to collect specimens of its natural history'.[1]

At Cape Town Grey chartered the schooner *Lynher*, loaded her with livestock – thirty-one sheep, nineteen goats and six dogs – and took aboard five more men. Of the party of explorers, just one had actually seen Australia before and then only from the deck of a ship. None of them had ever experienced the heat or seen the stretches of desert land which they were soon to face. The way in which Grey set out was typical of the man. The most sensitive and likeable of all the early explorers, he was also the most innocent and naïve, proposing to land on the coast of an unknown, unmapped continent with no idea whether or in what quantities water or food would be available, and with no conception of the rigours of the climate. The trials of the two expeditions he undertook revealed him as a natural leader whose slender frame belied his extraordinary strength, whose courage was high and whose sense of duty was unfailing.

On 2 December the *Lynher* reached Hanover Bay and Grey leaned over the side to see a sadly barren and arid shore. He and Lieutenant Lushington went ashore with three men and three of the dogs. Within a very short time they realised just how desperately unprepared they all were for their venture. They had left the ship carrying only two pints of water and they and the dogs soon disposed of that. After a long voyage without exercise, the heat quickly overcame the men, and two of the dogs dropped dead; they carried the third for a while, then he also died. At last they saw some water at the bottom of a ravine and climbed down to it, only to find that it was salt.

By this time night was falling and they were all exhausted, two of the men seriously so. Grey decided that he and the least fatigued of the soldiers should walk along the coast until they found the *Lynher* and send a boat for the others. After less than a mile, he and his companion, Corporal John Coles, came to a bay with an entrance about 500yd wide. Coles could not swim, but Grey decided to cross. He plunged in carrying his revolver, wearing his boots and a shirt and his military cap.

I found myself caught in a tideway so violent, that resistance to its force, so as either to get on or return, appeared at the moment hopeless. My left hand, in which I held the pistol, was called into requisition to save my life; for the stream washed the cap from my head, and the cap then filling with water, and being carried down by the strong current, the chin-strap caught round my neck and nearly throttled me as I dragged it after me through the water; whilst the loose folds of my shirt being washed out to seawards by the tide kept getting entangled with my arm.[2]

He had just managed to climb out on to the opposite side of the bay, his body cut and bruised by rocks, when he heard the cries of a number of Aboriginals. Clutching his wet and useless revolver, he walked as quietly as he could along the beach until he was opposite the *Lynher*. He called to her and in so doing attracted the attention of the natives. Defenceless, he crawled into a hole in the rocks, where despite the threatening situation he fell asleep, to be discovered the following morning by the schooner's mate. As it happened, the crew had launched a boat the previous day, found Coles, who had guided them to Lushington and the rest of the party, and they were all back in the comfort of the schooner while Grey was still struggling along the coast.

On 9 December Grey made a more formal landing, planting the Union Jack and claiming the territory 'in the name of Her Majesty and her heirs for ever'. While Lushington was sent off in the schooner to Timor to bring back some packhorses, Grey decided to make some short forays into the country to acclimatise himself and his men to the conditions under which they would have to explore it. If his first introduction to Australia had been rough, his enthusiasm was soon rekindled and on 17 December he set out with Coles and a Private Mustard.

They wondered at the strangeness of the landscape and animals – their first sight of a kangaroo delighted them – and quickly realised that the area was relatively thickly populated by Aboriginals. Their first real encounter was with a party of fourteen hunters, who brandished their spears in a definitely unfriendly manner. A single shot fired over their heads dispersed them, and Grey retreated to his base camp near the mouth of the Prince Regent river, which had been named in 1819 by the marine surveyor Philip Parker King.

The *Lynher* returned on 17 January with twenty-six ponies. These proved to be unbroken, and when they were brought ashore and tied together in a line they almost went mad with panic, bit and kicked each other and reduced the whole enterprise to confusion. Most of the men had no experience of horses and were terrified of going anywhere near them, except to hit or kick them. Eventually, the animals were mustered into a rough line, but when the party started to move off they all attempted to go in different directions and their ropes became entangled in rocks and trees – no two ponies ever passed a tree on the same side. It took Grey a whole day to get them anywhere near the base camp.

The explorers set off on 29 January 1838, coping with the wayward ponies as best they could, with the intention of plodding all the way down to Perth, some 1,600km to the south. Grey hoped to find plentiful rivers watering the land, perhaps even an inland sea, which would make settlement both possible and desirable. However, it soon became clear that this was not to be a comfortable expedition. Storms and heavy rain together with cold made it difficult for the men to get a good night's sleep and the climate had its effect on both sheep and ponies, which seemed to grow weaker by the day. The first major obstacle was a cliff which stood between their camp and the proposed route. Immediately, there was predictable trouble with the ponies. Grey led his about three-quarters of the way up the rough path, 'when turning one of the sharp corners round a rock, the load struck against it, and knocked the horse over on its side. I thought for a moment that the poor beast would have fallen down the precipice, but luckily its roll was checked in time to prevent this. There it lay, however, on a flat rock, four or five feet wide – a precipice of 150ft on one side of it, and the projecting rock against which it had struck on the other – while I sat upon its head to prevent it from moving. Its long tail streamed in the wind over the precipice; its wild and fiery eye gleamed from its shaggy mane and forelock; and, ignorant of its impending danger, it kicked and struggled violently, while it appeared to hang in mid-air over the gloomy depth of this tropical ravine.'

Maintaining his characteristic cool and calm demeanour, Grey took time to admire the view:

Anxious as I felt for the safety of my pony, I could not be unconscious of the singular beauty of the scene during the few minutes that elapsed whilst I was repressing its struggles, on a narrow ledge of rock, of which the dark brow projected threateningly above me, whilst the noise of a rushing torrent was audible far below. I cut the girths of the saddle, which then with its load rolled over the precipice, and pitched with a heavy crash on a rock far down. Even then, if the brute had not been a denizen of a wild and mountainous country, it must have been lost; but now, it no sooner felt itself freed from its incumbrance, than looking sagaciously around, and then raising itself cautiously up, it stood trembling by my side upon the narrow terrace.[3]

By now the wet season had set in, and day after day of torrential rain, often accompanied by storms, made progress a torture. The country was difficult and frequently impossible to penetrate: Grey took to surveying it himself, every day, before the party moved off, a procedure that sometimes took him hours, walking in heavy rain or at best under scorching sun, only to find impassable ravines. More animals died (they lost seven ponies within the first week). On some days they were unable to move at all, and when they did the weakened ponies often fell down and refused to get up. Their loads had to be lightened and gunpowder and cartridges, preserved meat, carpenters' tools and other supplies were jettisoned.

On 8 February they took a rest day, at the bottom of a ravine leading down to the sea. Grey looked, as always, on the bright side: 'The place I had chosen for our camp was a pretty spot; a sweet, short herbage had been raised, by the heavy rains, from the sandy soil, and amongst this the beauteous flowers, for which Australia is deservedly celebrated, were so scattered and intermixed that they gave the country an enamelled appearance.'[4] A clear stream ran through the ravine and for the first time for a week the explorers were able to bathe themselves. Next day they moved off, Grey realising that they had taken ten days to reach a spot which by an easier route should have taken one.

At least, he reflected, there had been no trouble with the Aboriginals. But on 11 February, Grey, Coles and another man set out to reconnoitre, leaving three men behind. Soon after he had left, some two hundred natives came out of the woods. The explorers retreated to a nearby hill while the Aboriginals examined their camp, spending two hours wondering at the ponies and the pieces of equipment. Meanwhile, Grey and his companions were unaware of anything unusual until suddenly they were surrounded by natives, who threatened them with throwing-sticks and spears.

Grey fired a shot over their heads, but they came on. While he was reloading, Coles found that the cloth case which had protected his rifle from the rain had become entangled, and he could not fire. The third man was completely panicked, and could only cry out 'Oh, God! Sir, look at them; look at them!' Spears were now being thrown – one struck the barrel of Grey's gun and damaged it – then three spears struck him. He fell, but staggered to his feet, then shot and seriously injured one of the natives. At this, the others immediately fled, 'and as I looked round upon the dark rocks and forest, now suddenly silent and lifeless, but for the sight of the unhappy being who lay on the ground before me, I could have thought that the whole affair had been a horrid dream'.[5] But then the wounded man stirred, and immediately several others emerged from shelter without their spears, came to him and carried him off into the trees.

Grey now found that one spear had slightly cut his right arm, another had been deflected by his water-flask, but the third had severely injured him in the hip. They bound up his wound as best they could and started back to camp, Grey increasingly weak and dizzy from loss of blood. It took him over two hours, his strength gone, to realise that they were lost. Coles volunteered to go on and attempt to find his way to the camp. Grey sat and waited.

I sat upon the rocky edge of a cool clear brook, supported by a small tree. The sun shone out brightly, the dark forest was alive with birds and insects – on such scenery I had loved to meditate when I was a boy, but now how changed I was; wounded, fatigued, and wandering in an unknown land. In momentary

Suddenly surrounded by Aboriginals armed with spears, Grey and his companions were forced to disperse them with firearms; even so, Grey was wounded in the hip. (*Grey's* Journals)

expectation of being attacked, my finger was on the trigger, my gun ready to be raised, my eyes and ears busily engaged in detecting the slightest sounds, that I might defend a life which I at that moment believed was ebbing with my blood away; the loveliness of nature was around me, the sun rejoicing in his cloudless career, the birds were filling the woods with their songs, and my friends far away and unapprehensive of my condition – whilst I felt that I was dying there. And in this way very many explorers yearly die.[6]

As might be expected, Grey's wound did not heal easily. For two weeks he lay in considerable pain on the hard ground in his tent with the temperature outside rising to 160°F. The men who accompanied him did their best to raise his spirits: one, Thomas Ruston, thought that perhaps he was conscience-stricken because he had killed one of the natives, and tried to comfort him: 'Well, Sir, I'm sure if I were you, I shouldn't think nothing at all of having shot that there black fellow; why, Sir, they're very thick and plentiful up the country.'[7]

Once Grey felt able to walk, there was nothing to do but press on across the eastern section of the MacDonnell Range. On 27 February he was heartened to come upon a splendid fertile plain, luxuriant lowland country which seemed to auger well for any settler. Those horses and sheep still alive were delighted at the ample food available, and the men recovered their spirits. On 2 March they saw some distance off a fine river, which Grey named the Glenelg; it seemed to run through a rich and fertile country, and in full flood to be perhaps as much as 6 or 8km wide. As they walked on, the country seemed more and more promising, the vegetation luxuriant, with large trees to provide timber and a plentiful supply of fresh water.

Grey was suffering not only from his still open wound but from rheumatism caused by continually sleeping on damp ground; the pain often made it difficult for him properly to observe the country through which they were passing. They came upon a mountain, which Grey named Mount Lyell, and from whose lower slopes he was able to observe again the promising country by which he was surrounded – 'as verdant and fertile a district as the eye of man ever rested on'[8] – with the Glenelg river to the south and the Prince Regent river to the north.

They explored the Glenelg and its tributaries, untroubled by the natives they occasionally saw in the distance. Then, on 26 March, Grey suddenly looked up at some sandstone rocks above him and, to his astonishment, saw a huge figure peering down at him. It was a drawing, guarding the entrance to a cave – a cave which, when he entered it, proved to contain even more extraordinary drawings on its walls. The main figure, brilliantly coloured in red and white, had a white face, the eyes encircled by red and yellow lines, the body, hands and arms outlined in red. Its head was surrounded by a sort of halo, and what was shown of its upper body was draped in a patterned dress. Below it was depicted a group of four other females – Grey thought they must be females 'from their mild expressions' – who seemed to be looking up at the first. Nearby was a strange, semi-abstract painting with spear-heads and a kangaroo; another of a native carrying a kangaroo. Also nearby, Grey came upon what is clearly a European head, carved on a limestone rock, and some days later, in a different cave, discovered another impressive figure, a 10ft-tall man clad in what looks like a monk's habit, and with what seems to be a halo around his head.

Grey sketched the paintings and made notes on them which he carried back to Perth. Some people thought he had invented the whole thing, but the paintings have since been thoroughly examined (the cave is now in the Kunmunya Aboriginal Reserve). No one has been able to offer a convincing interpretation of the drawings, though it may be reasonable to dismiss some theories – for instance, that they show visitors from another planet, wearing space helmets. The most likely explanation is that, though they bear little resemblance to conventional Aboriginal paintings, they are in fact representations drawn by natives of earlier European visitors to the area. Who these Europeans were, or when they came, it is impossible to conjecture.

Grey, weakened by his wounds, was conscious that he was unlikely to be able to venture much further; indeed he now felt that he had found what he had been looking for: good land capable of development. It was time to retreat to Hanover Bay. The march took a fortnight, often through heavy rain and with Grey's wound continuing to trouble him. On 15 April they were relieved and delighted to see the *Lynher* still lying at anchor in Hanover Bay; nearby lay the *Beagle*. Grey decided to turn the eleven remaining ponies loose; there were two mares among them, and he hoped that a valuable race of horses might result (a pious hope which from the first seemed unlikely, and proved so).

'Our whole residence in this country', Grey reflected, 'had been marked by toils and sufferings. Heat, wounds, hunger, thirst and many other things had combined to harass us.'[9] Yet as he looked at his ruined camp, he was sorry to leave; he would have liked to stay to see whether the single pumpkin he had planted would thrive, and the bread-fruit, the little coconut plant, and one or two others. But it was time to weigh anchor. Just as they were about to set sail, a dog appeared on the beach and barked forlornly after them. Grey sent a boat ashore to fetch him.

Grey spent four months recuperating in Mauritius, writing up his report on the area he had surveyed, and making plans for a return to the north-west coast of Australia. First, he thought, he would visit Perth and consult the governor there, then sail to a point on the coast near the estuaries of the Glenelg or the Fitzroy and trace those rivers as nearly as possible to their source.

The Governor of Western Australia, Sir James Sterling, approved of the plan, but a ship could not be made ready without delay, nor could necessary equipment be got together without difficulty, so this second expedition had to be postponed until mid-February, when with the assistance of a newly appointed Governor, John Hutt, Grey managed to acquire three whale-boats, and made an arrangement with an American whaler, the *Russell*, to take him and his party north of Shark Bay. He would take with him five months' provisions for his party, explore northward as far as the North-West Cape, and then return to Perth. He recruited eleven men, several of whom (among them Coles and Ruston) had been with him on the previous expedition, and included Kaiber, 'an intelligent native' from a tribe living around the Swan river. There was also the 19-year-old Frederick Smith, a young Englishman with a talent for drawing and a yen for exploration, who came along simply for the experience.

They sailed on 17 February 1839, at three in the afternoon, and a week later disembarked on Bernier Island and celebrated by catching three turtles, pickling much of their flesh, and enjoying turtle soup.

Rather typically, Grey had made no effort whatsoever to find out whether Bernier Island was a reasonable place to set up a base camp. Within twenty-four hours it had become clear that there was no water whatsoever there and that they would have to move on as quickly as possible. Having hastily buried some supplies which they left on the island as a hostage to fortune, Grey launched his boat and managed to bring it safely to shore on Dorre Island. The man steering the surgeon Mr Walker's boat panicked in heavy surf, let go of the rudder, and his boat was knocked to pieces on rocks. Fortunately no one was drowned, but all the stores in the boat were lost and the explorers spent an unpleasant night trying to sleep on the beach, tortured in turn by mosquitoes, ants and a land-crab, which bit several of them. Next morning, the third boat was loaded and launched, and the two surviving craft were rowed along the coast in heavy weather, half a ton of supplies in each. At three in the afternoon they found a sheltered cove protected by a reef. There was a small quantity of dirty water which they sucked up from holes in the rocks; they found turtles' eggs and killed and ate a kangaroo.

At eleven that night an even stronger gale sprang up and breakers poured over the reef. Grey, Walker and Frederick Smith stripped, swam out to the boats and baled furiously, but in the end they had to abandon both boats and swim to shore, badly cut by a half-submerged coral reef and fortunate to escape drowning. Walker's boat was eventually driven ashore, full of water and seaweed. Grey's could dimly be seen out at sea; in the morning, when the winds had died down somewhat, three men were ordered to swim out to her and bring her in. They all refused, terrified by the breakers, but fortunately she was driven on shore by the wind. The storm was clearly a frightening one: Grey himself said that it was one of the most fearful he had ever encountered.

On the morning of 1 March the storm abated, leaving the expedition in complete disarray: the boats were so wrecked that it seemed impossible that they could be salvaged, all the stores were spoilt (with the exception of some salted meat), the ammunition was damaged and Grey's chronometers had been lost. But the men set about repairing the boats, and in three days (working in broiling sun and with only half a pint of water to each man) managed to make them more or less seaworthy. They launched them, and half-sailed, half-rowed towards the mainland.

After spending one night at sea, they landed on the mainland on 4 March, and almost immediately found a pool of fresh water, which did much to recover their spirits. Despite setbacks which to many men would have sounded the expedition's death knell, Grey was still intent on exploration and set off along the coast in the damaged boats. Just south of the Tropic of Capricorn they came upon the mouth of what seemed a substantial river, and rowed up it until the water was only 2ft deep, when they made camp. The river course was almost completely dry, but it was surrounded by what seemed very fertile land, which Grey thought would lend itself well to the cultivation of cotton and sugar: 'I felt conscious,' he wrote, 'that within a few years of the moment at which I stood there, a British population, rich in civilization, and the means of trans-forming an unoccupied country to one teeming with inhabitants and produce, would have followed my steps, and be eagerly and anxiously examining *my* charts.'[10] He named the river the Gascoyne, and the area he first saw now supports flourishing plantations of tropical fruits and a wide variety of vegetables.

Returning to the coast on 7 March, Grey rowed 40km along the shore to the north of the Gascoyne before being overtaken by a storm; he managed to beach both boats, but not before they were swamped. Next morning he discovered that their supply of flour had been soaked with salt water; it was extremely unpleasant to eat, but all they now had. At least inland there was a large lake, presumably of fresh water, and they made for it. Unfortunately, as they approached it, it retreated from them; it was a mirage. They dug several wells, but only found salt water. Lack of food, scarcity of water and cold, wet nights had their effect, and many of the men were now sick; for some time both Grey and Smith had also felt weak and debilitated.

On the afternoon of Sunday 10 March they were taking refuge from the sun's glare in the shelter of the boats, resting after another miserable, cold, wet night and a meal of salty dough and rancid pork, when for no apparent reason they were suddenly attacked by natives. Before the explorers spotted them, the Aboriginals managed to steal a number of bags; when disturbed, they threw several spears, one of which wounded Ruston in the knee. A shot or two dispersed them, but pursued for 8km, they cannily delayed the explorers by dropping things from the stolen bags, and when the white men stopped to pick them up, the black men gained ground. The Aboriginals escaped, everything but the expedition's valuable fishing lines having been recovered.

The weather was now so stormy that it was impossible to launch the boats. Day after day for eight days the explorers sat forlornly on the beach, waiting for the wind to drop. On 16 March it did so, and the boats were launched through the breakers; but tide and wind were against them and in spite of the men rowing hard all day they only advanced 11km. They had to brave the breakers and beach once more. It was another four days before the weather allowed them to make an attempt to reach Bernier Island, where they hoped to recover some of the stores they had left there.

They were about halfway across the strait when the weather suddenly worsened. The boats were swamped again and again, but Grey was heartened by the determination of the men and the excitement of the moment: 'Great as our danger was, I do not recollect ever having a keener perception of the pleasure of excited feelings, or a more thorough revelry of joyous emotions, than I had during this perilous passage,' he wrote.[11] The sentiments were typical of the man: weak where planning was concerned, without the imagination to understand or foresee danger, time and time again he was carried away by his emotions and by his determination to 'see things through'. His tenacity, optimism and physical bravery sustained him again and again in the most challenging circumstances.

At last, from the peaks of tremendous waves, he caught sight of the island, and they made shore, dragged the boats as far up the beach as they could, and Grey with Smith and Coles started towards the place where the life-saving supplies had been buried. Within half a mile they began to come across broken staves which were obviously from the flour casks they had left, then a cask of salt meat, washed up on the beach; when they reached the area where the supplies should have been, they found everything had been washed away. They had buried the supplies below the high-water mark. Coles threw his spade to the ground.

'All lost, Sir! We are all lost, Sir!'

Smith remained calm.

'Nonsense, Coles, we shall do very well yet; why, there is a cask of salt provisions, and half a cask of flour still left.'[12]

But Smith and certainly Grey knew that this was little enough to sustain a dozen men on a 1,600km journey to Perth. Grey gave Coles a short lecture on the importance of remaining calm and composed, and not allowing the other men to see that he was in any way discouraged. Smith and Coles then carefully collected every trace of flour they could find while Grey sat down on a rock and considered their position. There was no water on the island, so aside from leaving a message there in case anyone should happen to land, perhaps in search of them, they must return to the mainland. Before leaving Perth, Grey had at least taken the precaution of arranging with the governor that if there was no news of the expedition within a designated time, a schooner should be sent to look for them; he knew, too, that an American whaler was due off the north-west coast at the end of July, so at the worst they might expect to be found in four months or so.

On the other hand there was a very slim chance of their being able to survive until then, so perhaps they should make for Timor in the boats? Or would it be better to turn south towards Perth? Grey produced his Bible from his pocket and looked for inspiration.

Whether or not he found it, while following Smith and Coles back to the other men he did happen upon a bag of flour half-buried under some seaweed. Soaked in sea-water for weeks, it had fermented and smelt like beer. He carried it back to the men, and immediately set out the position before them. Though dismayed, they took the news as well as could be expected, and set about searching for any more remnants of the stores which might be lying about.

Grey decided on the third alternative he had considered: to sail for the Swan river in the whale-boats. Added to the psychological advantage of actually travelling towards home was the fact that any search parties sent out would probably look for them south of their present position, and that if the boats should by any means be lost, it should not be impossible for them to walk to Perth. He told the men his plans, and none objected – what else, after all, could they do?

Next day, 21 March, Grey wrote a note which was placed in a tin can and firmly fixed to an oar stuck in the sand above the water-mark. On the following day they crossed to the mainland, and two days later started to row south, against a strong breeze and a heavy sea. The men got some relief when the wind changed and they were able to hoist sails. The coastline was beautiful, some fish were caught, the weather was good and they were making headway; they were all fairly cheerful.

But then on the afternoon of 26 March a tremendous gale blew up so suddenly that they barely had time to take down the sails. The men were set to the oars, and only just managed to control the boats and bring them to land. Their hands were so torn and damaged by their efforts that Grey had to give them a full day off to recover. When they set out once more, they again had to row against the wind, which gained in strength such that the ensuing storm forced them once more ashore. By this time they were all in a bad physical state, weak from lack of food, their hands almost useless, and with sores broken out on buttocks constantly galled by the wooden seats of the boats.

The day of 28 March started fine; but almost as soon as they had put to sea yet another storm let rip; they made for a dangerously rocky coast and managed to reach a small patch of sand, where they spent the night under torrential rain. They had virtually no clothes – these had been swept overboard in the storm at the end of February – and wore only shirts and trousers.

By the end of March it was clear to everyone that the coast was so tempestuous and the weather so unreliable that if they continued to attempt to sail towards Perth they would sooner or later be wrecked. The seamen in the party particularly implored Grey to stay on land and walk to Perth. He knew that for the next 200km the coast was relentlessly rocky and inhospitable; nor was there anywhere he could beach the boats in an emergency.

A general gloom now descended upon the party and there was a bad omen when, on Grey's issuing an order to one of the seamen, the latter quietly declined to obey on the grounds that he was virtually a dead man and had therefore decided to stop work. Grey's response was to order that the man's ration of water and food for the day be divided among the other men – he would receive no more until he returned to work. The man said that his leader might as well throw him overboard; Grey replied that that might well be a good idea; the man recanted, and after that became Grey's main supporter.

But the delay was obviously having a bad effect on the party. On the last day of March the boats were launched again, and rowed laboriously down the coast. They passed an uneasy night at sea; by dawn the men were completely worn out, and Grey decided to put ashore in Gantheaume Bay, though the surf was fearful. Seeing what seemed to be a quieter passage, Grey steered into it, but hit an even heavier surf:

> We were swept along at a terrific rate, and yet it appeared as if each following wave must engulph us, so lofty were they, and so rapidly did they pour on. At length we reached the point where the waves broke; the breaker that we were on curled up in the air, lifting the boat with it, and when we had gained the summit, I looked down from a great height, not upon water, but upon a bare, sharp, black rock. For one second the boat hung upon the top of the wave; in the next, I felt the sensation of falling rapidly,

then a tremendous shock and crash, which jerked me away amongst rocks and breakers, and for the few following seconds I heard nothing but the din of waves, whilst I was rolling about amongst men, and a torn boat, oars, and water-kegs . . .[13]

Extraordinarily, all the men survived, and none of the stores in the boat were lost. The second boat reached the shore more easily than the first. All the same, like the first, it was so badly damaged that both were clearly beyond repair. 'No resource was now left to us but to endeavour to reach Perth by walking,' concluded Grey; 'yet when I looked at the sickly faces of some of the party, and saw their wasted forms, I much doubted if they retained strength to execute such a task; but they themselves were in high spirits, and talked of the undertaking as a mere trifle.'[14]

The men insisted on clinging to belongings which they could well have left behind to lighten their loads – silly impedimenta such as lengths of canvas they thought they might be able to sell in Perth; more understandably, Smith was determined to preserve his sketch book and box of watercolour paints. Time and time again Grey tried to persuade them to jettison everything but necessities, but they refused, staggering on with their bits and pieces of plunder, which, with the additional weight of 20lb each of salty and almost inedible flour, made for a very considerable load to be carried through brush and banksia woods, over crevasses and level but rocky ground. There were plenty of springs of clear water, but there was no knowing whether or not this happy state of affairs would continue, so they set out each morning carrying as much water as they conveniently could.

After six days of steady but painfully slow progress several of the men were completely exhausted, and though Grey pointed out that they were so short of food that they really needed to travel as fast as they possibly could before supplies ran out altogether, they insisted on lying down for two or three hours at a time, complaining that Grey was 'killing them' by forcing them to walk every day.

Grey now believed that far from his killing the men, they seemed determined to commit suicide by dawdling until their supplies of food and water ran out. He decided that the only answer to the situation was for him and a few of the strongest men to leave the others and make as speedy as possible a forced march to Perth, whence a relief party could then be dispatched to find the others. He chose Corporals Auger and Coles, the two army men, H. Wood (one of the two seamen who shared the same name), Hackney, one of the convict volunteers, and the Aboriginal Kaiber to go with him. Walker, the surgeon, was left in charge of the others, who were to make what progress they could to a point on the Moore river, about 80km north of Perth and 19km inland. Grey would do his best to see that fresh supplies were sent there. Smith was now in a very bad way, but Walker seemed to be strong and confident, though whether he would be firm enough to persuade the men to make sufficiently quick progress was an open question.

On 10 April, Grey and his party set out. They made much better time now that the loiterers were no longer with them, sometimes as much as 30km in a morning, starting early before the heat set in. Soon, what little food they had began to run out. Grey had made up his last few ounces of flour into a rough dough cake known as a damper – only for a rat one night to gnaw a hole in the bag in which he kept it and eat more than half. He was left with the remainder and three tablespoons of arrowroot. Occasionally he and the men found some roots and nuts which Kaiber said were safe to eat; nevertheless as a result they almost invariably became ill and vomited. Completely out of food himself, one night Grey overheard the convict Hackney proposing to Wood that they should give him a little of their own.

'No,' said Wood, 'every one for himself; let Mr Grey do as well as he can, and I will do the same.'

'Well, then,' said Hackney, 'I shall give him some of mine at all events,' and offered Grey a piece of damper the size of a walnut, which he gratefully accepted.[15]

On 14 April they were fortunate enough to come across a number of holes in the ground in which Aboriginals had buried a store of nuts. After a lot of soul-searching, Grey decided he could justify taking the contents of one hole, leaving the rest untouched. Next day he shot a hawk, which he shared with Kaiber and Hackney. They were all growing steadily weaker and weaker. They then passed two days without any food or water at all, occasionally moistening their lips with a few drops of dew from the shrubs and reeds. Their progress became slower and slower; now it was Kaiber who continually bullied them into moving on, telling them that if they did not find water, they would die. Some of the men began to drink their own urine.

On 17 April, Kaiber took Grey aside, allegedly to hunt, and contrived to lose the rest of the party. Then he said, 'Mr Grey, today we can walk, and may yet not die, but drink water; tomorrow you and I will be two dead men, if we walk not now, for we shall then be weak and unable. The others sit down too much; they are weak, and cannot walk: if we remain with them, we shall all die; but we two are still strong; let us walk. . . . You must leave the others, for I know not where they are, and we shall die in trying to find them.'

'Do you see the sun and where it now stands?' asked Grey.

'Yes.'

'Then if you have not led me to the party before that sun falls behind the hills, I will shoot you; as it begins to sink, you die.'

'Surely, you play?' said the native. But Grey persuaded him that he was serious, and Kaiber led him back to the other men.[16]

Next morning he told the men that their situation was desperate, and desperate measures were called for. He himself intended to march on to Perth, not stopping until he either reached water or dropped. They could follow him, if they wanted, but they need not expect him to stop for them if they fell behind – though he did promise, if he found water, to do his best to carry some back to anyone who had been left behind. He set off, hearing the faltering steps and groans of the men behind him. In an hour and a quarter he had marched only 2 miles when suddenly he caught sight of Kaiber lying on the ground not far from him, his head apparently buried in the sandy soil.

The Aboriginal had found a hole full of moist mud and was half-eating, half-drinking it. The men, and Grey himself, followed his example. After three days without water, wet mud was astonishingly palatable; they cooked a little flour with it, which they ate. That night it rained hard; starved as they were, the cold and wet crippled them, and the following morning they could hardly get up; the flesh of their feet was so torn that walking was agony. On the morning of 20 April Grey woke wishing, quite literally, that he was dead. Believing that they were now about 43km from Perth, he managed to force himself to stagger on, followed by his men. Later that day they met some natives, one of whom, Imbat, was known to Grey.

Their ordeal was almost over. On the small amount of food the natives gave them, they struggled on, spent a night in a derelict hut and next morning Grey started alone for Perth. On the way he came upon a cottage where a settler's wife was sitting down to breakfast.

Would he like a cup of tea, she asked?

The Governor did not recognise the ruin of a man who told him his story. Within hours, a search party left to find the men Grey had left behind. The six who had been with him were all brought safely to Perth. Walker's party had had almost as hard a time of it as Grey's. Keeping close to the coast, they had never been completely without drinking water, and had lived on what fish they could catch and any dead birds they came across. Smith crawled into the bush and died, only four days before the relief party found them. His body was later found by one of Grey's West Australian Aboriginal companions, Warrup: 'Two sleeps had he been dead; greatly did I weep, and much I grieved. In his blanket folding him, we scrape the earth into the grave. No dogs can dig there, so much earth we throw up. The sun inclined to the westward as we laid him in the ground.'[17]

Of the men who explored unknown regions of Australia, several had little enough experience of the rigours of such undertakings, knew little of the conditions they would have to face or how to cope with them. Of them all, Grey was the most complete amateur, and there is a strong temptation to identify with the Aboriginal Imbat, who asked, 'What for do you who have plenty to eat, and much money, walk so far away in the bush? You had plenty to eat at home, why did you not stop there?'[18]

There are several answers, some to do with a young man's ambition and search for excitement – and in Grey's case an incurable romanticism combined with a fierce determination to achieve the often fanciful ambitions he conceived. One of these was the foundation of free states in Australia and later South Africa in which the natives (having been 'civilised') would enjoy equal rights with the white colonists.

No one gained much from Grey's expedition except perhaps from his description of the land through which he had passed, and of its flora and fauna. But he certainly succeeded in making his mark. As soon as he had recovered his strength, he was offered the post of Resident Magistrate at Albany, and shortly afterwards married. His later career was distinguished. In 1841 he became Governor of South Australia, was twice Governor of New Zealand, Governor of Cape Colony (South Africa) and Premier of New Zealand, and, eventually, in 1848, KCB. An excellent writer, his *Journals* read like the best Victorian adventure novel. He died in September 1898, and was buried in St Paul's Cathedral.

SEVEN

'The Heart of the Dark Continent'
Ludwig Leichhardt, 1844, 1846, 1848

Ludwig Leichhardt was determined to succeed in some noble enterprise; though he achieved the greatest overland expedition – a journey of over 3,000 miles – of any Australian explorer, he is perhaps best remembered for his final dramatic disappearance into the heart of the Outback.

On 27 September 1841, a Prussian music-teacher was surprised to receive a letter from his brother-in-law, Ludwig Leichhardt, then in London, announcing his intention of sailing immediately for Australia – 'the ends of the Earth' – in order to explore the unknown regions of New Holland (as New South Wales was then called).

'While the coasts are slowly being populated the nature of the interior remains completely in the dark,' Leichhardt wrote. 'Expeditions have been sent in, but they've made little more than comparatively short reconnoitring thrusts before either running short of provisions or being driven back by the hostility of the Aboriginals. The interior, the heart of this dark continent, is my goal, and I will never relinquish the quest for it until I get there.'[1]

Friedrich Wilhelm Ludwig Leichhardt was 28 when he made that decision. Born in Trebatsch, Prussia, he was the son of a farmer and minor civil servant. An intelligent boy, he was taught first by a private tutor then at a *Gymnasium* in Berlin. He had no particular ambition, but a conviction that he was marked out to achieve something special – in what way, he had for many years no idea. Encouraged by an English friend and medical student, William Nicholson, Leichhardt studied medicine, botany, geology and mineralogy.

He reached his early twenties still without any particular aim in life, but became convinced that his future lay outside Prussia, perhaps even outside Europe, and in time began to focus on the idea that he should mount expeditions to explore unknown lands in Africa, the West Indies or Australia. Summoned to compulsory military service in Prussia, he persuaded the authorities to allow him to postpone it, having no intention of allowing it to interfere with his life. In May 1837, he travelled to London to stay with his friend's family. He and Nicholson spent some months racketing around Europe, but the idea of Australia was taking hold in Leichhardt's mind, and on 16 September 1841 he drafted a letter to the Secretary of the Royal Geographical Society in London submitting a plan for an expedition of exploration to 'the interior of Australia', which he 'had the intention to execute under the condition, that the Geogr. Society would aid me in the enterprise'. He would, he mendaciously declared, 'spend with pleasure my unfortunately small fortune and even my life in such an expedition to which I have prepared myself these last five years'.[2] In truth, the decision was a relatively recent one; moreover he possessed not even a small fortune, living as he did on the generosity of his friend.

Though the Geographical Society did not reply to his letter,[3] he had made up his mind at last. He began to make serious preparations, reading up whatever information he could find about Australia, deciding on his precise destination (Port Phillip, Port Jackson or Sydney?), enquiring about a passage, persuading Nicholson to pay for it, and managing to coax a professor at the Royal College of Surgeons to furnish him with a letter of introduction to the distinguished explorer Sir Thomas Mitchell, whose account of his first expedition had just been published.

Leichhardt sailed from Gravesend aboard the *Sir Edward Paget* on 1 October 1841, calling at Cork to pick up 150 Irish migrants, and arriving at Sydney on 14 February 1842. No longer able to rely on the hospitality of Nicholson and his family, he ingratiated himself with a fellow passenger, a musician called Stephen Marsh and his wife (Marsh, a harpist, had impressed Leichhardt by improvising on the instrument an accompaniment to an immense Atlantic storm).

While living with them he lost no time in making himself known to anyone in Sydney who might help him to establish a reputation as a botanist and geologist – and to anyone who might recommend him as the possible leader of an expedition of exploration. Of these, Mitchell was of course one, though Leichhardt soon realised that for every friend Mitchell had, he also had an enemy.

During his first years in Australia, Leichhardt lived on money with which he had been provided by Nicholson, on his wits and on the kindness of new friends. He travelled around New South Wales, examining the coal seams in Newcastle and the fossilised forest at Awaaba, and surveying the agriculture of the region. Then, probably via Mitchell, he heard that the Governor, Sir George Gipps, was interested in the idea of discovering an overland route from Sydney to the north coast, which would open up a new trade route to India and the East Indies. Mitchell himself was eager to lead an expedition to investigate this possibility, and Leichhardt was no doubt eager to join it. But lacking an enthusiastic response from the Colonial Office in London, Gipps procrastinated and Leichhardt came to realise that it was unlikely that Mitchell's expedition would ever be approved. As a consequence, he began to discuss with a few friends the possibility of raising money to back an independent expedition. Although he had no money of his own, he was confident he could raise loans to support an expedition.

His plan was to survey the country between Toowoomba, on the Darling Downs in south-east Queensland, and Port Essington. Captain Philip Parker King, who had surveyed the Port Essington area a dozen years earlier, gave his support to Leichhardt's project, as did the colonists as a whole, who saw it as a stepping-off point for trade with the East. The construction of a road between Port Essington and Sydney also seemed a most valuable project. Contributions of cash flowed readily into Leichhardt's hands from settlers who saw the project as vital to the success of the colony, hoping not only for an established route to the north, but for the discovery of good grazing country on the way.

By September 1844 Leichhardt had received sufficient contributions and promises of aid to write telling Carl Friedrich Schmalfuss, his brother-in-law, that he had completed his preparations: 'My party consists of 9 persons, with 15 horses, and we may have 8 or 9 bullocks to carry the provisions. . . . I'm taking flour, tea, sugar and a few other provisions, but no meat, as our guns are to provide us with all the kangaroos, emus, bustards, pigeons, and so on, that we shall need. – If you recollect how ardently I used to look towards this unknown country you'll appreciate the delight I feel now I'm actually able to see and investigate the [still] unknown interior.'[4]

Leichhardt had originally chosen five men for his expedition, the most important to him being the 19-year-old James Calvert, another fellow passenger on the *Sir Edward Paget*, who had been eking out a living as a settler. Calvert was, or became, an enthusiastic botanist. Apart from him, there was John Roper, 20, John Murphy, only 16, with a talent for drawing, and a convict called William Phillips, 44, an ex-attorney transported for forgery. None of them had any idea of what lay before him. Leichhardt himself seems to have been somewhat uneasy; he told a friend: 'When you hear of me, it will be either that I am lost or dead, or that I have succeeded to penetrate through the interior to Port Essington', and suggested to another that he might leave his bones 'whitening on the plains, far inland'. He had well over 3,000km to cover if he was to be successful in reaching Port Essington, travelling the entire length of Queensland and on to the top of the Northern Territory – almost all the country between the two was completely unknown.

Offered free passage to Moreton Bay on the steamer *Sovereign*, the expedition's five original members (along with thirteen horses) left Sydney on 13 August 1844. They hoped to make Brisbane in three days, but storms delayed them for a week, and the horses suffered from want of food and water. Leichhardt was persuaded to recruit more men at Brisbane: Pemberton Hodgson, 23 and 'fond of botanical pursuits', joined the party, as did John Gilbert, an ornithologist and collector. From the start, Gilbert did not get on with Leichhardt, of whom he was jealous, believing that as 'a foreigner' he should not be first to discover anything at all about Australia. An American negro, Caleb, was engaged as cook, and two

Aboriginals were taken on, a native tracker called Charley Fisher (said once to have been a policeman) and another, Harry Brown.

When on 1 October 1844 they left Darling Downs for the unknown, the party was in good heart, joining lustily in a chorus of 'God Save the King' (though the tune was also that of a German popular song; so Leichhardt was expressing two patriotic sentiments at the same time). But they immediately ran into trouble. Rain had made the roads almost impassable, and as they struggled onward it was found that while Leichhardt had been told by the men from whom he bought the bullocks that each animal could carry 250lb in weight, they could actually only cope with 150lb, which meant that some of the horses had to be used as beasts of burden while the men took turns to walk.

Nevertheless, over the next weeks they made good progress, though Leichhardt soon found that running an expedition was no simple matter. Apart from the hard work of keeping the company of animals and men together, mapping their progress was not easy. He had a sextant and an artificial horizon, a hand-held compass, a watch and 'Arrowsmith's Map of the Continent of New Holland', which showed an outline of the coast, a few rivers, but otherwise was little but blank paper.[5]

Troubled by nothing more serious than mosquitoes and sandflies, they followed a chain of large ponds or small lagoons to the Condamine river, a tributary of the Darling. A serious setback came on 11 October, when forcing their way through a thicket the bullocks had their loads torn from their backs, and after 5 miles of coping with the beasts and trying to reattach the loads, the explorers found they had lost over 60kg (143lb) of flour. Then came more rain, and they were bogged down for several days. Young Murphy and Caleb the cook lost patience, took off into the wilderness, and were themselves lost. Leichhardt sent Roper and the Aboriginal, Charley, to try to find them; only after riding for three days and more than 112km were they successful.

Nevertheless, Leichhardt found the romance he had anticipated: like other explorers, and modern tourists who venture into the bush, he was continually fascinated by the strange flora and fauna, the alien sights and sounds, by 'the stillness of the moonlight night', for instance, 'not interrupted by the screeching of opossums and flying squirrels, nor by the monotonous note of the barking-bird and little owlet; no native dog is howling round our camp in the chilly morning: the cricket alone chirps along the water-holes; and the musical note of an unknown bird, sounding like "gluck gluck" frequently repeated, and ending in a shake, and the melancholy wail of the curlew, are heard from the neighbouring scrub'.[6]

By 3 November Leichhardt realised that he had been 'too sanguine' in believing that the party could live mainly off the game they were able to trap or shoot; they were already beginning to run short of food. He decided that the expedition must be reduced and that Hodgson and Caleb must return to Moreton Bay, although a result of this was that two valuable horses had to carry them, and were lost to him, their load redistributed among the others.

So far the party had covered not much more than 100km; now, Leichhardt set out determined to make serious progress. They crossed the Calvert Plains and the Dawson river (Leichhardt named both), then the Gilbert and Lynd Ranges, to reach Palm Tree Creek and a welcoming waterhole sheltered by coryphas and gumtrees, where they successfully fished for jewfish and eels, which they ate with what he called 'a wild vegetable known as "fat-hen" [the herb *atriplex*]', and which was rather like spinach.

On they went, managing from time to time to catch an emu or a kangaroo for food. They dried some of the meat by hanging it in the sun, and then overnight, to preserve it. Their festive fare on Christmas Day consisted of suet pudding and stewed cockatoo; on other occasions they also provided themselves with festive food, such as tarts made from wild lemons, 'rather like gooseberry-fool'. Culinary experiments with unknown plants usually proved disastrous, but interestingly, Leichhardt extracted oil from emu skins, which he found to be excellent for treating rheumatism.[7] Like all explorers, Leichhardt assumed the right to name features of the landscape as he discovered them – Robinson Creek, after one of the expedition's sponsors; Mount Nicholson after the politician who had first officially proposed the undertaking to the legislative

Above, left: John Oxley, the young Surveyor General who in 1817 explored the river systems of New South Wales in search of arable land. *(Anonymous watercolour miniature, Mitchell Library, New South Wales) Above, right:* Captain Charles Sturt, whose expeditions were dogged by bad luck, and who at the age of fifty struggled almost to his death through what was later called 'Sturt's Stony Desert'. *(Wood engraving, National Library of Australia)*

For more than five months Sturt and his colleagues, trapped in intense heat, lived in a rough underground dug-out, waiting for rain. *(Cassell's* Picturesque Australasia, *1889)*

Above, left: The irascible Major Thomas Mitchell saw himself as a professional explorer among bungling amateurs. His discoveries were undramatic but important – he found stretches of some of the best pastoral land yet located. *(Author's collection)*

Above, right: Edward John Eyre, drawn in 1845, four years after his astonishing trek around the Great Australian Bight. *(Drawing by Witkin; courtesy of the State Library of South Australia, reproduced by permission of the Speaker of the House of Assembly, South Australia)*

Left: Wylie, an Aboriginal of the King George Sound tribe, accompanied Eyre across the Bight, on several occasions saving his life. *(Eyre,* Journals, *1840–1)*

George Grey was one of the least competent but most intrepid and brave of early explorers, floundering down the West Australian coast, narrowly escaping death and accomplishing little. He later became a distinguished politician. *(Auckland City Art Gallery, artist not known)*

One of the extraordinary cave paintings found by George Grey near the head of the Glenelg river in Western Australia. *(Grey's* Journals, *1837–9)*

Above, left: Ludwig Leichhardt, whose disappearance – with all members of his expedition – was for over a century one of the great mysteries of Australian exploration history, and has never been satisfactorily resolved. *(Drawing by Isabel Fox, courtesy of Mitchell Library, New South Wales) Above, right:* J.F. Mann, a surveyor on Leichhardt's expedition, sketched him riding in his 'old greasy coat and moleskin trousers'. *(From J.F. Mann's sketchbook, Dixson Library, Sydney)*

Curious Aboriginals among the trees watch Leichhardt's camp at dawn, as the explorers watch their billy boil over a smoking fire. *(From J.F. Mann's sketchbook, Dixson Library, Sydney)*

John McDouall Stuart, a Scot who had been a member of Sturt's 1844 expedition, was the first man to succeed in traversing Australia from south to north. *(Drawing in Ian Mudie's* The Heroic Journey of J. McDouall Stuart, *Angus and Robertson, 1958. No provenance supplied.)*

On Stuart's triumphant return to Melbourne, the celebrations included a formal procession in which the Mayor's carriage was followed by the bedraggled explorers in their dirty, tattered and almost disintegrated clothing. *(Stuart's* Journals, *1865)*

Spade in hand, Stuart has just planted the Union Jack on the shore of the Indian ocean, at Chambers Bay, about 100km west of present-day Darwin. *(Stuart's* Journals, *1865)*

Burke, on horseback, leads his expedition out of Royal Park, Melbourne, followed by Landells on his camel and Becker (left) also on a camel. *(Painting by Nicholas Chevalier, 1860. M.J.M. Carter collection, Art Gallery of South Australia)*

Ludwig Becker, who accompanied Burke and Wills's expedition, was a skilled water-colourist; this sketch is of Dick, one of those Aboriginal guides invaluable to all explorers of Australia. *(La Trobe Library)*

Arriving at Cooper's Creek after an expedition to the north, Burke, Wills and King found buried beneath a tree a message telling them that they had missed their colleagues by only a few hours; they were too exhausted to follow them. *(Watercolour by Gill, Dixson Gallery, State Library of New South Wales)*

The sight of Ernest Giles's expedition riding into the city on camels astonished and delighted the citizens of Perth. *(From Giles,* Australia Twice Traversed, *1889)*

Members of Giles's expedition photographed on their arrival in Perth. Back row, Peter Nicholls, Alex Ross, Saleh Mahomet; middle row, Jesse Young, Ernest Giles, W.H. Tietkens; front, Tommy Oldham. *(J.S. Battye Library of West Australian History, Perth)*

council of New South Wales; and Murphy Range and Lake Murphy after his young companion.

The expedition's progress was, however, by no means completely smooth, the irritation suffered from black ants, flies and mosquitoes being the least of their problems. Flour was now running short, as was other food, and Leichhardt found that their clothes and the harnesses for the horses were rapidly becoming much the worse for wear. Eventually, they were forced to cannibalise their clothing, replacing tattered sleeves from the material of pockets, and using any surplus normally tucked inside their breeches to patch backs and sides.

There were also growing tensions within the party. Phillips, the convict, was frequently discovered stealing food; Roper seemed to consider himself joint leader of the expedition, with as much right to decision-making as Leichhardt himself; Murphy was impertinent and disobedient; the two Aboriginals took every opportunity to disobey any order of Leichhardt's which meant extra work for them; and the leader mistrusted Gilbert, the ornithologist, whom he suspected of setting Murphy against him, and of a worse conspiracy – intending to deprive him of credit for botanical and other discoveries. Only Calvert seemed to comply willingly and show the proper deference and respect.

Then, people kept getting lost. On 8 December Roper 'went to cut tent-poles, but, perhaps too intent on finding good ones, unfortunately lost his way, and wandered about the bush for about five miles before we were able to make him hear our cooees,' wrote Leichhardt. 'Accidents of this kind happen very easily in a wooded country . . . when sufficient care is not taken to mark and keep the direction of the camp.'[8] A week later, he himself got lost while out with Charley, the Aboriginal tracker, and they found themselves confused and bewildered, some 20km from camp. Luckily, Leichhardt's pony, Jim Crow, knew the way back, and guided them home. The following day, 16 December, Calvert, Murphy and Brown spent the night in the open, having lost their way in the dark.

The party had not, so far, had much contact with the Aboriginal tribes in the areas through which they were passing, but on

7 December and without warning some natives had attacked their horses, spearing one deeply in the shoulder. Fortunately, the beast recovered, but the incident prompted Leichhardt to keep a look-out for 'Blackfellows' even when their presence was not obvious. On the last day of 1844, they came across a large Aboriginal camp; as they rode up to it, the entire party of Aboriginals ran off, shouting in panic, and leaving behind a fire on which possums, bandicoots and iguanas were roasting, together with sweet potatoes and turkey eggs. Leichhardt inspected the camp, interested by the pipe-clay with which (he presumed) the men painted their bodies, by the cloaks made of possum skins, and the well-made fishing nets. The explorers then retreated, leaving the camp as they had found it.

The party slowly pressed on. On 18 January Leichhardt decided to take the two Aboriginals, Charley and Brown, and make a foray to the north-west, while the others concentrated on drying meat to replenish their dwindling stock. They spent a day riding forward through scrub, then camped for the night. In the morning Charley was sent back to bring up the other members of the expedition while Leichhardt and Brown rode on, again through dense scrub. Brown spent some time trying to catch an emu, which tantalised them by time and again allowing itself to be almost caught before scooting off once more. A thunderstorm then blew up, the ground quickly became muddy in the downpour, and their tracks disappeared so that they could not retrace their steps. They were lost, again. Drenched, they had carried no water and were forced to drink what they could catch in their blankets before falling into an exhausted sleep.

They spent the following day wandering about until they almost fell from their horses with fatigue. Without food, they managed to catch a pigeon, and were so hungry that they ate it, feet, bones and all. Brown became disconsolate, complained of pain in his legs and continually muttered, 'We are lost! We are lost!' until, after yet another day of aimless travel, he thought he recognised the way back to the camp; and so it was. Leichhardt was impressed, not for the first time, by 'the wonderful quickness and accuracy with which Brown as well as Charley were able to recognise localities which they had previously seen. The impressions on their retina seem to be naturally more intense than on that of the European; and their recollections are remarkably exact, even to the most minute details. Trees peculiarly formed or grouped, broken branches, slight elevations of the ground – in fact, a hundred things, which we should remark only when paying great attention to a place – seem to form a kind of Daguerreotype impression on their minds, every part of which is readily recollected.'[9]

By the end of January, traversing hilly country along the Comet river, the party had reached what is now Peak Range, east of Clermont, and was in a bad way: the horses were exhausted and had to be coaxed to make every step, Leichhardt himself suffered from bad diarrhoea, and shortage of water left all the men seriously dehydrated. The flour ration had been reduced to about 60g per day (1½lb) between all six men. Charley and Brown were particularly upset at what they thought were starvation rations, stole a batch of provisions and vanished – to return when they had eaten their fill, bringing some wild honey as a peace offering. Leichhardt wanted to chastise them, but had been kicked by a bullock and could not summon the strength.

Perhaps Charley thought that he had the upper hand, for later he went missing again, for twenty-four hours, and when Leichhardt threatened to deprive him of his food ration, cursed him and struck him in the face, loosening two of his teeth. Brown took Charley's side in the argument, and they both again walked off. A couple of days without more food than they could catch encouraged them to go back and apologise. Leichhardt had no option but to allow them to return, though threatening dire consequences should they misbehave again.

The party was now making very slow progress, following the course of the Isaac river, the principal tributary of the Mackenzie. After the Isaac they came to the Suttor, which joined another, larger river which Leichhardt named the Burdekin, after a widow who had financially supported the expedition. For the first time, the rivers of the area were at least being marked out, if not mapped. His journal diligently records, day after day, yet another trek through unknown country, noting the geology, the plant life, the occasional appearance of a kangaroo or an emu – there was little excitement to relieve the drudgery of trudging on, sometimes without water for twenty-four hours or more, and on rations which were just sufficient to sustain life. The occasional treats they allowed themselves were scarcely luxurious. Leichhardt's journal entry for 10 May reads:

It was the Queen's birth-day, and we celebrated it with what – as our only remaining luxury – we were accustomed to call a fat cake, made of four pounds of flour and some suet, which we had saved for the express purpose, and with a pot of sugared tea. We had for several months been without sugar, with the exception of about ten pounds, which was reserved for cases of illness and for festivals. So necessary does it appear to human nature to interrupt the monotony of life by marked days, on which we indulge in recollections of the past, or in meditations on the future, that we all enjoyed these days as much, and even more, than when surrounded with all the blessings of civilized society; although I am free to admit, that fat-cake and sugared tea *in prospectu* might induce us to watch with more eagerness for the approach of these days of feasting . . .

He also recorded vividly the psychological ups and downs experienced by all explorers:

Much, indeed the greatest portion, of my journey had been occupied in long reconnoitring rides, and he who is thus occupied is in a continued state of excitement, now buoyant with hope, as he urges on his horse towards some distant range or blue mountain, or as he follows the favourable bend of a river; now all despairing and miserable, as he approaches the foot of the range without finding water from which he could start again with renewed strength, or as the river turns in an unfavourable direction, and slips out of his course. Evening approaches, the sun has sunk below the horizon for some time, but still he strains his eyes through the gloom for the dark verdure of a creek, or strives to follow the arrow-like flight of a pigeon, the flapping of whose wings has filled him with a sudden hope, from which he relapses again into a still greater sadness; with a sickened heart he drops his head to a broken and interrupted rest, whilst his horse is standing hobbled at his side, unwilling from excessive thirst to feed on the dry grass.

How often have I found myself in these different states of the brightest hope and the deepest misery, riding along, thirsty, almost lifeless and ready to drop from my saddle with fatigue; the poor horse tired like his rider, footsore, stumbling over every stone, running heedlessly against the trees, and wounding my knees! But suddenly, the note of *Grallina Australis*, the call of cockatoos, or the croaking of frogs, is heard, and hopes are bright again; water is certainly at hand; the spur is applied to the flank of the tired beast, which already partakes in his rider's anticipations, and quickens his pace – and a lagoon, a creek or a river is before him. The horse is soon unsaddled, hobbled, and well washed; a fire is made, the teapot is put to the fire, the meat is dressed, the enjoyment of the poor reconnoiterer is perfect, and a prayer of thankfulness to the Almighty God who protects the wanderer on his journey, bursts from his grateful lips.[10]

Leichhardt now believed that following the course of rivers was one of the best – and perhaps least troublesome – ways of making progress. Aiming to continue towards the south-eastern coast of the Gulf of Carpentaria, he followed a new river which he named the Lynd, finding that it joined another, which he named the Mitchell (after his acquaintance, Sir Thomas); this led him on to the north-west.

On 27 June, he was disturbed by a report from Charley and Brown. Out hunting, they had noticed a local Aboriginal creeping up towards the explorers' bullocks, obviously with the intention of driving them towards a number of his companions who, spears at the ready, seemed likely to attempt to kill them. Charley fired his gun, and the men fled. At the end of the next day, only a few miles further on, they made camp and were just settled down for the night when out of the darkness came a shower of spears. In the ensuing chaos, Roper and Calvert received spear wounds, and Gilbert was killed by a spear in the chest. Fortunately, the natives fled at the first reports of the guns which Charley and Brown quickly seized.

At first light it was clear that both Roper and Calvert were seriously hurt: Roper had several wounds in his head, a spear was right through his left arm, another had pierced his cheek and injured his eye, yet another had struck him in the loin. Calvert had received a spear in his groin and one in his knee, and both men had also been injured by stones and other missiles. The spears were barbed and difficult to extract from the flesh: Leichhardt had to pull one right through Roper's arm.

Calvert and Roper 'recovered wonderfully, considering the severe injuries they had received',[11] although they were subsequently weak for some time and for almost a month had to be treated more or less as inactive passengers. It is highly likely that their recovery was aided by Leichhardt's care. While he had never completed a medical degree in Berlin, clearly he had some medical knowledge (he always liked to be addressed as 'Doctor' Leichhardt), which on this occasion proved invaluable. The party was able to move off again as early as 1 July, and four days later sighted the Gulf of Carpentaria and the sea. The men broke into cheers and 'all the pains and privations we had endured were, for the moment, forgotten, as if we had arrived at the end of the journey'.

Their euphoria and pride were understandable. As Leichhardt put it, 'We had discovered a line of communication by land, between the eastern coast of Australia and the gulf of Carpentaria: we had travelled along never failing, and, for the greater part over an excellent country, available, almost in its whole extent, for pastoral purposes.'[12] But they did not rest on their laurels. The party turned south-west around the gulf, and on 12 July discovered a river running through pleasant and placid country. They named it after Gilbert.

The coast of the gulf was marshy, the mudflats criss-crossed by many small streams and larger rivers, some of which at least had been observed and named by earlier explorers – the Flinders river, for instance, had been discovered and named by Lieutenant John Lort Stokes, sailing in the area on the *Beagle* in 1838. One river which Leichhardt crossed, he left unnamed, thinking that it was probably the Albert or Maet Suyker. In 1856 a later explorer, A.C. Gregory, named it the Leichhardt.

Leichhardt kept inland, travelling at a distance of between 25 and 50km from the coast, and made good progress. The explorers now had a daily routine. When the kookaburra roused Leichhardt in the morning, he would waken the other men while Harry Brown renewed the fire, which had burned all night, and brewed tea. Time and again Leichhardt mentions in his journal the vital importance of tea. In early September the possibility of having to cut the tea ration sent him into what, for this cool-headed man, was almost a panic:

Our tea bag was getting very low, and as I was afraid that we should have to go a long time without this most useful article, I thought it advisable to make a more saving arrangement. We had, consequently, a pot of good tea at luncheon, when we arrived at our camp tired and exhausted, and most in want of an exciting and refreshing beverage. The tea-leaves remaining in the pot, were saved and boiled up for supper, allowing a pint to each person. In the morning, we had our soup, and drank water. . . . Tea is unquestionably one of the most important provisions of such an expedition; sugar is of very little consequence, and I believe that one does even better without it.[13]

A cauldron of stew simmered all night, and they breakfasted on it. Then young Murphy and Charley would collect together the horses and bullocks, and the march would begin – usually four hours' steady walking, then a rest in the afternoon. In the evening, there would be more tea and next day's stew would be made, containing about a kilo of meat (about 2lb) for each man – sometimes dried meat, sometimes fresh cockatoo, emu or, more rarely, kangaroo meat, together with about 600g (18oz) of flour to make a suet 'fat cake' which cooked while Leichhardt wrote up his journal. They picked and consumed a good deal of wild fruit and berries, perhaps rather incautiously; sometimes they suffered from diarrhoea, but unlike other explorers completely avoided the scurvy.

Occasionally they made contact with local Aboriginals, and once with a group that, unlike others they had encountered, seemed to know how to use a gun and a knife. That was on 21 September, the day on which Leichhardt came to the largest river they had yet discovered, which he named the Macarthur. A number of natives approached the party and seemed friendly, although many of them held boomerangs ready to throw. They appeared to want to tell the explorers something, but no one could understand their gestures or language. They must, Leichhardt concluded, have met white men before, 'for they knew the use of a knife, and valued it so highly that one of them offered a *gin* [a woman] for one. They appeared equally acquainted with the use of our fire-arms.'[14] It seems likely that they were not Aboriginals at all, but Macassans, from one of the islands of the narrow strait between Borneo and Celebes, possibly Laut or Sebuku.

It was at this moment that one of the bullocks lay down and refused to move, and Leichhardt realised that he must slaughter it. They left the beast while they went on for a few miles and found a suitable campsite (where, lighting a fire, Leichhardt set his hat alight – a serious matter in the strong sun – and had thereafter to make do with a small canvas bag). The bullock was then brought in and killed. Leichhardt was glad that he had not been called upon to slaughter his pet bullock, to which he was particularly attached: 'Throughout the journey I used to load him myself. He was wild and unmanageable at first, but he gradually became tame and quiet, though now and then he'd give me a friendly kick with a hind foot, which made me lame for a day or two.'[15] His favourite was the only bullock to survive the journey. The meat of its companion was unfortunately tough and tasteless, though their dog, Spring, enjoyed it. With the meal, they drank their last pot of tea.

The party marched on, over what is now Rosie Creek (Leichhardt called it Red Kangaroo river because of the large number of the beasts he saw there) and then the Limmen Bight river. The whole party was depressed by the sudden death of Spring, and not only because he had been a good hunting dog. As Leichhardt noted, every animal on the expedition had its own character and personality and had become a companion. Brown didn't help, whistling as he did a doleful, funereal tune as he marched. On 19 October, they reached a fine river, at least 460m wide, which Leichhardt named after Roper, who had been the first to set eyes on it two days earlier when on a scouting ride. So plentiful was game along its banks that one day Charley had no difficulty in shooting twenty duck for lunch. Fruit bats were less palatable.

The horses were set loose to graze in the rich grass, but three of them inexplicably managed to drown themselves. Leichhardt was literally dizzy with dismay. He had no alternative but to dump most of his collection of botanical specimens, which amounted to between four and five thousand samples of flowers, fruit and seeds and which one of the horses had carried: 'The fruit of many a day's work was consigned to the fire; and tears were in my eyes when I saw one of the most interesting results of my expedition vanish into smoke,' he wrote.[16] That disaster had been on 21 October; two days later, another horse slipped into the river. After several hours they managed to haul him out, but in his panic he plunged in again, became entangled in the tether rope and drowned. The nine remaining horses were now almost dangerously overburdened, and soon showed signs of weakening. The party had to stop frequently to rest them (on one occasion only just managing to scare off some Aboriginals who were threatening to spear them).

The whole expedition, men and beasts, was now exhausted. Their failing strength showed itself in various ways – the beasts were incapable of sustained effort while the men were weak, and troubled by boils and skin rashes, no doubt a result of their debilitated physical state. The heat was such that at every sign of water the bullocks and horses could not be restrained from rushing to it; on one such occasion one of the bullocks swam happily about in a pond while Leichhardt almost wept with vexation because it was carrying the precious remains of his botanical collection, which were getting soaked.

The country was now rocky and barren and progress distressingly slow. Another horse died in an accident; one of the two remaining bullocks had to be slaughtered (until they moved on, Leichhardt noted, its companion returned again and again to the spot where it had been killed). On 2 December they were heartened to meet a tribe of over two hundred natives, most of whom spoke some English – a sign surely that the end of their journey might be within reach. Plagued by boils and prickly heat, with festering cuts and sores on their hands, all they now wanted was for their ordeal to end. And on 17 December, it did. First, they reached a simple cart track, next what might be called a road; they then passed a cultivated garden with well-kept bushes and palms, thereafter a row of thatched cottages, and finally came to the house of the Commandant of Port Essington.

The Commandant, John McArthur, had had no hope of their arrival; they had been due at Port Essington eight months previously and he had assumed that they had either died in the bush or been killed by natives.

Back in Sydney, having travelled there comfortably by schooner, they were greeted with incredulous joy. Isaac Nathan, friend of Lord Byron and composer of Australia's first opera, had written for Sydney's Royal Victoria Theatre an elegy, 'Leichhardt's Grave' – he had rapidly to change it to a paean, 'Thy Greeting Home Again'. A public collection on the explorer's behalf raised £1,500, to which the governor added a grant of £1,000. The Speaker of the Legislative Council paid tribute to the expedition, and Leichhardt sat for his bust, which was placed in the public museum. He settled down to sorting out his specimens and preparing his journal for publication, which occurred in 1847. It is an interesting and vivid account of the journey, although it was obviously carefully edited to give the impression of complete accord among the explorers. But Leichhardt seems to have spoken freely to friends in Sydney about the shortcomings of the other members of the expedition. A poem written to celebrate his accomplishments included the lines:

Oft in the silent wilderness, when meaner spirits quail'd,
Have thy unfailing energies, to cheer and sooth prevailed.

The 'meaner spirits', especially Roper, were not amused and began in turn to criticise Leichhardt's behaviour. The latter was forced to put him right:

You know well Mr Roper how little satisfied I was with your behaviour and you will remember that I expressed even two days before reaching Pt Essington my ardent wish, not so much of being at the end of my journey, as being rid of companions who did take so little trouble to please me . . . I assure you that even now in reading over my journal I feel frequently most miserable. – But let it pass. I think you acted very wrong, but I am ready to excuse you.[17]

As he wrote that letter, not content with having just returned from a 4,827km trek, Leichhardt was already planning another expedition.

On 7 December 1846 Leichhardt and eight men departed from Jimbour, in Queensland, with the intention of crossing the whole continent, to the Swan river on the west coast. Gathering his party together, he took care this time to make sure recruits knew what they were letting themselves in for, 'how necessary it was that every one, who went with me, should share equally in the general work'. He pointed out

how harassing and fatiguing [the] work frequently was, the loading and unloading of the bullocks, which became frequently restive and upset their load during the day's stage, the saddling, hobbling, tethering of horses, the watching at night, collecting firewood, the killing of bullocks, cutting up their meat, drying it by frequent turning, the mending of saddles and pack-saddles, and many other little things, every one of which in a tropical climate becomes troublesome and fatiguing. There is even the chance of increased difficulties, as we take four different kinds of animals, goats, bullocks, horses and mules, every one of which has its peculiar habits and requires attention . . .

I advise you to consider all these points well, and to remember that the fatigues of our solitary bush life will render us taciturn and morose; every one wants a stock of good humour and cheerfulness; but more than this is the interest in the success of the expedition, and the perfect willingness to submit to every thing which is required for that purpose. Do never think of joining such an expedition if you find it difficult to obey; you would render yourself as well as the whole party miserable.[18]

The expedition was to be even more miserable than Leichhardt had suggested. At the very start, only two days out, something frightened the animals during the night, and the whole lot took off; at daybreak, only four mules and two horses could be found. Three weeks were spent searching for the missing beasts and it was past Christmas before most of them had been recovered. In the meantime the explorers were troubled by the worst plague of flies and mosquitoes anyone had ever experienced. The roast goat which made their Christmas dinner seemed to consist as much of flies as of meat.

At last, the venture really got under way. One of the explorers, the surveyor John Frederick Mann, left in his notebook the best description we have of Leichhardt's appearance as he led the group into the wilderness:

The Doctor was a tall man, six feet in height; he had lost a considerable amount of flesh since leaving Sydney which gave him the appearance of greater height. He wore at this time a Malay hat of conical shape, a most serviceable covering; the lower part of his face was hidden by a bushy, light-brown beard and moustache; a very old, greasy, long tweed coat, which had seen service on a former occasion, partly hid a red woollen shirt; his moleskin trousers did not quite reach to his low boots; these were tied with string. He preferred to carry a sword, as he could not use a gun; this was slung in such a manner – the handle projecting behind him – that he would have found it a difficult matter to grasp it in case he required to do so. Being now troubled with boils, he had one stirrup as long and the other as short as possible.[19]

It soon became crystal clear to everyone but Leichhardt that the expedition was doomed. The wet season was upon them, and it rained and rained and rained. The tents proved to be too light-weight and tore, so that the men were soaked through during the night. Tensions made themselves felt among the company, the men were seriously stung by hornets, sandflies made life miserable, the mules became bogged down in river mud and it was found that the spade needed to dig them out had been left behind. Then everyone fell sick and the whole party came to a halt for three weeks, reduced to lying in what shade could be found, feverish and delirious. Daniel Bunce, the botanist (who seems to have been suffering from venereal disease as well as fever) called repeatedly for snuff, which in fact he never took, then hysterically accused Leichhardt of eating a whole bed of mustard and cress which he had sown. Leichhardt had certainly eaten some, but Bunce in his fever exaggerated, as he did when, the following day, he accused his leader of eating too much of a stew he had made from a sheep's head.

Time and again Leichhardt tried to get the party moving, but the men were too sick. On Easter Monday they made a serious attempt to march on, but were still too weak to manage the animals. During the second half of April they made some progress, but by the beginning of May Leichhardt himself was ill, and also suffering from severe toothache. They struggled on, though everyone but he realised that the situation was impossible. Finally, on 9 June 1847, with his men still weak and still attacked every day by sandflies, the horses' limbs streaming with blood from the bites; with the humidity and heat a torment during the day, and the temperature almost freezing at night, he finally gave up. The disconsolate party straggled home.

Leichhardt's confidence and ambitions remained unscathed by the kind of experience which would have put many people off the whole idea of exploring for life. As with his first expedition, he blamed his companions for the failure of the second, or rather himself for choosing them, writing to Schmalfuss:

Here I am, back again from a journey of exploration, but not in the least like a conqueror marching in with banners flying to the jubilation of the multitude. On the contrary, I've been compelled to return worn out by illness and with disgruntled companions whom I've had to lead back to the fleshpots of Egypt before I had even set foot in unexplored country.

The probable reasons why I failed are these: the young men I took with me were from Sydney; they were accustomed not to the hard life in the bush but to the soft, easy-going life in town; in both mind and body they lacked that resilience which enables one to recover quickly even from illness; and in disposition they lacked the calmness and pliancy that help one to keep his eyes fixed on present considerations instead of gazing hopefully into the distance or regretfully back towards the pleasures of the old life. Their interests were mundane and mercenary, nothing more.[20]

The new expedition set out from Cogoon, in the Western Downs of Queensland, on 5 April 1848. Led by Leichhardt were Arthur Hendig, a station manager who would know how to control the beasts; August Classen, a distant relative; three 'working men', Kelly, Stewart and Hands; and two Aboriginal men, Jimmy and Billy. The procession, including fifty bullocks, twenty mules and seven horses, set off towards the Warrego river. Nothing of men or beasts was ever seen again: they all vanished without trace.

Over the following thirty years and more efforts were continually made to discover what had happened to Leichhardt and his companions. In 1852 an official enquiry concluded that they had probably been killed by Aboriginals somewhere in Western Queensland. Throughout the 1850s, here and there from the Barcoo river to the Flinders and Arltunga, east of Alice Springs, and at Glenormiston on the Georgina river, trees were found with the letter L carved into their bark. In 1871 skeletons were discovered on the banks of the Diamantina river, which were very possibly those of the explorers.

The mystery remains, as does Leichhardt's reputation as one of the great explorers of the Australian interior. He was a man who

Leichhardt's initials, carved into the bark of a tree at Cooper's Creek, persuaded some of those enquiring into his expedition's disappearance that they might have been swept to their deaths in 1848 by flash flooding. *(Illustrated Australian News supplement)*

had overcome almost insuperable obstacles, had done so without any loss of life until the last, and whose limitations were those of his companions rather than his own. In a letter to Schmalfuss written just before he set out on his last expedition, he promised on his return to visit his relatives in Europe. Meanwhile, he quoted Schiller's poem *Sehnsucht*, or 'Longing':

> *Du must hoffen, Du must wagen,*
> *Denn die Götter leihn kein Pfand*
> *Nur ein Wunder kann Dich tragen*
> *In das schöne Wunderland —*
>
> [You shall trust and you shall venture
> Pledges to the gods are banned;
> Nought but Wonder's wings can bear you
> To the far-off Wonderland.]

* * *

While Sir Thomas Mitchell was at home in England preparing his journals for publication, he instructed his 27-year-old assistant, the surveyor Edmund Kennedy, to attempt to trace the Barcoo river to its mouth, which Mitchell had supposed was in the Gulf of Carpentaria (the possibility of finding a practicable route to the north coast was of course in both their minds). The expedition failed, but Kennedy impressed the Governor, Sir Charles Fitzroy, who appointed him to head an expedition to explore the eastern coast to the north as far as Port Albany, mainly in the hope of finding a good site for a port where ships could replenish their coal supplies as they sailed between Sydney and Singapore.

Kennedy set out from Sydney on the barque Tam O'Shanter *in April 1848, with twelve men, twenty-eight horses and a hundred sheep, and landed at Rockingham Bay, between Townsville and Cairns, to face a journey as hard as that attempted by any Australian explorer before or since. He and his men fought their way through salt-water creeks, marshes and thick scrub, their clothes and flesh torn by the lawyer vine* (Calamus australis), *with its long hooks and spurs like barbed wire, and tortured by the stinging tree* (Laportea) *whose leaves painfully stung men and horses.*

By 18 July they had been forced to abandon their carts and fifty of their sheep, and their horses were dying, one by one. For four months they wandered about the north Queensland jungle and toiled up and down its mountains, increasingly short of provisions, and growing weaker and weaker. On 9 November Kennedy decided that he must leave eight of his party behind and with three white men, an Aboriginal boy, Jacky Jacky, and seven of the healthiest horses make for Port Albany, from where he intended to send a ship back to rescue the others.

The five men cut their way again through thick scrub until one of them became violently ill and another accidentally shot himself. Kennedy left them, and a third man to care for them, and himself pressed on with Jacky. They had almost reached Albany when a number of local tribesmen appeared and trailed them all day before suddenly throwing spears, hitting Kennedy in the back. Jacky fired and hit one of them, and while they retreated cut the barbed spear out; but they came back, spearing several of the horses, which bolted, hitting Kennedy again, this time in the leg and side, and Jacky in the eye.

Jacky again cut the spear-heads out of their flesh, but Kennedy was obviously severely wounded. He ordered Jacky to take care of his journals, which they had been carrying, and attempted to write a last message, but was too weak. Then he died.

'I caught him as he fell back, and held him,' Jacky later said, 'and I then turned round myself and cried. I was crying a good while until I got well, that was about an hour, and then I buried him. I digged up the ground with a tomahawk, and covered him over with logs and grass and my shirt and trousers.'[21]

Pursued by his attackers, Jacky managed to evade them; but it was thirteen days before he reached Port Albany. The three men who had accompanied Kennedy were never found; only two of the party left behind survived.

There were other expeditions in Western Australia in the early 1850s, searching as usual for good grazing land. In 1854, Robert Austin, Assistant Surveyor-General, set out to look for grazing land and also for gold, for the gold rush was now in full swing. His expedition was crippled almost from the start, when his horses ate poisonous weeds; almost all fell sick and fourteen died. He found a gold field, at Mount Magnet, 350km inland from present-day Geraldton, but it was too remote to be developed (it later became a gold town and now has an excellent pastoral museum). He and two Aboriginal guides attempted to find the way to the Murchison river and water, living for several days on half a rat each and tormented by mirages holding out the promise of non-existent lakes (the Aboriginals called this 'walk-away and tell lie water'). The Murchison, when they reached it, was dry. On the way there, over rocky and intransigent country, one of Austin's party *accidentally shot himself in the arm, the wound became infected and the unfortunate man died in agony. The ten remaining men marched on, largely at night to avoid the fearful heat, and survived to reach Perth after two months. They had discovered only desert.*

The following year a large expedition funded by the British government set out from Moreton Bay in Queensland to seek out land for potential development in Northern Australia. A surveyor from Western Australia, Augustus Gregory, led a team of eighteen men, with fifty horses and two hundred sheep. The barque taking them north ran aground, but on 24 September 1855 they landed at Treachery Bay, near the mouths of the Fitzmaurice and Victoria rivers. The landing was not without difficulty: the horses had to swim over 3km through mangrove swamps before they reached solid ground during which arduous journey three were drowned, one was sucked down into the mud, and one simply disappeared. The rest were almost totally exhausted.

Problems continued as they travelled south: crocodiles attacked three of the horses and killed a dog, and several others died for lack of food, as did many of the sheep. The drunken captain of one of the support boats ran her aground, losing valuable supplies including fifty sheep, which had been in pens on the deck. Gregory's collapsible rubber boat melted in the heat. Tension among the men meant that disagreements and quarrels broke out as they continued south for 500km until, at Mount Wilson (named after the expedition's geologist), Gregory was forced to conclude that there was nothing within human reach but what he called the Great Australian Desert.

At the end of June he and six men began to trek east, over ground much of which had been traversed by Leichhardt in his 1844–5 expedition. In July trouble struck again: two of the best horses ate poisonous plants and died as the party rode through the sandy, arid country bordering the McArthur river, and by the end of August, his horses almost completely exhausted and many of the party suffering from scurvy,

Gregory was again forced to recognise the enormous size of the northern desert country.

They tramped on towards the Gulf of Carpentaria, past the Flinders river, then the Gilbert river, where they were forced to kill one of their horses for food. On 15 November at the Mackenzie river they found a tree still incised with Leichhardt's initial. On 21 November 1856 they reached the Dawson river and the outermost reaches of civilisation. Gregory had travelled 3,000km by sea and 8,000 by land, and though he had found some pastoral land, most of his journey had only confirmed the fact that much of north Australia consisted of desert.

The pace of exploration was now quickening. It was also in 1856 that the geologist Benjamin Herschel Babbage discovered excellent grazing country north of the Flinders Ranges in South Australia; two years after Augustus Gregory had tramped through that desert, his brother Francis found good pastoral land north of Perth, in West Australia, during a 3,000-km expedition from the Murchison river to the De Grey, over the Kennedy and Hamersley Ranges.

EIGHT

Seven Months Underground
Charles Sturt, 1844–5

A decade after his first, successful expedition, Charles Sturt set out again in search of the Great Inland Sea. Inevitably, since it did not exist, his endeavour failed; he barely survived the adventure, he and his fellows suffering privations as great as any experienced by the other Australian explorers.

Sturt hoped for considerable advancement in the wake of his achievements of 1827–30, but he was to be disappointed. He was sent to the notorious Norfolk Island, a penal settlement for the most intransigent of convicts, who lived there under one of the harshest and most brutal regimes ever inflicted on British prisoners. It is not known just what position Sturt held, but he seems to have successfully discouraged the convicts from mutiny against the brutality of their warders. In the meantime he enjoyed exploring and recording the wildlife on the island.

Deteriorating eyesight and indifferent health led to his return to London, where he arrived, almost completely blind, in 1832. He retired from the army and wrote up the journal of his expedition. On 20 September 1834 he married, and he and his wife left England almost immediately for Australia, where he intended to settle down as a farmer. For a time he was content, his only venture into open country being in April 1837 when he drove cattle and sheep from Sydney to Adelaide. This had been done before, but was nevertheless an adventure. The Aboriginals were far from friendly, and there was almost a fight with them (characteristically, Sturt went out of his way to avoid bloodshed). Wild dogs attacked the sheep and crossing the Murray river required ingenious planning, but the journey was successfully accomplished.

Despite his poor eyesight, Sturt was unhappy at having to lead a relatively sedentary life, and in 1844, when he was 49 years old – almost an old man by the standards of the time – he managed with the help of his old friend the former Governor Darling to persuade the Colonial Office in London to authorise him one more expedition in search of the Great Inland Sea. (He may have seen the map published in London in 1830, which showed a 'Great River or the Desired Blessing' flowing from a 'Great Lake' in the middle of the Simpson Desert.[1]) Lord Stanley, the Secretary of State for the Colonies agreed that he could select a team and set out immediately. The discovery of the Inland Sea was not the main purpose of the expedition: it was more important thoroughly to map the area, particularly the rivers, around the 28th Parallel. Privately, Sturt hoped to reach the very centre of the continent, an ambition which had preoccupied his fellow explorer Edward Eyre.

Sturt selected seventeen men from among more than three hundred applicants, all eager to join such a renowned explorer in his new adventure. James Poole, an Irishman, was appointed as Sturt's right-hand man, John Harris Browne as the expedition's doctor, and the 29-year-old John McDouall Stuart as draughtsman. Among the humbler members were the Devonshire-born Methodist Daniel Brock – a deeply egocentric and unlikeable man with a religious mania who was to look after the guns; Robert Flood as head stockman (he had accompanied Sturt on his overlanding to Adelaide); and an Aboriginal named Tampanang ('Bob'). Six wagons carried 7 tonnes of stores; there were 30 bullocks, 11 horses, 200 sheep, 6 dogs, a portable boat, a great number of warm blankets (against the freezing cold of the nights), 200kg of bacon (to augment the supply of fresh meat provided by the sheep) and a Union Jack which Sturt intended to plant in a suitable spot.

Well-wishers lined the streets of Adelaide on Sunday 10 August 1844 as the party set out, having partaken of a celebratory breakfast with some of the city's notables, two hundred of whom rode out to accompany Sturt and his men for the first few kilometres. Sturt was pensive. 'I watched [the party] with anxiety which made one forgetful of everything else,' he wrote in his journal; 'and I naturally turned my thoughts to the future. How many of those who had just passed me so full of hope and in such exuberant spirits would be permitted to return to their homes? Should I, their leader, be one of those destined to remain in the desert . . . ?'[2] He also wrote to his wife warning her in so many words that his days might be numbered.

Two months of steady plodding brought the expedition to Moorundi and the banks of the Murray. There, they were met by Eyre, the Protector of Aboriginals, and in his presence Sturt addressed the whole party on the importance of treating any native they might meet with kindness, but warning them to be careful to have nothing to do with their women.[3] The men bent their heads over their bullock whips as he read a prayer, reminding them that they 'were perhaps *for ever* to pass away into the unknown interior and [face] dangers of many characters'.[4] Eyre persuaded Sturt to add two more Aboriginals to his party, Camboli and Nadbuck, both strong and willing, although Nadbuck could be too easily distracted by the appearance of any handsome *gin*. Eyre also accompanied the expedition for a while, carrying a supply of blankets to distribute to any Aboriginals they met, items that would be welcome against the cold of the nights.

Passing Lakes Bonney and Victoria, and measuring their circumference, the expedition pressed on to the Darling river. The Aboriginals they encountered were friendly, although Sturt was wary of them: 'Although I was always disposed to be kind to the natives,' he wrote, 'I still felt it right to shew them that they were not to be unruly. Neither is it without great satisfaction that I look back to the intercourse I have had with these people, from the fact of my never having had any occasion to raise my arm in hostility against them.'[5]

Eyre left the expedition as it marched on up the Darling to Menindee, and set up a depot at Lake Cawndilla. Sturt lived in daily expectation of catching sight of his 'Mediterranean', the inland sea. Indeed, Stuart and another man, James Poole, came back after a short trek to the north with an excited report of a huge lake which, alas, proved to be a mirage. The expedition moved on northwards and set up another camp at Flood Creek, which seemed to be the only reliable source of water for hundreds of kilometres around. Christmas was a melancholy occasion, with several of the men suffering from mild dysentery and almost everyone from sore eyes. Poole had developed scurvy and Sturt noticed the same symptoms in himself: 'We had swollen gums, taste of copper in the mouth, and violent headaches, and I had what perhaps did me good – constant but not profuse bleeding at the nose . . .'.[6] Some 200 miles west of the Darling, Sturt contemplated his surroundings and thought he must be at the end of the world: 'It appeared as if we were the last of creation amid the desolation and destruction of the world. There was a solemn stillness around, not a living thing to be seen, not an ant, not a cricket, or a grasshopper. The horizon was unbroken from north all round to north again, nor was there a shadow of hope in that dreary and monotonous wilderness.'[7]

On 27 January 1845, he made a camp at what he called Preservation Creek, about 40km from Mount Hopeless, which seemed to have an ample supply of water. It was now midsummer and there was unlikely to be any rain for several months. For safety's sake Sturt decided to stay there until rain came. For seven months they did not move. They dug an underground shelter, a hole in the ground roofed with brushwood coated with mud, on top of which earth was piled. This offered some protection from the glare of the sun, and the temperature in the small 'room' (which measured about 2m high by 5m wide and 4m long – 7ft × 16ft × 12ft) was some 4 degrees cooler than outside, where it sometimes rose as high as 157°F in the sun.

'Our hair, as well as the wool on the sheep, ceased to grow,' Sturt recorded; 'and our nails had become as brittle as glass. The flour lost more than eight per cent of its original weight, and the other provisions in still greater proportion. The bran in which our bacon had been packed, was perfectly saturated, and weighed almost as heavy as the meat; we were obliged to bury our wax candles; a bottle of citric acid in Mr Brown's box became fluid, and escaping, burnt a quantity of his linen; and we found it difficult to write or draw, so rapidly did the ink dry in our pens and brushes.'[8]

There was nothing much to do, although Sturt made several excursions in order to prepare really detailed maps of the surrounding area. Conditions deteriorated: in the intense heat the water of the creek visibly shrank every day, becoming stagnant and almost impossible to drink. Sturt rode out in search of a waterhole, but found only a small puddle of water, so muddy that when Punch, his horse, tried to drink his nose became coated with mud. The heat was remorseless.

Everyone was now in poor health. Scurvy had attacked them all: they could not relish their food because of the coppery taste in their mouths (though a monotonous diet of damper, mutton, bacon and tea was not in any event very palatable). Poole was in the worst state: 'The scurvy seized him with the grip of a tiger. He lost the use of his lower extremities, the skin of his legs turned black, large pieces of flesh hung down from the roof of his mouth, and he was at once reduced to perfect helplessness. . . . On 26 March he took to his bed, and never rose from it again. . . .'[9] Sturt prepared to send Poole back to Adelaide on a dray as soon as the rain came, and at last, on 12 July, it did, but too late for Poole. On 14 July he died and was buried, rolled up in a blanket and placed on his mattress, under a grevillia tree on which Sturt carved 'J.P., 1845'.

Now, with the rain, came the possibility of moving. Sturt sent six men – those in the worst health – back to Adelaide under the care of his storekeeper, Piesse; he himself, with nine others, set off to the north-west, chaining their way to Lake Pinnaroo. He was ambitious to reach the centre of the continent, apart from which, almost unbelievably, he still clung tenaciously to the idea that the inland sea must be somewhere yet to be discovered. Conditions in the rain brought their own trials: the horses pulling the wagons sank 6 inches into mud and when, infrequently, they did reach dry ground it was so sandy that it brought almost the same problem. At Lake Pinnaroo he built a stockade, which he named Fort Grey, for the sixty-eight remaining sheep and from there pressed on with three men, ten horses and a supply of provisions which he calculated would last fifteen weeks.

The heat was now more bearable – indeed, there was frost at dawn, but there was a wind that muddied any water pools the party found. They reached one of the most arid and threatening places in the continent, the south-east corner of what is now called the Simpson Desert, a corner which became known as Sturt's Stony Desert. Here, an immeasurable barren plain stretched away into the distance, covered with stones, scarcely any vegetation; a satanic landscape. The explorers staggered on for 80km, their horses, frantic for food, gnawing desperately at the bark of the few stunted trees they found.

Sturt was now, he judged, within 240km of the very centre of Australia; yet to go further would be suicide – it was near the end of the rainy season and the prospect of being caught so far from civilisation without enough water was a horrific one. 'We have seen no change in this fearful and unparalleled Desert,' he wrote. 'I have now lost all hope of finding any body of water or of making my discovery, and feel that I am subjecting myself and others to all this exposure & privation solely to discharge my duty conscientiously [yet] weeks have yet to transpire ere I can feel myself justified in giving up this most difficult and most anxious task.'[10]

Back the party dragged, over the Stony Desert, Sturt's journal recording day after day his concern to find fresh water and his fear that quite apart from himself and his companions, the horses could not long endure without a proper supply. Any natives they encountered were almost equally dehydrated. On 30 September they reached Fort Grey. Sturt wrote: 'We had ridden from first to last a distance of 963 miles [some 1,500km], and had generally been on horse-back from the earliest dawn to 3 or 4 often to 6 o'clock, having no shelter of any kind from the tremendous heat of the fiery deserts in which we had been wandering, subsisting on an insufficient supply of food, and drinking water that pigs would have refused.'[11]

But having survived a journey which few men could have endured, Sturt was deeply depressed: 'I had the painful reflection before me that whatever my exertions had been, I had made no discovery to entitle me to credit or reward, and that therefore I should fail in the only object for which I sought and undertook this tremendous and anxious task . . . difficulties and disappointments have overwhelmed me from first to last.'[12] Even now, he wanted to turn about once more and attempt, travelling north-east, to reach the centre of the continent.

Browne, the doctor, was in very poor health and Sturt attempted to order him back to Adelaide. However, Browne had promised Sturt's wife not to leave him and resolutely refused to go. Sturt reluctantly agreed, placed Browne in charge of Fort Grey and set out again, with Stuart and two others, eight horses and provisions for ten weeks. They reached Cooper's Creek, but trying to force their way onward were confronted with yet more relentless, arid desert. At first, water had been relatively plentiful; but soon the old problem returned of finding a bare minimum to ensure survival. By early November 1845, after just over five weeks, the party was in a sorry state. One of the men had been careless in replacing the bungs of the water kegs, which had run dry, and the nearest known supply of water was 50 miles away. The horses, unshod, had worn their hooves down to the quick. Sturt had travelled 1,475km before his thermometer burst, two horses died and he was finally forced to retreat. Having lurched back to the depot at Fort Grey, they found it deserted; dysentery had afflicted all the men so severely that Browne had retired to Preservation Creek. Sturt and his men had to follow, reaching the depot on 17 November. There, he collapsed with scurvy and, protesting at not being allowed to ride, was carried on a litter as they started out on the 450km journey to Menindee, where there would be ample food supplies. Browne collected quantities of berries which he had seen the Aboriginals eat and fed them to Sturt; these countered the effects of scurvy, and the leader's health gradually improved. At Moorundi he was provided with a carriage and rode back to Adelaide, arriving at midnight on 19 July. His wife fainted when she opened the door to him.

Sturt was given a public dinner in Adelaide, and the Royal Geographical Society awarded him the Founder's Medal. He was appointed Colonial Treasurer, returning to England in 1853 after his retirement still lamenting his failure to discover the Great Inland

Sea, but resigned to the fact that 'it is of no avail regretting what it was not in one's destiny to fulfil'.[13] He died in 1869.

Attempts have been made to denigrate Sturt, pointing out with some justice that he was inclined to boast, sometimes made chronological errors in his books, and neglected his men. Most of these accusations are based on material in a book by the Methodist Brock,[14] who was with him on his last expedition. Whatever the criticisms, of all Australia's explorers Sturt remains the most sympathetic, both for his attitude to and treatment of his men, and for his attitude to the Aboriginals, which contrasted markedly not only with that of other explorers, but with the behaviour of a great number of Australians of his day and, indeed, of the subsequent thirty or forty years.

NINE

To the Very Centre
John McDouall Stuart, 1858, 1859, 1862

The most cautious, best-prepared and one of the most determined of the great Australian explorers, Stuart in his unostentatious, modest way accomplished as much as Leichhardt or Burke, but remains perhaps the least celebrated of them all. His ambition was to be the first person to cross Australia from south to north, and he accomplished it – though in the process 'enduring the greatest pain that it is possible for a man to suffer'.

John McDouall Stuart's first sight of Adelaide, when in 1838 he arrived, aged 23, on the barque *Indus*, cannot have been particularly impressive. Most of the dwellings were thatched hovels with mud walls and the 'streets' little better than rough tracks which in winter were churned into rivers of mud. On the other hand, the town was growing fast and it quickly became apparent to him that his decision to come to Australia had been the right one, as was his choice of a town which, although then barely more than a rough settlement, was growing more substantial by the day.

Born on 7 September 1815, the fifth son of a Scottish customs officer who worked in the port of Dysart, on the Firth of Forth, Stuart had trained in Edinburgh as a civil engineer and so had no difficulty in gaining employment as a surveyor and draughtsman, working out in the bush around the Onkaparinga river 30km outside Adelaide.

It was in 1844 that he heard that Captain Charles Sturt was forming a new expedition to seek out the Inland Sea which everyone believed must exist somewhere in the centre of the country, and applied to join it as surveyor. His application was accepted, and he is listed among the members of Sturt's expedition as 'draughtsman'.

He accepted the fearful hardships of the expedition[1] with equanimity, and proved so reliable that for the latter part of it he was appointed Sturt's second in command. When the party returned to Adelaide and Sturt wrote his final report, it included a tribute to his colleague: 'I should be sorry to close without recording the valuable and cheerful assistance I received from Mr. Stuart, whose zeal and spirit were equally conspicuous, and whose labour on the charts did him much credit.'[2]

The torments of their undertaking had failed to dampen Stuart's enthusiasm for exploration, which if anything was stimulated by the experience. Eager to mount his own expedition, it was to be fourteen years before he was able to fulfil his ambition. In 1858, with the help of a patron who had made a fortune in copper mining, he managed to get a small expedition together to search for good pastoral land in South Australia, at the same time keeping his eyes open for evidence of the inland sea, which had still not been discovered.

On 14 May he set out with five horses and two companions, a George Forster (of whom nothing is known but his name) and a young Aboriginal; apart from food supplies, the only equipment he took with him was a pocket compass and a watch. It was a valuable experience, which served him well later on his major expedition. The three men tramped doggedly to the north-west of Adelaide, from station to station, waterhole to waterhole, over bleak, stony country which badly wore the horses' shoes – and he had brought no spares (a mistake he never made again). By 26 June he had passed north of Lake Torrens and come upon a large and handsome creek which he called Chambers Creek (it is now sometimes called Stuart Creek), a valuable discovery which alone justified the expedition. It was to be the place where Stuart himself, and many later travellers, would rest and recuperate before tackling the desolate country ahead.

In early July rain came, making the ground boggy and difficult to negotiate, the horses up to their knees in mud and increasingly lame.

All their rations and everything they had were soaked through. There was not much game about, and when they did see it they found it difficult to kill – they seem to have been indifferent shots. Occasionally, they dined off opossum and wallaby. On 3 August, the Aboriginal deserted, simply vanishing into the landscape. Stuart was untroubled: he had been of very little use and presumably would join up with a native tribe somewhere in the area. The country remained largely barren, worse even than Sturt's desert. By the middle of the month Stuart was discouraged: 'I almost give up hopes of a good country; this is very disheartening, after all that I have done to find it,' he wrote in his journal.[3] A few days later, on 11 August, he seemed on the brink of despair: 'Today's few miles have been through the same *dreary, dreadful, dismal desert* of heavy sand hills and spinifex [a rough grass] with mallee [woody shrubs and trees] very dense, scarcely a mouthful for the horses to eat. When will it have an end?'[4] He had now travelled over 1,600km. From natives, he heard stories of Wingillpin, a legendary freshwater lake surrounded by gum trees, where crowds of kangaroos congregated to graze on rich grass.[5] They never found it.

Prospects were not good. Stuart was now making for Streaky Bay, but on 17 August only had left enough food for two meals. For some time he and Forster had been living on one meal a day of a little flour-cake, occasionally made more interesting by roast kangaroo-mice ('elegant little creatures', Stuart noted), and lack of food had exhausted them. It took them three days to cover the 160km to Miller's Water, near the coast of the Great Australian Bight, where a settler gave them some food. They rested for a day, then made on for the Maryvale station on the southern tip of Streaky Bay. After ten days there they were able to travel on to Adelaide.

At the settlement, there was much praise for Stuart's effort, which had indeed been remarkable. He had travelled over 12,000km through previously unexplored country, with no means of discovering his longitude, yet equipped with only a small pocket compass had found his way to a spot so insignificant that it was just a dot on the map. The Governor, Sir Richard MacDonnell, wrote home to the Secretary of State for the Colonies to extol the explorer as a man 'with a moral courage and hardihood of the highest description'.[6] The Secretary immediately dispatched a gold watch as a token of his congratulations and approval. Sturt, too, who was now living in retirement in Cheltenham, sent his good wishes.

Stuart's second expedition set out on 2 April 1859, financed by two friends. This time he took some proper instruments with him: a good compass, a sextant and an artificial horizon. He also had three companions – David Herrgott, a Bavarian botanist, Louis Miller, a miner, and Campbell, a stockman. It was a successful but relatively uneventful survey lasting only three months, their plans cut short because of difficulty with the horses; ironically, although this time he had taken spare shoes for them, he had not taken enough. He discovered new springs, which he named Herrgott Springs after his botanist companion. But more important to him was his first sight of the native melon, *cucumis melo*, which he mistakenly called a cucumber; recognising it in later expeditions, he was able to take advantage of what, when boiled, constituted a valuable food. And the Governor was again impressed; in particular he considered that the route Stuart had taken to the north might well represent the best line for an 'electric Wire' which might eventually connect Australia with India and Europe.

The third expedition was somewhat similar, except that to the hope of finding pastoral land was added that of finding gold. But Stuart was seriously let down by some of his companions, who either absconded or were sent packing; the only positive result was the surveying of no less than 20,700 sq km of countryside, among which was some good farming land. One positive aspect of the expedition was the presence as a member of William Darton Kekwick, an amateur botanist who had come to Australia in 1840 and had had experience as a surveyor. Vigorous and dependable, he was to become second in command on Stuart's fourth expedition, which was mounted in 1860 and had as its aim nothing less than a trek right up through the centre of the continent to the Gulf of Carpentaria.

The government had offered a reward of £2,000 to 'the person who shall succeed in crossing through the country lately discovered by Mr Stuart either to the North or North-western shores of the Australian continent'. Unsurprisingly, Stuart himself decided to compete and on 2 March once again led a team into the unknown. It was a small party, comprising Stuart, William Kekwick and Benjamin 'Ben' Head, a Cornish lad of only 18 who had come from Hayle to Adelaide in 1854, where he had worked in the railway yards. Substantial and muscular of physique, he was over 6ft tall and weighed almost 15st. Setting out with these two companions and thirteen horses, Stuart planned a journey of no less than 3,200km, most of it through unexplored country and, as it turned out, through a country where the native inhabitants were almost universally hostile.

On 1 April, after a fairly successful month's progress, there was an ominous sign of trouble to come: Stuart had for some time found his sight to be deteriorating and noted that 'my right eye . . . is become useless to me for taking observations. I now see two suns instead of one, which has led me into an error of a few miles. I trust to goodness my other eye will not become the same; as long as it remains good, I can do.'[7] A less determined man, fearing blindness, might have turned back. Not Stuart; for some time now he had been passing through entirely unexplored country, and was steadily marching towards the centre of the continent.

Rain slowed their progress at first. One old horse, which had been on Stuart's previous expedition, got bogged down and had to be left behind, while the rain spoiled half their supply of dried meat. The country varied between the rocky and difficult, and stretches of excellent well-watered grassland. He followed the usual practice of naming features of the landscape after his friends and supporters – the MacDonnell Range after the Governor, Brunkley Bluff and Hanson Bluff after friends in Adelaide, Anna's Reservoir after the child of another friend, and Mount Leichhardt 'in memory of that unfortunate explorer, whose fate is still a mystery'.[8] Perhaps the most remarkable feature was something which, from the distance, looked like 'a locomotive engine with its funnel'. When he came up to it, he found it to be a 'pillar of a sandstone 120 feet high [in reality 167ft], quite perpendicular; and it is twenty feet wide by ten feet deep, with two small peaks on the top'.[9] He named it Chambers Pillar, after one of his most generous supporters. It remains an uncommon feature, situated some 150km south of Alice Springs and 60km east of the Stuart Highway.

Stuart, the first white man to come this way, found the landscape through which he passed fascinating in its changes of colour and texture. Not for nothing is the area now known as 'the red centre', a tourist attraction, renowned for its gorges and waterholes, craggy red sandstone outcrops and limpid creeks. He pressed on along the Hugh river, west of what is now Alice Springs, until on 22 April he was able to write in his journal: 'Today I find from my observations of the sun, 111°00′30″, that I am now camped in the centre of Australia. I have marked a tree and planted the British flag there. There is a high mount about two miles and a half to the north-north-east. I wish it had been in the centre; but on it tomorrow I will raise a cone of stones, and plant the flag there, and name it "Central Mount Stuart".'[10]

It is an unemotional entry apart from the fact that the words 'Centre of Australia' are heavily underlined; but his feeling of satisfaction must have been great. Sturt had badly wanted to reach the 'centre', but drought had forced him back. Now, the three men, their hands torn by scrub, their limbs – through clothing so rent that they were nearly naked – bitten raw by flies, Stuart's little mare, Polly, lame from an injured fetlock, enjoyed a moment of triumph perhaps unequalled by any other explorer. Next day they climbed Mount Stuart – 'much higher and more difficult of ascent than I experienced' – and looked down over a landscape considerably more colourful and interesting than they had anticipated. Below them was a plain with gum trees, mulga and spinifex, watercourses running freely through it, a creek winding round the hill and flowing on to the north, broken ranges of hills visible in the distance.

Then Stuart 'built a large cone of stones, in the centre of which I placed a pole with the British flag nailed to it. Near the top of the cone I placed a small bottle, in which there is a slip of paper, with our signatures to it, stating by whom it was raised. We then gave three hearty cheers for the flag, the emblem of civil and religious liberty, and may it be a sign to the natives that the dawn of liberty, civilisation and Christianity is about to break upon them.'[11] In the original manuscript of his journal, he has added: 'I then named the mount Sturt [after] the Father of Australian Exploration, for whom we also gave three hearty cheers and one more for Mrs Sturt and family.' By the time the journal was published, the Governor had decided to name the hill after Stuart himself, and the moving tribute to his friend was deleted.[12]

On 25 April the three men started their final journey towards the north-west coast. Five days later they ran into trouble. Stuart had guided the party to the west, making as he hoped for the Victoria river, but water became increasingly scarce – on one occasion it could only be found in a well so deep they had to draw it up in separate pots to water the horses. By 3 May Stuart was afraid that ambition had drawn him too far on the wrong track. They turned back to the well they had previously used, their horses now so thirsty they almost threw themselves into it: 'The quantity some of them drank was enormous,' Stuart recalled; 'I had no idea that a horse could hold so much, and still want more.'[13]

They rested for some days, Stuart now additionally worried by the fact that they were all beginning to suffer the effects of scurvy, himself worst of all: his mouth and gums were raw with sores. Kekwick was similarly plagued, though not so badly. Then, as they resumed their journey, worse followed: on 13 May he recorded in his journal: 'My attention being engaged looking for water, my horse took fright at a wallaby, and rushed into some scrub, which pulled me from the saddle, my foot and the staff that I carry for placing my compass on catching in the stirrup-iron. Finding that he was dragging me, he commenced kicking at a fearful rate; he struck me on the shoulder joint, knocked my hat off, and grazed my forehead. I soon got clear, but found the kick on my shoulder very painful.'[14]

They retired to Mount Stuart to recover their strength; there, Stuart became even more unwell; his bruises were yellow and black, his muscles excruciatingly painful, his hands a mass of sores which would not heal and his mouth so painful he could scarcely swallow. But they must make the effort to move on or die where they were.

This time, moving to the north-east, they found a way through less arduous country, and on 1 June arrived at a fine creek, the Bonney, with plentiful fish. They pressed on over what Stuart named the Murchison Range and Mount Samuel to Tennant and Bishop Creeks, once more traversing arid land where no water was to be found. Stuart climbed a tree, but could see nothing as far as the horizon other than the familiar scrub. One horse was 'knocked up' and had to be left to die, and the little bay mare Polly seemed to be running mad, kicking every living thing that came near her. Still, Stuart continued his observations, climbing painfully to the top of every hill in order to make notes of the surrounding landscape – 'killing work', as he observed.

After travelling for over 160km in a hundred hours without water they made camp at Bishop Creek, staying there for six weeks, exploring the land to the north-west. Two days after their arrival, a small group of Aboriginals appeared; they were different from the previous tribesmen the party had encountered in that they were well-nourished, powerful men, 6ft tall, with long hair, wearing only nets cast around their shoulders. They were armed with boomerangs, spears and sharp, scimitar-like weapons and looked prepared to use them. Stuart, by holding out a branch of green leaves and bowing his head, managed to ingratiate himself, and they left the explorers alone.

On 23 June, when, after having found only tracts of barren waterless land, Stuart made camp at a series of small ponds they had fortuitously come across in the desert, other Aboriginals appeared and, astonishingly, one old man seemed to make a Masonic sign. Stuart repeated it, whereupon the old man was highly pleased, stroking Stuart's beard and patting him on the shoulder. The accident aroused much speculation – could the 'Masonic gesture' have been taught him by a member of the lost Leichhardt expedition? It seems more likely that the old man was merely trying to communicate and Stuart misread his gesture.

He had always taken care to treat the Aboriginals with courtesy, if also with firmness – they had eager hands for anything which they could make off with; so far, although he felt a problem might arise, the relationship had been untroubled. But things now turned nasty. On 26 June, three powerful armed men suddenly appeared, and seemed to be angry. Stuart's journal records what happened.

I faced them, making every sign of friendship I could think of. They seemed to be in a great fury, moving their boomerangs above their heads, bawling at the top of their voices, and performing some sort of dance. They were now joined by more of their tribe, so that in a few minutes their numbers had increased to upwards of thirty; every bush seemed to produce a man . . . I told my men to make their guns ready, for I could see they were determined upon mischief. They paid no regard to all the signs of friendship I kept constantly making, but were still gradually approaching nearer and nearer to us.

I felt very unwilling to fire upon them, and still continued making signs of peace and friendship, but all to no purpose. Their leader, an old man, who was in advance, made signs with his boomerang, which we took as a signal for us to be off. They were, however, intended as tokens of defiance, for I had no sooner turned my horse's head to comply with what I thought were their wishes, than we received a shower of boomerangs, accompanied by a fearful yell; they then set fire to the grass, and commenced jumping, dancing, yelling, and throwing their arms into all sorts of postures, like so many fiends.

In addition to the thirty that already confronted us, I could now see many others getting up from behind the bushes. Still I felt unwilling to fire upon them, and tried again to make them understand that we wished to do them no harm. Having now approached within about forty yards of us, they made another charge, and threw their boomerangs, which came whistling and whizzing past our ears, one of them striking my brow. I then gave orders to fire, which stayed their mad career for a little. Our pack-horses, which were on before us, took fright when they heard the firing and fearful yelling, and made off for the creek. Seeing some of the blacks running from bush to bush, with the intention of cutting us off from our horses, while those in front were still yelling, throwing their boomerangs, and coming nearer to us, we gave them another reception, and I sent Ben after the horses to drive them on to a more favourable place, while Kekwick and I remained to cover our rear. We soon got in advance of those who were endeavouring to cut us off, but they still kept following, though beyond the reach of our guns, the fearful yelling still continuing from more numerous voices, and fires springing up in every direction.[15]

It was a perilous situation, for though Stuart had guns, the odds were at least ten to one against him, and he knew that if he made a stand the probability was that the Aboriginals would cut them off from their horses, whereupon they would become easy prey. He made camp, naming the place Attack Creek. The night was undisturbed, though there were fires all around. He decided he must give up any idea of reaching the Gulf of Carpentaria. The Aboriginals seemed determined to put an end to the expedition; they knew where water was to be had, and could no doubt cut the white men off from it. Stuart and his companions had been living on restricted rations and were far from strong; Stuart himself could scarcely sit in the saddle while the animals were in an equally sorry state and at the point of total exhaustion.

The explorers collected themselves together and prepared to retreat to Bishop Creek. On the way they passed a macabre sight – many bodies hanging in the branches of trees, where the Aboriginals placed their dead. The sheer number of these corpses suggested that the area was surprisingly highly populated. It was as well that Stuart had, albeit reluctantly, decided to abandon all hope of reaching the north coast.

On 3 July they reached Bonney Creek, at which they had stopped on their way north. The water there was much diminished, and seemed to be falling at the rate of 6in a day. Nor was there any rain, and little prospect of any – tantalising rain clouds would seem to gather only to break up and disperse. Rations were quickly shrinking; Ben, whose weight was down to 10st, turned out to have been systematically pilfering extra food, and Stuart now reckoned that for some time he had been eating double his ration. There was little he could do about it. At least there were supplies of 'cucumber' nearby, and by eating plenty of these they managed to lessen the effects of scurvy. They left the Bonney on 9 July, depressed by their failure to achieve their aim; the disappointment added a psychological burden to the physical hardships they continued to endure as they trekked south over the arid MacDonnell and James Ranges.

The conditions were now as bad as those any explorers had ever faced. 'My men', wrote Stuart in his journal, 'have lost all their former energy and activity, and move about as if they were a hundred years old; it is sad to see them.'[16] The horses were exhausted, their bodies covered with open sores. By the first week of August, Stuart doubted whether Kekwick could continue, he was so ill; yet he had to steel himself against showing too overt a sympathy, for fear Ben Head would altogether lose heart.

Just as it seemed possible that the horses would prove too weak to proceed and the fatigued men would have no option but to walk almost another 300km, things unexpectedly took a turn for the better: water became more plentiful, they discovered some native food, and then, on 26 August, they came across another human being, a Mr Brodie, encamped near Mount Hamilton. They rested at his camp for six days during which time their horses, delighted by plentiful supplies of food and water, strayed away and were never recaptured. From Mt Hamilton the weary three were able to get to Chambers Creek, thence to Port Augusta and onwards by ship to Adelaide.

They were greeted with enormous enthusiasm. They might not have reached the north coast, but their accomplishment had been staggering enough – and offered comfort to the South Australians, who had listened enviously to tales of the elaborate expedition mounted by Burke and Wills, which had left Melbourne a short while earlier. Surely, with a properly equipped party, Stuart could be counted upon to make another successful journey to the north, perhaps reaching the coast before Burke and Wills. He was even offered encouragement in verse:

To the Very Centre

Haste ye, Stuart, do not sleep; in
Settled districts never lurk.
Onward! or you're surely beaten
By the great O'Hara Burke.[17]

Stuart, himself scarcely rested, barely had time to acknowledge the honour of being awarded the Gold Medal of the Royal Geographical Society (and an accompanying gold watch) before starting out on his next expedition, this time supported by the state government, which promised to supply an escort of ten armed men and offered £2,500 to equip the venture. An advance party set out to the north on 10 October 1860, and on 24 October 400 people paid 5s each to attend a public breakfast to bid Stuart farewell, at which he was presented with two rifles, one a gift from a wealthy patron, the other bought from the proceeds raised by subscription from a hundred admirers.

The main body of Stuart's fifth expedition left Adelaide on 31 October, led by Kekwick and including Ben Head. Stuart departed by train the following day and the explorers were reunited at Clare, and were cheered off by a small crowd, one member of which read a farewell poem, warning the explorer again of the threat that Burke might outdo him:

> Haste ye Stuart! Brave Caledonian,
>   Onward to the tropic clime,
> Haste ye, ere that proud Victorian
>   Shares the glories should be thine.

This time Stuart was at the head of a dozen men and led them with a firm but friendly discipline which was a great deal more effective than, for instance, Sturt's military strictness. The men addressed him as 'Mr Stuart', he used their forenames, and there was a complete lack of the tensions which bedevilled so many other expeditions. (He allowed all the men 4oz of tobacco a week, a luxury bought dearly when food was strictly rationed in order to keep down the weight to be carried by the horses. But then, Stuart was an enthusiastic pipe-smoker.)

After a slight delay due to some difficulty in acquiring horses, the expedition set out in earnest at the very beginning of 1861, and from the start made excellent progress, though detained a little by torrential rain (at least there was no shortage of water). On 16 February the faithful Polly had a foal, Stuart naming the place Polly Springs to commemorate the event.

They marched steadily on, following for a while Stuart's earlier route, making – as he hoped – for the Victoria river. During the following weeks there were demonstrations of hostility from small groups of Aboriginals. On 7 February F.W. Thring, Stuart's third in command, was attacked with a boomerang and had to fire over the attacker's head to frighten him off. On 5 March seven Aboriginals attacked, and it proved more difficult to disperse them, for when Stuart fired above their heads they took absolutely no notice. However, no substantial attack materialised. Later, the explorers found that a simple way of dissuading the Aboriginals from hanging about the camp was simply to introduce them to the horses – these were unfamiliar animals to them, and they did not at all like the look of their teeth.

They marched steadily on until the end of April, passing Attack Creek on the 24th, the northernmost point from where Stuart's previous expedition had turned back. Then they came up against the Sturt Plain – parched, desolate country which seemed impassable. The ground was rough and riddled with numerous holes and cracks into which the horses continually stumbled, unable to see them under the long grass. Polly fell, throwing Stuart heavily. Despite the lushness of the grass, water was extremely short. After plodding on for 70km without water and under a blazing sun, the horses were completely 'knocked up'. There was also some trouble with the Aboriginals. At first they seemed friendly enough, but then began setting fires near the explorers' camp, and finding one of the men, Woodeforde, alone at some distance from the camp, attacked him with boomerangs and stones. When one man aimed a boomerang at him from only a couple

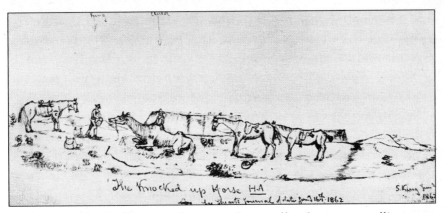

'The Knocked up Horse H.A'
from the Stuart Journal of date Jun 16th 1862
S. King Junr 1863

Explorers suffered – but their horses perhaps suffered more, travelling great distances without adequate water, and when they became exhausted (or 'knocked up') were often killed for food. *(Sketch by King, from Stuart's Journals)*

of yards away, Woodeforde shot him in the face and made for the camp. Nothing more was heard from the natives.

Retreating to the Ashburton Range, Stuart followed the McKinlay Creek, which he named, north-west; only to be again faced with a vast stretch of featureless country, with no sign of water. He returned to Burke Creek (named after his fellow explorer who, though he could not have known it, was already lying dead at Cooper's Creek). Setting out once more, the party was soon desperate for water – the men dug down for 5ft without finding so much as a trace of moisture.

The expedition seemed almost to be falling to pieces. The explorers were always thirsty, on short rations and, wrote Stuart on 10 July, 'almost naked, the scrub has been so severe on our clothes; one can scarcely tell the original colour of a single garment, everything is so patched. Our boots are also gone.' At a conservative estimate they were now ten weeks' tramp from the nearest station, with provisions for only four weeks. 'It is with great reluctance that I am forced to return without a further trial,' he concluded.[18]

The journey home was dispiriting, a sense of failure adding to the rigours of the season – there was now heavy frost, ice on the water buckets in the morning, biting winds making it cold even at midday. Though he regarded the expedition as a failure, Stuart was greeted in Adelaide as a hero – 'the Napoleon of Explorers' as the Adelaide Register *called him. The Governor presented him with the Royal Geographical Society's medal, which had arrived in Australia, and anxiously enquired when he was setting out once more. Stuart needed no prompting: all he wanted was to re-equip, and start again. And indeed, by April 1862 he was once more heading north, with between forty and fifty horses (among them the indomitable Polly) and a force which included Kekwick, Thring and John Woodeforde, the son of Stuart's doctor. There were the usual farewell demonstrations – the presentation of a Union Jack to raise on the north coast – and then the expedition set off, the horses panicking at the cheers and running amok, one breaking into a front garden, the owner of which appeared wielding a broom and offering a farewell greeting of her own.*

That Stuart was able to lead the sixth expedition at all was a token of the toughness of his mind and body: as he went to leave Adelaide, he attempted to unravel a tangled halter of one of the horses, which reared and struck him unconscious, then trampled on him, damaging an arm and breaking a finger. His injuries delayed him for six weeks, but even so he insisted on leaving the town before he was really fit – he never regained proper use of his right hand.

While hardly a quiet country walk, the journey northward was aggravated only by the sort of troubles which might be expected – minor interruptions such as when, on 16 December, a flock of emus inquisitively approached the horses, which immediately stampeded. The major disappointment for Stuart was the defection of Woodeforde, who surprisingly regarded the leader as a martinet and declined to accept his orders. On the face of it this seems unjust – no one else made similar allegations and it seems likely that there was a simple clash of personalities, though Kekwick always maintained that Woodeforde had only joined the expedition to please his father. More serious, as the long march continued, was the condition of the horses; in one way or another eight were lost during the trek north, mainly through weakness and inability to cope with the hard going on meagre rations of food.

At the start there was no real trouble with the Aboriginals except when, understandably, a group became annoyed when one of the men began reflecting the sun's beams at them with a mirror. But on 3 March, near Mount Hay, while the explorers were watering the horses at a creek, six Aboriginals appeared, fully armed and obviously intent on attacking. Stuart ordered the men to fire over their heads, but the natives took no notice other than to beckon to more of their companions to come out of the bushes where they had been hiding. Altogether, there were now about a hundred of them. More shots were fired, and eventually, perhaps realising for the first time that rifle fire could injure them from a greater distance than they could throw a spear or a boomerang, they retreated; nothing more was seen of them.

On the expedition pressed, passing Central Mount Stuart, crossing the Roper river, discovering the Katherine river and, on 10 July, the Mary. For once, Stuart was able to write in his journal of the beauty of the country, rather than to complain of its aridity and impassability:

The view was beautiful. Standing on the edge of a precipice, we could see underneath, lower down, a deep creek thickly wooded running on our course; then the picturesque precipitous gorge in the distance; to the north-west were ranges of hills. The grass on the table land is coarse, mixed with a little spinifex; about half of it had been burnt by the natives some time ago. We had to search for a place to descend, and had great difficulty in doing so, but at last accomplished it without accident. The valley near the creek, which is a running stream, is very thickly wooded with tall stringy-bark, gums, and other kinds of palm trees, which are very beautiful, the stem growing upwards of fifty feet high, the leaves from eight to ten feet in length, with a number of long smaller ones growing from each side, resembling an immense feather; a great number of these shooting out from the top of the high stems, and falling gracefully over, has a very pretty, light, and elegant appearance. Followed the creek for about two miles down this gorge, and camped on an open piece of ground. . . . In the valley is growing an immense crop of grass, upwards of four feet high; the cabbage palm is still in the creek. The cliffs, from the camp in the valley, seem to be from two hundred and fifty to three hundred feet high. Beyond all doubt we are now on the Adelaide river.[19]

He believed they must be approaching the coast, though Stuart said nothing of that to his companions. Then, on 24 July, one of the men, riding ahead, called out: 'The Sea!'

This, Stuart wrote, 'took [the men] all by surprise, and they were so astonished, that he had to repeat the call before they fully understood what was meant. Then they immediately gave three long and hearty cheers . . . I dipped my feet, and washed my face and hands in the sea, as I had promised the late Governor Sir Richard MacDonnell I would do if I reached it.'[20] He raised the Union Jack at the mouth of the Mary river, about 100km south-west of where Darwin now stands. Underneath it, in a tin, he placed a note of their accomplishment, signed by every member of the expedition.

After his triumph, the return journey proved a harrowing one for Stuart. Success seemed somehow to have robbed him of his remaining strength. One of the expedition's members, Pat Auld, later recalled that his leader seemed to collapse after reaching the coast and 'went about as if he had no ambition in his life'.[21] His eyes, which had troubled him for the past two years, had reacted so badly to the glare of the sun – and probably to the effects of scurvy – that he had become almost blind. By August he was in so much pain that he had to take laudanum to enable himself to continue. He was almost permanently worried by the state of the horses; if anything, they were suffering more than the men. He was forced to lighten their loads, leaving all sorts of equipment behind including many specimens of flora and fauna which had been collected during the expedition.

The men, too, were continually hungry, their meagre rations only occasionally augmented when they were able to catch a lizard, or pick some edible fruits or berries. By mid-October Stuart was vomiting blood, was no longer able to eat anything but a little boiled flour, and had lost the use of his legs: 'I was then enduring the greatest pain and agony that it is possible for a man to suffer,' wrote this normally uncomplaining man. 'On being lifted from the horse, all power was gone out of my legs, and when I attempted to put the weight of my body on them the pain was most excruciating. . . . My feet and legs are now very much swollen; round the ankles they are quite black, and the pain is dreadful.'[22] He was so exhausted he could neither sleep nor eat. Once, they killed a horse and made some jelly from its lips, which gave Stuart a little energy to continue.

When he could no longer bear to sit on Polly's back, a stretcher was improvised and slung between two horses, which worked well until a horse kicked it to pieces. On 28 October his voice failed and he could no longer give orders. He was just alive when the party reached Mount Margaret on 27 November.

The excitement with which the news of the expedition's success was received in Adelaide was scarcely short of hysteria. The train in which Stuart arrived on 17 December was met by an enthusiastic crowd, and he was forced to make a short speech, though the onlookers closest to him were startled by his weak and disabled appearance. For a fortnight, doctors allowed him to see no one, but he was able to work on preparing his journal for publication; it began to appear in instalments in the local press as early as 26 December.[23] He also set about making a detailed plan for the laying down of a telegraph line from Adelaide to the north coast.

On 21 January 1869 occurred one of the most memorable days in Adelaide's history, the day of the Great Stuart Demonstration. The streets were decorated with flags and bunting – flags were flown all over the city – and there were generous displays of tartan, in tribute to Stuart's Scottish lineage. The *South Australian Chronicle* described how 'from the Treasury, along King William-street to Government House, thence down the City Bridge-road and into North Adelaide, as far as the eye could trace, were dense crowds of people – men, women and children – together with hundreds of vehicles of every description and crowds of horsemen and horsewomen. The windows of the principal houses on the route of the procession were chiefly occupied by the female members of the various gentlemen who formed the procession; balconies were crowded, and even the roofs of the houses were well sprinkled with ambitious spectators anxious to get a "bird's-eye view" of the whole demonstration.'[24]

Ministers of the government, Members of Parliament, five mayors, two bands, mounted police and cavalry – and in the middle of the procession Stuart and his men and their forty-one remaining packhorses (he had set out with seventy-one). The men wore the clothes in which they had completed their expedition, clothes which barely hung together; a reporter counted thirty-nine patches on one pair of trousers.

On a platform set up outside the Treasury, Stuart almost collapsed several times during the interminable tributes paid him; his reply was quite inaudible, though at the banquet that evening he was heard to declare, if weakly, that he would rather have died than failed in his enterprise. With the irony of fate, that very day, in Melbourne, the bones of two men who had failed – Burke and Wills – were carried in procession to their graves.

Awarded a state pension, Stuart never fully recovered his health nor, indeed, his spirits. He seems to have been lonely and dejected during his last years, and in the end barely remembered his great feat. He returned to England, to London, where he died aged only 50 – in a house at 9 Campden Hill Square, Notting Hill, on 4 June 1866. His funeral was attended by seven people. Stuart never received the financial rewards which were surely his due; his memorial lies in the fact that, as he had recommended, the overland telephone line connecting south to north almost precisely followed the line of his progress, as does the railway line along which tourists now travel from Adelaide to Darwin.

Between Stuart's first expedition in 1858 and his last in 1862, others were also at work opening up previously unexplored areas of the country. George Elphinstone Dalrymple raised money for a private expedition in north Queensland in 1859, by which time it had become a colony in its own right with a governor if its own, who was eager that the whole area should be properly surveyed. A fellow Scot, William Landsborough, opened up almost 4,000 sq km of excellent grazing land and his Irish friend Nathaniel Buchanan was the first to drive stock the 500km from Rockhampton to Bowen. Meanwhile two brothers, John and Peter MacDonald, explored the bushland around the Nogoa and Belyando rivers, 250km from the coast.

TEN

'Unburied as I lie'
Robert O'Hara Burke and William John Wills, 1860

*Error and incompetence dogged the great expedition tasked
with solving once and for all the mystery of the continent's
interior, and either finding the Inland Sea or totally disproving
its existence. Brave men made their way right across the
continent, from south to north, but achieved nothing, and the
expedition ended in the deaths of its leaders.*

The most iconic and best known of all Australian expeditions
into the country's interior was the result of the whim of some
members of a small, somewhat patrician Melbourne club, the
Philosophical Institute of Victoria.

By the 1860s Melbourne was already established as the
commercial, social and administrative centre of Victoria, which itself
had only become a separate colony in 1851, after discontent with
the government in Sydney had come to a head. The Philosophical
Institute was formed in 1855 as one of a number of similar bodies
which were to dignify the city and give its wealthier and more
intellectual inhabitants the feeling that they were taking their place
in the wider world of science, art and literature. The Institute was
the chief centre of scientific and cultural thought, and membership
was imperative for any respectable denizen of Melbourne who
believed himself of consequence.

One of those members, Dr David Wilkie, put forward in 1857 the
idea that the Institute should sponsor an expedition into the interior
of Australia, crossing it from east to west along the Tropic of
Capricorn. This had been the unfulfilled ambition of Ludwig
Leichhardt, who in 1848 had vanished in the attempt. Explorers

160

equipped and financed by the Melbourne Institute should, Wilkie suggested, endeavour to achieve what Leichhardt had failed to do, and in the process might be able to discover what had happened to the earlier explorer – there were some people who still optimistically hoped that he might have survived and, after nine years, still be wandering through the sunbaked desert 800km from civilisation. The expedition would also hope to discover great stretches of pastoral land which could be profitably farmed, map out a route for an overland telegraph line and set up a base for later expeditions.

The members of the Institute greeted the idea with enthusiasm and formed an Exploration Committee consisting of a number of Melbourne worthies. While most of them knew nothing about exploration, one or two had real experience, among them Ferdinand von Mueller, a botanist who had been a member of an expedition to 'the great Australian desert' led by Augustus Gregory[1] only a year previously, and was eager for the blank spaces on the maps of that remote and barren area to be filled in. The committee began seriously to discuss plans. The local press became excited, the Governor of Victoria, Sir Henry Barkly, was equally enthusiastic, and local businessmen began to offer financial support: there was one anonymous donation of £1,000. An Englishman, George Landells, was about to sail for India with horses for the British army and offered to secure and bring back a number of camels. Camels were not unknown in Australia, but had never been used for exploration. Landells explained that they would be a great deal more useful in desert country than packhorses or mules, and the Exploration Committee duly commissioned him to buy several dozen and bring them back to Melbourne.

The Victorian Parliament voted £6,000 to support the project, the Institute received a royal charter, became the Royal Society, and began to look for someone to lead the expedition.

Robert O'Hara Burke was not an obvious candidate. An Irish Protestant whose elder brother had inherited the family's estate in Galway, in the way of younger sons he was sent for a soldier, and in 1840, at the age of 20, like a number of young Irishmen, joined the Austrian army, eventually becoming a first lieutenant in the 7th

Hussars stationed in Italy. He left the army unceremoniously in 1847, only just escaping a court martial for desertion (perhaps by the exercise of the Irish charm which endeared him to almost everyone he met). After five years' service in the Irish Constabulary he decided that he was in a dead-end job and took off for Australia. Arriving in Melbourne with excellent references (family influence had secured him letters of commendation from such dignitaries as the British First Lord of the Admiralty and the Solicitor-General for Ireland), he had no difficulty in joining the Victorian police force, becoming by 1858 a senior inspector at three times the salary he had commanded in Ireland.

Burke was a well-built, fit man and made himself popular in the town of Beechworth, near the rolling hills of the Ovens Valley at the foot of the Victorian Alps. Gold had been discovered there in 1852, and the population of the area had rocketed; there was little serious crime to preoccupy the police, but it was an interesting and lively posting at a time when the town was establishing itself, with heavy drinking (in which Burke often joined) at the timber-built Tanswell's Commercial Hotel. Burke was in control of over a hundred men and sat on the local bench in the roughly constructed courthouse (the handsome courthouse and gaol which can still be seen at Beechworth were not built until just after he had left the town). Outside working hours, when not relaxing in a sort of jacuzzi – a hole in the ground which he ordered his men to dig near the police house and in which on the hottest days he would sit up to his waist in water clad only in his police helmet – he took an interest in local goings-on and helped to set up the local Literary and Scientific Institute. He was personable and friendly, and when his transfer was announced, a petition was set up asking him to stay at Beechworth.

However, he moved on to Castlemaine, some 250km from Melbourne, where he swiftly became as popular as he had been in Beechworth. His new posting was very similar. The town was another gold-mining centre, and once again there was little for Burke to do: perhaps the miners were far too busy making their fortunes to engage much in the way of crime, and policing offered few opportunities for action outside the arrest of a drunk or two and the occasional prosecution for adultery.

Burke's superiors thought well of him – the Chief Police Commissioner of Victoria considering that he possessed 'indomitable pluck, energy, great powers of endurance, and the by no means useless talent of making himself beloved by those serving with or under him, without relaxing the rules of discipline'.[2] If he had a fault, it was that he was volatile and emotional, and occasionally followed his emotions without a great deal of forethought. One cannot blame a man for falling in love, but for a policeman to fall for an actress, at a time when the very noun suggested immorality, was perhaps a mistake. Burke followed the young dancer Julia Matthews from theatre to theatre around the state, courting her and paying attention to her mother, who did not care for him. Finally, he even proposed marriage; but the girl refused him.

While he was at Castlemaine, he met the railway magnate and member of the Royal Society J.V.A. Bruce, who was busy supervising the building of the railway from Melbourne to Bendigo. It was Bruce who in 1860 persuaded Burke to put his name forward as the leader of the proposed expedition. It may have been boredom, together with the realisation that marriage to Miss Matthews was not on the cards, that persuaded Burke to accept Bruce's advice and allow the financier to drive him to Melbourne to meet other members of the Exploration Committee. With only Bruce's recommendation to support his candidature, they agreed to put his name forward.

Though Burke was strong and in good health, he had no experience which might be useful to the leader of an expedition into hard, unknown country, nor had he the calm practicality and forceful nature required of a man who must make plans and ensure that others follow him. He knew nothing of Australia outside Melbourne and the two towns where he had served, and was incapable of undertaking a survey or drawing a map (indeed, it was said of him that he frequently lost his way in the streets of the city). He was, too, unfamiliar with literature, and wrote only with some difficulty – the reason, no doubt, that, unlike the other Australian explorers, he left no journals. Entering his house, visitors were surprised to see the walls covered with scraps of paper on which were written in his unformed, childish hand brief reminders to do this or that; he even went so far as to put up a notice asking people to be so good as not to read the walls. One of the members of the expedition spoke of him as 'an ordinary person . . . in no way adequate to his office. Leader of an expedition, but completely ignorant of the land, totally blind as to geography and astronomy.'[3]

Nevertheless, a public dinner celebrated his appointment. A little later, Landells arrived back in Melbourne from Karachi with eight camel-drivers and their beasts, which were driven through the crowded streets of the city followed by their proud escort dressed in a somewhat theatrical explorer's costume. Later Landells bought ten more beasts from the well-known showman George Coppin, who had been exhibiting them in his pleasure-ground, Cremorne Gardens (one of the beasts, particularly troublesome, was later nicknamed 'Master Coppin').

Burke invited Landells to join the expedition. He would clearly be an advantage; he understood camels, and would keep the sepoys (Indians employed to attend to these animals) under strict control – he had already knocked one down for swearing in public. The camels were wary, stubborn, intelligent beasts that needed careful supervision by those who understood their ways. After some negotiation – Landells initially wanted too much money and too much authority – an agreement was reached, and he agreed to serve under Burke.

Among the other appointments, by far the most important was that of William Wills as surveyor. Wills had been born at Totnes, in Devon, in 1834. He was educated at a grammar school at Ashburton, began to study medicine with his father, a surgeon, then went on to medical school in London. At 16, without completing his studies, he sailed for Australia with one of his younger brothers. There, until his father arrived to start a medical practice, he passed the time for three years as a 'shepherd', which really meant a menial servant to any smallholder who would employ him. He worked for his father for a while, but, disillusioned with medicine, moved on to open a gold office at Ballarat.

By 1855, a slender, rather diffident, stammering young man of 21, slightly feminine in the delicacy of his features, he was smitten by the idea of becoming an explorer. When his mother, to whom he perhaps unwisely confided his hopes, complained that he was likely to run into danger, he pointed out that 'if every one had such ideas we should have no one going to sea for fear of being drowned, no one would go in a railway train for fear the engine should burst, and all would live in the open air for fear of the houses falling in',[4] though in a previous letter he had admitted, prophetically, that it would be 'rather disagreeable' to die of starvation in the bush.

Failing to find any expedition which would employ him, Wills decided to train as a surveyor and subsequently worked in the bush before conceiving a passion for astronomy and finding a place at the Sydney Observatory under its director, Georg Neumayer. Neumayer took a strong interest in the proposed expedition and suggested that Wills might join it as surveyor. Though Burke had his doubts as to whether Wills would stand up to the hardships involved, he was interested in the idea of a surveyor with some medical knowledge, and not only appointed him Surveyor and Astronomical Observer, but made him third in command after Burke and Landells, and gave him the important task of mapping out the route the expedition should take.[5]

The next appointments, of Hermann Beckler and Ludwig Becker, gave rise to some irritation. Racial tension showed its ugly face. The two men were German, and Germans were not specially popular in Melbourne. Moreover, they were relatively unknown in the city. Beckler was a Bavarian who had set up a medical practice in New South Wales in 1855. He found the profession not only unremunerative but also boring, and conceiving a passion for natural history made himself known to Neumayer, moved to Melbourne and took a job at the Botanical Gardens. He had done a little botanical work in the field, and applied to join Burke's expedition both as botanist and doctor. The Exploration Committee had some doubts about his medical ability – and indeed no one could have thoroughly recommended him on the basis of his experience in that discipline – but Burke was conscious that Wills had little real knowledge of medicine, and the economy of employing another man in two posts appealed to the Committee, which strengthened Beckler's appointment.

Becker, born in Darmstadt in 1808, was an artist, a scientist of slightly dubious credentials (though, to do him justice, he had written a considerable number of scientific papers which had been published and admired in Europe), a friend of Mueller and Neumayer, and a member of the Royal Society. He was particularly celebrated for the pet bat to which he was devoted, and for his vocal imitations of birdsong. He applied for a position with the expedition as an artist and naturalist. As a fellow German, Beckler particularly welcomed his application.

Burke seems not to have been eager to admit Becker as a member of his party, and left him off the list which he submitted to the Exploration Committee. However, Beckler and his other friends exerted their influence, and Burke gave way. Other appointments followed swiftly. Charles Ferguson, said to be one of the best horse-breakers in the country, was surprised to receive a letter asking if he would care to apply for the position of foreman. He did, and was accepted. In other cases, it was a matter of weeding out the likeliest applicants from a field of over seven hundred, three hundred of whom turned up for interview at the headquarters of the Royal Society. Burke ignored most of these, understandably preferring men of whom he had some personal knowledge, or who had been personally recommended to him.

The final selection was made by the middle of 1859, and including the sepoys the company consisted of nineteen men. Burke gave them, or some of them, a taste of things to come by setting up a camp in the park where the camels were corralled – less a park, in fact, than a piece of bushland just outside Melbourne. There he got them up at break of day for physical exercises, target practice and long, arduous tramps around the countryside – all of which were easier than learning how to manage the camels. He began to endear himself to most of the men under his command: 'His good natured character and his direct, open, simple nature won him the devotion and trust of both officers and subordinates', Beckler wrote.[6] Meanwhile, he was getting together the stores the expedition would need. He acquired a large oak desk with two stools, in order that the expedition's leaders should be able to sit comfortably while recording progress. He secured a waterproof sheet lined with flannel for each horse and camel (though they were heading for blistering heat, the nights could be extremely cold). There were also special camel shoes, made to protect the beasts' feet from injury on stony ground (these proved impossible to fit and were discarded at an early stage).

Burke also unwisely allowed each member of the expedition to order the stores he thought would be necessary. So Landells ordered several cartons of pepper, 6 gallons of vinegar and packets of alum and sulphur together with 20 gallons of rum which would cheer the camels up when they were disheartened by the rigours of the journey. His own personal equipment weighed no less than 86kg (192lb). Becker ordered an inordinate number of sketchbooks, notebooks, steel nibs and pencils. The farrier carried into the camp a portable forge, bellows and anvil. One day a large grindstone together with its frame, stand and crank appeared. Beckler's medical equipment consisted of eight boxes each weighing 36kg (80lb).

Burke made plenty of provision for defending the party against attack by spear-carrying Aboriginals by packing a hundredweight of powder and 226kg (500lb) of balls and bullets for revolvers and shotguns. He was less generous in the provision of food, for the amount turned out to be considerably underestimated, though there was more than enough to make carriage an additional problem. Some thought went into the ordering, which comprised not only basic foodstuffs but dried fruit and lime juice to prevent scurvy. There was plenty of fatty salt pork (Beckler said that this was eaten 'with relish' even in the scorching heat of the interior in summer), and preserved meat to be mixed with flour and baked to make a sort of meaty biscuit. The usual victuals – flour, rice, sugar – were accompanied by 166kg (371lb) of tea, 10kg (22lb) of coffee, 45kg (100lb) of dried Californian apples, 227 litres (15gal) of grapes and

50 litres (60lb) of raisins, 27kg (61lb) of mustard and 13kg (30lb) of pepper. There was also curry powder, presumably for the 'Indians' (the sepoys) since Beckler had clearly never heard of it, describing it as 'a mixture of Indian spices'.

This mass of equipment was not only extremely cumbersome, but cost a great deal more than the Exploration Committee had bargained for; Beckler commented that several other expeditions had been mounted for half of what it would cost to transport Burke's equipment.

All these preparations went ahead while the Exploration Committee was still deliberating the expedition's purpose and direction. It had been generally agreed that in order to discover 'if there really existed within their great continent a Sahara . . . great lakes . . . or watered plains which might tempt men to build new cities',[7] the explorers should tramp 1,300km north from Melbourne to Cooper's Creek, which since its discovery by Stuart in the summer of 1844 had become the acknowledged base for the exploration of the great, unknown north country. What direction Burke should take after reaching the creek was left to him; there were any number of alternatives; goodness knows there was enough unmapped country to explore. Sentimentalists still favoured the idea that there should be a search for any trace of Leichhardt's expedition, though no one seriously suggested that there was any chance of survivors. Or almost no one: a speaker at one of the farewell dinners laid on for the explorers in Melbourne hoped that Burke might find his great predecessor, perhaps kept prisoner by the inhabitants of the wild unknown interior.

After all the discussion and argument, it was at last time to make a move; and Burke set Monday 20 August 1860 as the day on which the expedition would set out. Three days earlier he invited his most prominent supporters to Royal Park to inspect the expedition: the camels were on show together with their useless shoes, and the men, colourful in flannel trousers and bright red jackets. On the following day there was a more public display at the Exploration Committee's headquarters, when congratulatory speeches and toasts seemed to go on for ever.

On Monday morning half the population of Melbourne gathered to bid the party farewell – or was prepared to do so had the expedition been ready to leave. As it was, the public simply got in the way of the explorers as they struggled to complete their packing and discovered that there was insufficient room for all their supplies in the wagons which Burke had hired. Beckler said it was 'the sourest day' of his life: most of the supplies 'lay all open in the tents. No member of the expedition could work with another, no one could even call to another – such was the crush among the thousands who thronged to see our departure. With great exertion it was finally possible to load the wagons, but only after the mounted police had cleared some free space.'[8]

Burke attempted to load supplies on to the camels, but Landells told him the animals must conserve their strength for the long trek, so Burke reluctantly bought another wagon (these were expensive both in terms of money and the energy needed to shift them, and he was determined to discard them at the first opportunity). After the Mayor of Melbourne had addressed the crowd from the top of one of those wagons and three cheers had been given, Burke mounted his grey horse, Billy, and led a train of twenty-six camels and a few horses out of the park, leaving behind the wagons, several of which were still half empty, and one of which broke down before it had even got out of the park. Two more broke down on the road not far from the city, and one of the horses drawing them bolted. But at least, and at last, Burke and his expedition were on their way.

The muddle which characterised the start of the expedition persisted as far as Essendon, not 10km distant, by which time it was clear that everything was so disorganised that no real progress could be made. Burke halted, waited for all the wagons to catch up, and ordered them all to be unloaded and repacked. With the trail of camels and wagons more rationally ordered, the expedition set off again, the camels with their strangely attired sepoys attracting a great deal of attention, not only from human onlookers but from horses and cattle, which fled at their approach (there was trouble with the expedition's own horses, which viewed their exotic companions with deep mistrust and tended to buck and rear whenever one came too close).

Despite this, and though they were not yet bearing real loads, in every other way the camels were at first a great success; Wills found their motion so steady that he could write his journal and take notes while riding one. Landells cared for them assiduously, and the only untoward incident occurred when Becker, who had offered to help him, was seized by the seat of his trousers, the camel 'raising and lowering him, to the height of not less than ten feet, the doctor kicking and swinging his hands and calling for help, when at last his pants gave way, and just at the moment when the doctor was highest in the air, down he came upon his hands and knees'.[9]

Soon, however, there was trouble: subjected to continual rain, the camels developed catarrh and diarrhoea, and from time to time proved incapable of bearing even light loads, which had to be placed in the already overloaded wagons. As a consequence, these lagged even further behind as the expedition pressed on, and there had to be frequent halts in order to allow them to catch up. Then the road became so bad that the wagons began to shake and list, and had to be unloaded and repacked once more. When, one day, the expedition succeeded in travelling 40km, it was a record; the normal rate of travel was more like 16km a day.

Otherwise, the first 320km or so of the long trek northward proved rather pleasant. As they left the coastal area, Beckler was delighted at the change of scenery; now they were travelling through dense forests of tall eucalyptus, tree-ferns and palms, mighty fig trees and cedars – some of the tallest trees he had ever seen. This in turn gave way to open bushland with only small patches of forest and thickets, hard red soil perforated by rocks and hundreds of kilometres of sand. Climbing to the highest point of Mount Hope, he looked down with awe at the magnificent panorama of the flat landscape, broken only by an outcrop they called the Pyramid, with Mount Korong in the distance, and a horizon so faint that the eye could scarcely see it: 'The play of sunlight and clouds produced wonderful effects on the wide plain; light and shadow alternated in quick succession as in a diorama,' he wrote.[10] 'Miles of land were lit

As his expedition crossed the Terrik-Terrik Plains, Burke rode his favourite horse Billy between the ranks of camels (on the left) and horses: it had been found wise to separate the animals which were incompatible. *(La Trobe Library)*

up, only to be cast into deepest shadow within a few seconds. Huge clouds sailed across the sky and their shadows rolled over the land like the tatters of a gigantic, torn veil. Like the rotating light of a lighthouse, the Pyramid was alternately illuminated and in deep shadow.' On the Terrik-Terrik Plains, he was also fascinated by the nightly apparition of a mirage which promised large lakes of water (a delightful but tantalising sight as the party was growing increasingly short of water).

When they moved on from Mount Hope, however, the situation deteriorated. A biting northerly wind blew up and it began to pour with rain. Soon, wrote Beckler, 'the wagons could not keep pace with the camels, as the ground, soft and porous at the best of times, was now such a quagmire that the horses could hardly move the heavy wagons at all. Even we sank inches deep at every step. The poor camels, completely soaked and shivering with cold, slipped at almost every step and sank deep into the mud. One could not but feel for the animals when they stopped now and then for a moment to rest. They looked at us so miserably.'[11] A number of the horses made off, and Charles Ferguson, the party's American foreman, got lost somewhere between the camels and the wagons, fell into a pit and suffered concussion.

Eventually they reached a homestead, and were made welcome. Landells gave the camels tidy doses of rum to warm them, and the humans enjoyed some hot food and their own measures of grog. This welcome was not uncharacteristic. Almost every small town or farm along the way greeted the expedition enthusiastically, sometimes inviting the explorers to heavy drinking bouts, sometimes praying over them, and on at least one occasion handing out religious tracts – improving reading for those long days crossing the desert land ahead.

When they set off again the landscape opened out and it was time for Wills, Beckler and Becker to start making serious observations. While Becker sketched, Beckler collected botanical specimens and Wills noted astronomical and meteorological phenomena. If any of them had any doubts about Burke's leadership they did not express them, though it must have been clear to them by now that he had not yet decided just where he was leading his team. The expedition paused for a few days at Swan Hill, then a tiny hamlet on the banks of the Murray river of only a dozen houses.[12] The party pitched their tents and enjoyed the entertainment offered by the locals; considering the size of the place this was astonishing: they dined out almost every night in a different house, were given a substantial parting luncheon by the local doctor, and even what Beckler described as 'a small ball' at the one hotel in the place. As they continued their march Beckler wondered at the cheerfulness of the men and women who chose to live so far from civilisation. Even the 'towns' often consisted of only a single row of houses – Balranald, for instance, considered a promising township, had only two rows of cottages, a store and two hotels. The 'stations' they passed usually consisted only of a single half-derelict hut or perhaps even just a tent.

They left Swan Hill after a 'champagne' breakfast to the cheers of the inhabitants, who threw old boots and shoes after them for luck.

Burke had now decided on his next course: he would make for Menindee, 160km north of the junction of the Murray and Darling rivers. As Landells still argued that the camels were not well enough to carry anything heavier than a man, Burke decided to retain the hired wagons, although they were expensive, cumbersome and frequently broke down. However, he had been warned by Swan Hill men that he would be forced to abandon them within a week or two, because he could not possibly carry enough food and water for the horses; and in any event the road would become impassable due to rain.

Three days later, at Balranald, Burke decided he must lighten the load in the wagons as the horses were beginning to tire. Since Landells insisted that the camels were still not ready to bear a full load, Burke jettisoned a lot of supplies, including all the lime juice he had brought to prevent scurvy, four bags of sugar intended for the camels, the blacksmith's anvil and bellows, many miscellaneous hammers, nails and other tools, and some firearms. He ordered the men severely to restrict their personal belongings: they were allowed just one pair of shoes, three shirts, two pairs of flannel trousers and one canvas pair, a poncho and a blanket and piece of oilcloth. He also dismissed three men, including, surprisingly, his foreman Ferguson. No one knew quite why he did this, though there had been tensions between himself and Ferguson.

Deciding to split the expedition into two, Burke rode on to the Darling river, leaving Beckler to make his way in the same direction, but more slowly, with the wagons. Burke made good progress, but Beckler's party dragged on much more slowly than anyone had planned. Water became more and more scarce, and it was soon clear that nowhere near enough fodder had been carried for the horses, which lost weight and became weaker and weaker. They were so thirsty that when they came to a waterhole, they drank it dry, leaving the local shepherd to drive his sheep elsewhere. The poor horses, dragging the loaded wagons, had to plod through loose red sand, while overhanging branches tore the wagon covers to shreds. Recalling the episode, Beckler provided the following graphic description:

The wagon wheels sank deep into the soil as did the horses and we were often forced to come to the aid of one or the other half-buried wagon wheel with a shovel. After minutes of gradually increasing shouting and yelling, often to the point of despair, the horses were perhaps able to pull together, only then to stop exhausted a few paces further on . . . dozens of times the horses had to be unharnessed from one wagon in order to help another out of a particularly difficult spot. In addition, they hardly had a drop of refreshing water to drink all day.[13]

Then, when they stopped for the night, a hurricane blew up, and men and beasts were all drenched and shivering. Beckler's tent was blown down, and he spent the night cowering under a wagon. They rested for four days, then pressed on; eventually, with enormous relief, reaching the Darling river. Beckler reflected, quite rightly, that if the necessary supplies had been sent there by water, they could have accomplished the journey much more easily and speedily. The pleasure the men felt at reaching the relatively lush riverbank was enhanced by the fact that they tramped alongside it for some miles, and were able from time to time to take cooling baths in its clear water.

In one way and another rumours reached the Exploration Committee that things were not going well. Several men whom Burke had dismissed got back to Melbourne and told their tales; the committee had also discovered that Burke had spent more money than was available on equipping the expedition. Though Neumayer, who had travelled with Burke from Swan Hill to the Darling, did his best to reassure everyone that things were going well, pessimistic paragraphs began to appear in the press. Meanwhile, Landells had more trouble with the camels. The major problem was that they were both male and female, with inevitable results: they periodically fought and chased each other, ran away and had themselves to be chased and caught by Beckler and the two remaining sepoys. Beckler was terrified of Matvala, a camel with a ferocious temper that several times attacked him, decided that the animal was nothing but a menace, and wanted nothing more to do with him. This was perhaps one motive for his resignation from the expedition when it reached Menindee. Landells also resigned, partly because Burke accused him of entirely losing control of the camels (which was true) and partly because Burke had decided to dump the rum which Landells believed was essential to keep the beasts going.

Various people have provided different accounts of the Burke–Landells dispute. According to some, Burke burst out sobbing and clutched Landells saying that he could not do without him; others claimed that Wills had continually complained to Burke about Landells's behaviour, and wore him down. At any event, Landells's resignation was accepted, and he and Beckler (who had badly injured his foot) remained behind at the tiny settlement of Menindee, watching as Burke and the rest of the party trudged on into the unknown. When the news of their resignations reached Melbourne, it did nothing to increase confidence there that the expedition would be a success, though publicly sympathy was still with Burke – Beckler was, after all, German, and Landells had probably only joined the expedition to safeguard his investment in the camels.

By October 1860, Burke had appointed Wills as his second in command, and the rest of his party consisted of four other Europeans, one sepoy (Dost Mahomet), fifteen camels and nineteen horses. The wagons were finally abandoned, and Burke had decided that the horses and camels must be reserved for carrying stores. The humans, he said, must march every step of the way, for as far as the expedition went. The rule was not strictly enforced; certainly Burke himself often rode his grey, Billy, and from time to time would invite some other member of the party to ride, while he walked.

At first, travelling was easier than it had been for a long time. The weather was mild, a wet season had meant there was plenty of grass, and there was no shortage of water. The expedition at last made good progress, often marching until eleven at night. It only took them twenty-three days to reach Cooper's Creek, on 11 November. The famous name described what was only a series of waterholes, with the cooling shade of eucalyptus and mulga trees. But for over a week the explorers allowed their beasts some respite from the hard march, to graze and drink their fill. The only disadvantage of the place was that it was swarming with rats.

Burke now had to decide on the best route forward. Initially, his idea was to press on in a straight line directly to the Gulf of Carpentaria, but first he must reconnoitre to ensure as far as possible that there would be water for the humans, camels and horses. Wills and a companion, Thomas McDonough, rode out to the north, then, mistakenly believing their camels to be exhausted, allowed the beasts their freedom, at which they took off and were never seen again, leaving the two men to make their way on foot the 140km back to Cooper's Creek.

Burke now decided to split the party again, taking with him William Wills, Charles Gray, a middle-aged Scottish ex-seaman and ostler, and John King, an Irishman who had served in India as a soldier, and whose constitution had been weakened by bad bouts of fever. The latter, still under 20 years old, had been an enthusiastic member of the expedition from the beginning – indeed, hearing of it (possibly from Landells) he had travelled to Australia especially to join it. The others were left at the creek, where Burke established what he called Depot LXV (he had carefully numbered all his halts). In charge, he left William Brahé, a young digger and stock-keeper whose experience had been invaluable in getting the wagons through the worst of the rough country. He gave Brahé careful instructions: he and the others should build a timber stockade (which they did, calling it Fort Wills) and wait for three months, or longer if their supplies held out. If after that time Burke and his companions had not returned, they should assume that there had been a disaster, and should themselves retreat to Menindee. Wills privately suggested to Brahé that it would be well if he could hold on for four months. But no instructions were ever set down on paper.

Burke took with him six of the twelve camels, one of the eleven horses (two horses had been killed for meat), and enough supplies to last twelve weeks. He and his men would have to walk for most of the journey, however long and arduous it might be. On 16 December they set out with remarkable equanimity into the parched, unknown country. In a letter to his sister, Wills told her the whole expedition was more like a picnic than anything else, while Burke said that though he might experience some small difficulty, he was in good health and expected to be back in Melbourne by August.

Although the temperature was often over 100°F in the shade (when there was any shade, which was not often), Burke and his small party crossed Sturt's Stony Desert and without much difficulty reached the Diamantina river on Christmas Day. The camels had once had to go without water for three days and the men's ration was reduced to under 3 litres (5 pints) a day, but for the most part they were well supplied by many fine waterholes, some almost big enough to be called lakes. They occasionally saw Aboriginals in the distance, but they seemed to be too frightened by the unfamiliar sight of camels to approach. A group did come up to them on New Year's Eve, when they were camped by a waterhole not far from King Creek (Burke named it after his colleague),[14] and there was a nasty moment when their leader, carrying a 25ft-long spear, seemed threatening. However, though unpacified by the gift of some beads and baubles, the natives (as the white men referred to them) retreated when shots were fired over their heads.

Despite what might have been regarded as an unfriendly act, the Aboriginals returned, gave good advice about a route which would guide the explorers from waterhole to waterhole, brought gifts of fish and pestered the men to go to their camp, have a dance and make use of their women. The fish were accepted with gratitude, the other offers politely declined. The party pressed on, starting each day at five in the morning and only stopping briefly until five in the evening, marching at a punishing rate of between 30 to 50km a day. Wills had the added burden of writing up his journal (Burke kept none, only occasionally scribbling a phrase or two in his notebook), of planning the expedition's route and recording their position and meteorological phenomena.[15] The journal suffered somewhat from Wills's exhaustion during the march; there are several long gaps, when it is impossible to work out the party's precise movements.

After they had marched for six weeks, crossing the Tropic of Capricorn, the gulf still lay somewhere ahead. They crossed a luxuriantly green plain, with plentiful ducks and pigeons. (Surprisingly, they did not take the opportunity to shoot some to supplement their dwindling food supply, although Burke had always asserted that killing game would be essential to bolster their rations.) They plodded on over the De Little Range, the hills sadly taxing the strength of the camels (one, Golah, became so exhausted they had to leave it behind). On 9 February they reached the Bynoe river, a tributary of the Flinders, and tasting the water, found it salty. The coast must be near. It was just as well: they were almost at the end of their strength. Burke made a note: 'I am satisfied that the frame of man never was more sorely taxed.'[16] He took Wills and pressed on, taking his horse, Billy, but leaving King and Gray with the camels, hoping that men and beasts would recuperate with a good rest. With the temperature over 100°F the going was sticky and taxing. Billy sank to his knees in salty marsh mud. The two men and their horse plodded on for perhaps 24km (15 miles), not entirely sure where they were; Wills was unable accurately to determine their latitude, for one of the camels had rolled over on to its back, damaging the few instruments he had been allowed to retain. On 11 February they reached a tidal channel where mangrove swamps made further progress impossible. They reluctantly gave up before actually reaching the coast, turned back and, on 12 February, rejoined their colleagues.

There was no celebration. Though Burke believed that the Exploration Committee would be satisfied with the fact that he had crossed the continent from south to north, during the latter part of the journey through previously unexplored country he felt a sense of disappointment at not being able to say that he had reached the coast. 'It would be well to say', he wrote in his notebook, 'that we reached the sea, but that we could not obtain a view of the open ocean, though we made every endeavour to do so.'[17]

And now they had to face the journey back to Cooper's Creek, which they must reach before Brahé decided to return to Menindee. They had already taken over two weeks longer than Burke had allowed for the tramp to the coast, and three-quarters of their food supply was gone.

With each man's daily rations reduced to 125g (4oz) of flour and a tiny portion of meat, Burke and his three companions began the return journey to Cooper's Creek. Severe storms and heavy rain made the going soft, slow and strenuous; the temperature rose every day into the low hundreds, and fell to a chilling extent at night; high humidity sapped their energy. The names Burke gave to their camps tell their own story: Muddy Camp, Humid Camp, Mosquito Camp. . . . They were glad to come across the camel Golah, still alive and apparently much recovered, and were even happier when Gray killed a large snake (2.5m long and 18cm in girth), which provided a welcome addition to their larder, although after eating too eagerly Burke was ill for two days with dysentery. Early in March, having already killed two camels for food, they shot Billy and preserved what little flesh there was on him (so little, indeed, the poor beast could not have survived much longer). Burke took the decision to kill his own horse because he did not want to leave him to die slowly and ignominiously from hunger. The men's diet was supplemented by portulaca (*Portulaca oleracea* or pigweed), which they had seen the Aboriginals eat; Wills noted that without it he thought they would never have made it back to Cooper's Creek.

On 13 March, when there were more storms and more heavy rain, Golah gave up again and simply refused to attempt to negotiate the thick, slippery mud over which they had to make their way. Wills wrote in his notebook: 'Another of the camels having given up today and been left on the road, or rather on the plain, order has been given for leaving everything behind but the grub and just what we carry on our backs, so the instruments being planted[18] no more observations can be made.'[19]

The four men now had almost 27kg (60lb) less weight to carry, but their physical condition continued to deteriorate. Gray, in particular, quickly lost strength and eventually, after being beaten by Burke for stealing extra food, was unable to walk; they tied him on the back of one of the camels, muttering among themselves about his 'gammoning' (pretending to be ill). But on 17 April, Wills recorded: 'This morning, about sunrise, Gray died. He had not spoken a word distinctly since his first attack, which was just as we were about to start.'[20] The remaining three men were so weak that it took them a whole day to dig a shallow grave. Four days later, they staggered into the camp at Cooper's Creek, expecting to be greeted with generous supplies and the opportunity to rest and recuperate. But they had been away for ten and a half weeks, and after waiting for considerably longer than he had been instructed to do, Brahé and his party had departed. The terrible irony was that they had left Cooper's Creek only nine hours before Burke and his companions' return.

Brahé had come to the conclusion that Burke and his party could not have survived, but in case they *had* done so, he wanted to leave at least a small amount of food for them, but needed enough to sustain himself and his party as far as Menindee. He left what food he could spare buried under a large coolibah tree, carving into the trunk the words

DIG

3 FT   NW

APR 21 1861

Seeing the date, Burke realised that Brahé must have left the camp early that very day; but he and his companions were simply too exhausted to make the huge effort of trying to catch them up. Wills's weariness can be seen in the scribbled words of his notebook:

After four months of the severest travelling and privation our legs almost paralysed so that each of us found it a most trying task only to walk a few yards. Such leg-bound feeling I never before experienced, and I hope I never shall again. The exertion required to get up a slight piece of rising ground, even without any load, induces an indescribable sensation of pain and helplessness, and the general lassitude makes one unfit for anything. Poor Gray must have suffered very much many times when we thought him shamming. It is more fortunate for us that these symptoms, which so early affected him, did not come on us until we were reduced to an exclusively animal diet of such inferior description as that offered by the flesh of a worn-out and exhausted horse.[21]

Digging, the exhausted men found a small quantity of flour, rice, oatmeal, sugar and dried meat. It was little enough, but they felt considerably restored after eating. They rested for two days, during which Burke wrote his last report to the Exploration Committee:

Depôt No. 2, Cooper's Creek. . . . We have discovered a practicable route to Carpentaria, the chief portion of which lies on the 140th deg. of E. longitude. There is some good country between this and the Stony Desert. From there to the tropics the country is dry and stony. Between the tropics and Carpentaria a considerable portion is rangy, but it is well watered and richly grassed. We reached the shores of Carpentaria on February 11, 1861. Greatly disappointed at finding the party here gone.

Robert O'Hara Burke, Leader,
April 22, 1861.

P.S. The camels cannot travel, and we cannot walk, or we should follow the other party. We shall move very slowly down the creek.[22]

Rather than chasing after Brahé's party, which would be making far better time travelling south than they could hope to do, Burke had decided to follow Cooper's Creek towards Mount Hopeless and then struggle on to Blanchewater, 240km away, where he believed there was a sheep station. They broke camp on 23 April after burying a message under the coolibah tree recording this plan, though they had no real hope that Brahé or a rescue party would discover it; indeed, they carefully disguised the place where they left it, to avoid curious Aboriginals digging it up.

At first, they thought the journey to Blanchewater would be relatively easy. They felt stronger after eating the food left by Brahé, and even the two remaining camels seemed to have had heart put into them and worked well. The Aboriginals they met gave them fish, and Burke believed that they should have no difficulty in reaching their goal. But then one of the camels, Landa, became bogged down in quicksand at the side of a waterhole.

Though we tried every means in our power, we found it impossible to get him out all the ground beneath the surface was a bottomless quicksand through which the beast sank too rapidly for us to get bushes or timber fairly beneath him, and being of a very sluggish and stupid nature he could never be got to make sufficiently strenuous efforts towards extricating himself. in the evening as a last chance we let the water in from the creek so as to buoy him up and at the same time soften the ground about his legs but it was of no avail. the Brute lay quietly in it as if he quite enjoyed his position.[23]

Next day, they found Landa still happily reclining in the quicksand. They made a few more attempts to extricate him; their efforts proving useless, they shot him and cut the carcass up for meat, drying it in the sun over the next few days. When they went on, they found they were unable to carry all the supplies he had carried. Despite loading themselves with 11kg (25lb) of supplies each, they were forced to leave some behind. The creek which they had been following dried up, and they began to think they would have to return to Cooper's Creek and wait there in the hope that sooner or later a rescue party would arrive. By now they had lost all idea of walking in any particular direction.

On 6 May Wills wrote in his notebook: 'The present state of things is not calculated to raise our spirits much the rations are rapidly diminishing our clothing, especially the boots are all going to pieces and we have not the materials for repairing them properly. the Camel is completely done up and can scarcely get along, although he has the best of feed and is resting half his time I suppose this will end with us having to live like the blacks for a few months.'[24]

'The blacks' were giving them food – fish and 'a couple of nice fat rats, the latter found most delicious'. But then the Aboriginal family moved on, leaving the explorers to fend for themselves, which they were utterly unable to do. They killed the one remaining camel, Rajah, who was in any event on the point of death, and managed to find and collect quantities of nardoo (the seed of a fern, which the Aboriginals ate ground into a sort of flour, sometimes cooked, sometimes made into a sort of gruel). But nardoo contained almost no protein or starch, and they did not realise that it needed to be accompanied by meat of some sort; because it filled their stomachs they thought it was doing them good. Heartened, they set out again towards Mount Hopeless; but lack of water forced them to turn back. For unfathomable reasons, they made no attempt to catch fish, though fish were plentiful and they had an ample supply of fish-hooks; nor did they attempt to shoot game, though this too was plentiful and they had arms and ammunition. Wills seemed to have some idea of doing so: 'I must devise some means for trapping the birds and rats,' he wrote. 'What a pleasant prospect, after our dashing trip to Carpentaria, having to hang about Cooper creek living like the blacks.'[25] But they never made the necessary effort.

Wills struggled back alone to Cooper's Creek in order to leave a note explaining that the party was to be found nearby, rather than attempting to reach Blanchewater. He came across the family of 'blacks', who continued to be friendly. They plied him with so much food that he could scarcely consume it all; but he did, eating 'until I was so full as to be unable to eat any more . . . I was then invited to stop the night there but this I declined and proceeded on my way home.'[26]

On his return 'home', almost unbelievably, he learned that Burke and King had fired on the Aboriginals, once above the head of a man who had attempted to steal a valueless piece of oilcloth and once (with what seems the most complete stupidity) because Burke believed the natives were becoming 'too friendly'. Naturally, the supply of free fish dried up. Wills did his best to repair relations, but in the end was unsuccessful; the Aboriginals left, and though Burke realised his mistake and made attempts to locate them, they could not be found.

By 10 June lack of nourishment – for they still made no attempt to supplement the nardoo with meat – had rendered Wills so weak he could scarcely stir. He still scrawled almost daily weather observations in his notebook, but the entries grew shorter and shorter. 'I feel much weaker than ever, and can scarcely crawl. . . . Unless relief comes in some form or other, I cannot possibly last more than a fortnight.' Three days later he barely had the strength to crawl to the waterhole to drink. On 20 June, a warm day, he made the effort to sponge his body with water, 'but it seemed to do little good beyond the cleaning effects for my weakness is great but I could not do it with proper expedition'. At night it was cold, often with a cutting wind which sometimes persisted throughout the day. 'The Cold plays the Deuce with us from the small amount of clothing we have my wardrobe consists of a wideawake, a merino shirt, a regatta shirt without sleeves, the remains of a pair of flannel trousers, two pairs of socks in rags, and a waistcoat of which I have managed to keep the pockets together. The others are no better off. Besides these we have between us for bedding two small camel pads, some horsehair two or three little bits of rug, & pieces of oilcloth. . . .'[27]

He clung to the belief that the failure of the expedition was due to the neglect of others, rather than to any shortcomings in Burke's planning:

> It is a great consolation at least in this position of ours to know that we we [*sic*] have done all we could and that our deaths will rather be the result of the mismanagement of others than of any rash acts of our own. had we come to grief elsewhere we could only have blamed ourselves but here we are returned to Cooper's Creek where we had every reason to look for provisions & clothing, and yet we have to die of starvation in spite of the explicit instructions given by Mr Burke 'That the depot party should await our return' and the strong recommendation to the committee 'that we should be followed up by a party from Mininda'.[28]

Neither Wills nor Burke was able to leave the camp, and King no longer had enough strength to gather nardoo for himself and his companions. But at last Burke and King decided they must make one final almost superhuman attempt to find the Aboriginals, who would surely not let them die. As Wills wrote, 'it is the only chance we have of being saved from starvation. . . . Nothing now but the greatest good luck can save any of us . . . I can only look out, like

Mr Micawber, "for something to turn up".' That entry was dated 29 June. Probably two days later, some way from their camp, Burke told King that he did not feel he could last much longer. He gave King his watch, which he said was the property of the Exploration Committee, and his pocket-book, and then said: 'I hope you will remain with me here till I am quite dead – it is a comfort to know that someone is by; but, when I am dying, it is my wish that you should place the pistol in my right hand, and that you leave me unburied as I lie.'[29]

At eight o'clock the following morning, he died. As his leader had instructed him, King left him unburied, lying in the desert, his revolver in his hand. Later, his notebook was found near his body. In it was scribbled a note:

> I hope we shall be done justice to. We fulfilled our task, but were [aban–] not followed up as I expected. The depôt party abandoned their post. R. O'HARA BURKE
> For the Committee.
> Cooper's Creek, 26th June, 1861
> King has stayed with me till the last. He has left me, at my own request, unburied, and with my pistol in my hand.[30]

For a while, King struggled on alone still looking for the Aboriginals; four days later, when he returned to the camp, he found Wills dead. Some Aboriginals had disturbed the body and stolen some clothes. King managed to scrape some sand over the corpse.

By following their tracks, he found 'the natives', and they fed him. They made it clear that it was they who had found 'the Whitefellow', Wills. He curried favour by shooting crows and hawks (why on earth had he not done so earlier, to feed himself and his companions?) and by bathing the injured arm of one of the women. Eventually, they accepted him as a sort of honorary member of their tribe. They insisted that he show them Burke's body, over which they wept before covering it with brushwood.

Meanwhile, at Menindee, provisions had been made ready for sending on to Cooper's Creek, and on 26 January a party set out, led by William Wright, an experienced man familiar with the land at least halfway from Menindee to Cooper's Creek. Charles Stone was another experienced bushman, and Becker and Beckler (who approved of Wright and agreed to serve under him) were among the party, with thirteen horses and ten camels, together with six men including a bushman, half European and half Aboriginal, and Dick, a full-blooded Aboriginal.

From the first, they were distressed by mosquitoes and, when camped, by rats: 'Sleep was impossible except as the effect of complete weariness, for soon after sunset when the numberless swarms of flies which had tormented them during the day began to disperse, the undisputable owners of those dreary grounds, "the rats", kept up the wildest and most unhowley [*sic*] noise . . . gnawing through every pack bag, and absolutely biting the men when at rest.'[31]

The horses frequently bolted and had to be chased and caught; the intense heat worried the camels. Water ran short, and a number of the men, including Becker, fell ill. They took seventeen days to get halfway to Cooper's Creek, when Burke had covered the same ground in eleven. As they pressed on, there was trouble with the Aboriginals. At first they seemed friendly and even generous: three approached the party offering the Europeans their women. When the offer was refused, the entire tribe turned up to show their contempt, carrying shields and brandishing spears and boomerangs. Clearly, they wanted the explorers to get off their land forthwith. But speed was impossible when the men were almost dead with thirst, hunger and fatigue.

The natives became more and more threatening. Rousing himself from his bed, Charles Stone, who spoke an Aboriginal language (though it is not clear that it was one understood by the tribe that threatened them), tried to explain that the party would move on in due course, but would not be frightened into doing so. Over fifty Aboriginals replied by throwing sticks and making threatening gestures. Gunfire, over their heads, dispersed them. The following day, Stone and another member of the party died; they were buried together on 24 April.

Five days later, they were surprised to see Brahé and his party on their way from Cooper's Creek. Neither company was sufficiently healthy to take comfort from the presence of the other. Becker was unable to recognise Brahé, and died the day after they met. His excellent drawings and paintings of the expedition, the flora and fauna and the country through which the explorers passed, often produced in the most difficult circumstances, survived him. The two parties set up camp together while Brahé and Wright returned to Cooper's Creek to check one last time that there was no sign of Burke and Wills. Because the latter had so carefully disguised the place where he left the message, it was assumed that they had not arrived. In fact, they were camped a little more than 50km away.

Wright and Brahé returned to their combined group of explorers. In their absence the camels and horses had strayed, and it took five days to round them all up and begin the journey back to Menindee. They lost one more man, who died from scurvy, before they reached the camp on 18 June.[32]

Back in Melbourne, the Exploration Committee had grown increasingly concerned at the lack of news from Burke, and urged on by the newspapers, a number of prominent people – including Wills's father – argued for a second expedition to discover what had befallen the first. On 26 June 1861 such an expedition set out from Melbourne led by Alfred William Howitt, an experienced bushman and himself an explorer – he had previously led various expeditions in search of either gold or good farming land.

While the rescue expedition was still at the planning stage, Brahé returned to Melbourne, and immediately offered to accompany Howitt back to Cooper's Creek. What news he had was deeply depressing, but a few people still clung to the hope that Burke and Wills and their party might yet be trudging on through some obscure part of the north. At any event, even if they had perished it was necessary to confirm their fate.

On 13 September the rescue expedition reached Cooper's Creek. Nothing there had changed, but horse and camel tracks that seemed to run randomly about the campsite suggested that someone had been there since Brahé's departure. Cautiously, the rescuers began to explore. Edwin Welch, a surveyor and second in command of Howitt's party, rode out along the creek and came upon a group of Aboriginals. As he approached, they retreated, leaving one solitary figure, apparently covered with some scarecrow rags and part of a hat, alone in the sand.

'Before I could pull up,' Welch later wrote, 'I had passed it, and as I passed it, it tottered, threw up its hands in the attitude of prayer, and fell on the ground . . . when I turned round, the figure had partially risen. Hastily dismounting, I was soon beside it, excitedly asking, "Who, in the name of wonder, are you?" He answered, "I am King, sir." For a moment I did not grasp the thought that the object of our search was attained, for King being only one of the undistinguished members of the party, his name was unfamiliar to me. "King," I repeated. "Yes," he said; "the last man of the exploring expedition." "What, Burke's?" "Yes." "Where is he – and Wills?" "Dead – both dead, long ago"; and again he fell to the ground. Then I knew who was before me.'[33]

King led Howitt and Brahé to the place where he had buried Wills; dingoes had dug the body from its shallow grave, but Wills's journals, buried with him, survived. Burke's body, also savaged by dingoes, was also recovered. Both were reinterred in deeper graves, and the now ironically entitled 'rescue party' returned to Melbourne with their news.

Amid the furore which followed, almost everyone was blamed for the tragedy – Burke for making the wrong decisions, the Exploration Committee for not mounting a follow-up, Aboriginals for obstructing the expedition, attacking and even killing and eating some of its members. Hysteria was rife, and rival parties either extolled or criticised Burke. Julia Matthews, still appearing in the state's less salubrious theatres, emerged to claim his dying affection; others accused him of murdering Gray, beating him to death for stealing flour.

It was not sufficient to put the failure of the expedition and the death of so many of its members down to the harshness of the terrain, the lack of food and water, and general misunderstanding of what was required for the success of the venture. Someone must be

The incomplete remains of Burke and Wills were given a grandiloquent funeral in Melbourne, borne through the streets on a carriage modelled on that used at the funeral of the Duke of Wellington. *(National Library of Australia)*

to blame. A Commission of Enquiry found Burke culpable, even if his faults were excessive bravery and determination. Brahé was also condemned, for leaving Cooper's Creek too early. Wright was blamed for indecision and sluggishness. The Exploration Committee had been ridiculously inactive.

The ordinary people of Melbourne, however, continued to regard the explorers as heroes. On 21 January 1863, Burke and Wills (whose remains various people were allowed to handle, even taking teeth as souvenirs) were returned to the city and lay in state at the Hall of the Royal Society, through which some hundred thousand people passed to pay their respects. There was then an impressive funeral. A huge carriage had been designed for the occasion, based on the one that had carried the body of the Duke of Wellington through the streets of London. Between fifty and a hundred thousand people stood in silence beneath houses hung with crepe as, drawn by six black horses, it passed by. A rough-hewn block of granite weighing a formidable 36 tonnes was hauled more than 100km and placed over the grave, later to bear the names of the two men, 'comrades in a great achievement, companions in death, and associates in renown'. In Totnes, in Devon, an obelisk erected near his family home commemorates Wills.

The survivors of the expedition dispersed. Beckler returned to Germany, where he wrote an account of his experiences, in particular defending Brahé, who he believed had been maligned by the Commission. The public subscribed £3,135 to support King, who never fully recovered from his experience, never regained his health and died of tuberculosis nine years after his rescue.

The expedition on which so many men lost their lives had cost over £6,000. Burke left debts of £18 5s 3d and an estate of 7s 8d.

ELEVEN

The Last Australian Explorer
Ernest Giles, 1872, 1873, 1875, 1876

Giles forced his way twice right across the forbidding continent from east to west, with the most terrible effort and an unflinching determination scarcely equalled by his great predecessors. Alas, his bravery was unrewarded with even a single discovery of importance.

Like many a youngster in the mid-nineteenth century, at the age of 15 Ernest Giles found himself on his way from the relatively civilised surroundings of his school in London to a future in a country so far away as to be almost unimaginable.

When his parents emigrated to Australia in 1848, the 13-year-old boy had been left behind in order to continue his education at Christ's Hospital, a well-endowed charitable school for the more intelligent sons of indigent parents. After a long voyage, he joined them in 1851, in Adelaide. When, soon after his arrival, his father died, they moved to Melbourne. Eventually, he found himself a job as a clerk in the post office. His career there did not last long; he was made redundant just over a year later, after which he vanishes from our sight for over fifteen years. It has been suggested[1] that he probably spent these years helping to open up the land around the Darling river and that it was during his time there that he conceived the idea of becoming an explorer.

The second of these suppositions is certainly true, and his ambition had been formed by the time he met a young man after his own heart, William Harry Tietkens, another ex-pupil of Christ's. Tietkens had left the school in 1859, also aged 15, and travelled to Australia in the care of an itinerant actor, a friend of his mother, who abandoned him soon after their arrival. After managing to eke out a living by doing odd jobs, he found a position as a ticket clerk at St Kilda railway station, a post he still held when, at the end of 1864, he met Giles, who had been commissioned by some stockmen to journey into the outback in search of likely country to support their livestock. Though there was ten years between them, Giles immediately felt drawn to Tietkens, and invited him along. No doubt their memories of Christ's were an important bond.

That first expedition was short and relatively unsuccessful. For some years Giles seems to have returned to a life of wandering, finding employment where he could, while Tietkens became manager of a sheep station. It was to be some time before they went on a major expedition together.

Seven years after his first expedition, in 1872, Giles was given the opportunity to lead a real foray into the unknown. His patron was Baron Ferdinand von Mueller, a chemist who had been appointed Government Botanist in Victoria, and later became Director of the Botanic Gardens. Von Mueller had himself travelled extensively through the Flinders Ranges and as far as Tasmania, collecting specimens of flora (he recognised and collated almost five hundred previously unknown species).

Von Mueller was preoccupied with the whole idea of exploration. He had been a member of the organising committee which had set up the Burke and Wills expedition of 1860, and expended much time and energy trying to discover their fate. One of his great ambitions was to see an overland telegraph line laid from Melbourne to Perth, and he fixed on Giles as the man to attempt to open up the country with an eye to that proposition. Though he failed to obtain a government grant, together with contributions from Giles's brother-in-law and Giles himself he raised enough money to mount an expedition.

With him, Giles took a young friend, Samuel Carmichael; another companion, a young Irishman, Alex Robinson, who was to do service as cook; and an Aboriginal boy, Dick. Giles's black-and-tan terrier, Monkey, was also a member of the expedition. Explorers almost always took dogs with them, not only as hunters but as companions, for they often found it difficult to confide in the men they were leading.

Dick deserted the expedition almost before it had started, but the other three men began their trek on 22 August 1872 at Chambers Pillar, named twelve years earlier by Stuart. They set out to the north-west, following the course of the Finke river, and were almost immediately troubled by both heat and cold – during the day a hot wind blew dust in their faces, while at night their blankets were covered with a thick coating of ice, and when they woke they found that the mugs of tea they had left ready for the morning were frozen solid. At first the going was fairly easy, but the ground around the Finke often became treacherous, and firm ground could give way in an instant to treacherous quicksand – sometimes they had to use their stockwhips to urge the horses on before they had time to get bogged down.

At the end of August, in the middle of what seemed very un-promising country, the explorers came upon what Giles called Palm Glen, a place surrounded by cliffs where the river was flanked by magnificent tall fan and red cabbage palm trees, beneath which grew a profusion of the most beautiful wild flowers.[2] 'Though this glen was rough and rocky,' Giles wrote in his journal, 'yet the purling of the water over its stony bed was always a delightful sound to me; and when the winds of evening fanned us to repose, it seemed as though some kindly spirit whispered that it would guard us while we slept, and when the sun declined the swift stream echoed on.'[3] (Giles was of a poetical bent and never travelled without several books of poetry; he was particularly fond of Edgar Allan Poe and Byron, could quote Shakespeare and Spenser from memory, and was himself given to composing the occasional verse. In his journal he rarely foregoes the opportunity to lapse into hyperbole. A great romantic at heart, he often talked to his favourite horse, Cocky, and much of his journal describes the antics of his dog.)

They marched on westward without major difficulty, other than the usual explorers' nightmare, the flies, and what Giles called 'the hideous spinifex', the sharp barbs of which were a torture both to men and horses. They rode through this inhospitable growth for almost

300km, their horses' feet bleeding and the explorers' clothes torn and their flesh punctured by its barbs whenever they dismounted.

On 21 September they reached Mount Udor (as Giles named it), and ahead, to the west, lay dense scrub through which it was clear they would literally have to cut their way if they wished to pass. Giles decided to retreat, and on 1 October turned westward, 'only too thankful to get out of this horrible region'.[4] One of the horses dropped a foal; it was too young to walk, and had to be killed ('the mare looked the picture of misery', Giles wrote), but they were cheered by the fact that the way soon became much easier; moreover they found trees bearing luscious quandong (native peaches), and others with mulga apples, and enjoyed the fruit. Water was another matter – it remained scarce and they once went without it for two days before reaching what had obviously been a large Aboriginal encampment, the walls of a cave nearby covered with red, white and black drawings and hand-prints with a spectacular drawing of a snake. Nearby was a tarn which refreshed both men and horses. Giles named it the Tarn of Auber, after an Edgar Allan Poe poem, 'Ulalume'.

When they moved on, water remained scarce. They travelled over 200km before they came upon another tree-lined pool, which he called Glen Edith, after one of his nieces. Giles was fortunate in finding several beauty spots as he continued south, the last of which was the Vale of Tempe, with excellent grassland and fruitful fig trees, which he reached on 11 October. But ahead to the south there was more barren land, where the party became bogged down in an expanse of salt marsh; they tried to pass around it, then to cross it, but the moment the horses set foot upon what seemed a hard white surface they began to 'flounder about in the bottomless bed of the infernal lake'.

We were powerless to help them for we could not get near owing to the bog, and we sank up over our knees, where the crust was broken, in hot salt mud. All I could do was to crack my whip to prevent the horses from ceasing to exert themselves, and although it was but a few moments that they were in this danger, to me it

seemed an eternity. They staggered at last out of the quagmire,
heads, back, saddles, everything covered with blue mud, their
mouths were filled with salt mud also, and they were completely
exhausted when they reached firm ground.[5]

As so often, it was the horses that were tortured by a thirst
perhaps even more severe than that of the men; it was still a rarity to
come across a clear stream or waterhole; one day they plodded for
120km without water in a temperature of 104°F in the shade (not
that it was possible to find substantial shade). When they did locate
water it was impossible to persuade the horses to drink moderately,
and Giles was afraid they would kill themselves with over-
indulgence. They spent some time circling round one waterhole,
which he called Glen Thirsty, then decided that they must retreat.
But there was to be one final trial, an encounter with hostile
Aboriginals. They left their overnight camp to go on a recon-
naissance, and first came across two warriors, armed with shields
and enormously long spears. These kept their distance, but gradually
more men appeared, also armed, and kept pace with them as they
marched. They had a distinctive appearance, different from that of
any other tribesmen Giles had seen. The first two

> had their hair tied up in a kind of chignon at the back of the head,
> the hair being dragged back off the forehead from infancy. This
> mode gave them a wild though somewhat effeminate appearance;
> others, again, wore their hair in long thick curls reaching down to
> shoulders beautifully elaborated with iguanas' or emus' fat and
> red ochre.[6]

The Aboriginals shouted demoniacally, brandishing their spears;
Giles knew that, well aimed, they could be thrown with precision
for at least 100 yards. The men gestured to them to depart in the
direction from which they had come. Giles and Carmichael had only
their revolvers, since they had left their rifles with Robinson at the
camp, so began to retreat, at which the natives began to cheer, the
noise so loud it could be heard even after they were well out of

sight. The explorers broke camp and set off to the east, but soon came across more Aboriginals, all of whom seemed antagonistic. However, as soon as Giles unstrapped his rifle and held it up, they dispersed, to the explorer's surprise.

That evening, 6 November, Carmichael and Robinson announced that they had had enough. They wanted to go home. Giles would not have regretted losing Robinson, who he thought was lazy, not really interested in the expedition, and had just come along 'for the ride' (albeit not an easy ride). In fact, he had discussed with Carmichael the possibility of dismissing their colleague, if some way could be found of sending him safely home. But he was surprised and hurt when Carmichael also announced that he no longer wanted to go on. However, he could do nothing but accept the situation, but did so with ill grace, and henceforth the three men, childishly if understandably, only spoke to each other when it was absolutely necessary.

Giles made one last, solo excursion in search of water with which to fill up the water-bottles – and had a narrow escape from more Aboriginals. He found himself in a narrow gorge, and on the cliffs on either side suddenly appeared a horde of men, standing like statues, spears poised to throw. He turned his horse, 'one of the best and fastest I have. He knew exactly what I wanted because he wished it also, and that was to be gone. I mounted slowly with my face to the enemy, but the instant I was on he sprang round and was away with a bound that almost left me behind; then such demoniacal yells greeted my ears as I had never heard before and do not wish to hear again . . . we went out of that glen faster, oh! ever so much faster, than we went in. I heard a horrid sound of spears, sticks, and other weapons, striking violently upon the ground behind me, but I did not stop to pick up any of them, or even to look round to see what caused it.'[7]

When he got back to camp, the others asked why his horse was in such a lather. He advised them to ride back and see for themselves. Wisely they declined. Giles called the place Escape Glen. By 1 December 1872 he and his companions were back in relative civilisation, at the telegraph station at Charlotte Waters, on what is now the border between South Australia and the Northern Territory. He considered that he had failed, though he had crossed 16,000km of country previously unknown to any white man.

Once bitten by the exploring bug, as we have so often seen, men seem helpless to resist. At the end of his book *Australia Twice Traversed*, Giles writes that 'an explorer is an explorer from love, and it is nature, not art, that makes him so', and no sooner did he get back to Adelaide than he set to work to put together another expedition, once again sponsored by von Mueller (the South Australian government contributed £250). This time he summoned Tietkens, who travelled from Melbourne to act as second in command, bringing with him a young man called James 'Jimmy' Andrews. The three men drove in a four-wheeled trap from Adelaide to Port Augusta, the most northerly point on the Spencer Gulf, later known as 'the cross-roads of Australia'. They collected horses as they went, and on 4 August 1873 were once again off, to the west with another companion, Alf Gibson, twenty-four horses and two dogs (Monkey and another terrier, Toby, belonging to Gibson).

By 30 August they had arrived at a pleasant creek, with good grass for the horses and plentiful fresh water. It being Tietkens's twenty-ninth birthday, they opened a bottle of brandy from the medical stores, enjoyed some parrot soup, and Giles named the place Tietkens Birthday Creek. They then went on to explore Officer Creek, south of the Musgrave Ranges, when the sudden appearance of Giles and Tietkens startled a tribe of about two hundred Aboriginals. While the explorers were careful to show no sign of unfriendliness, their horses became very restless, especially when some spears were thrown and struck the ground nearby. Giles was forced to fire a shot over the natives' heads. This quietened them for a while, but when the explorers dismounted they again became agitated – Giles thought they had previously believed man and horse to be one – and launched a proper attack.

The explorers fired at the ground in front of their attackers' feet ('it was no use waiting to be speared first', as Giles later remarked)[8] and the sand and gravel flew up into the eyes of the Aboriginals in the front rank; this, and the noise of the guns, made them pause, so affording an opportunity for Giles and Tietkens to make a run for it, firing their revolvers as they went. The natives retreated out of sight, but the men could hear them shouting in the distance. Within the hour they again appeared, and again were sent packing by gunfire, although the fact that the explorers were careful not to hit any of them resulted in the Aboriginals laughing, jeering and slapping their bare bottoms in derision. Eventually, a few very close shots convinced them that their situation was not altogether safe, and they finally retired; for some time, however, Giles was uncomfortably aware that they were not far away.

'It is next to impossible in Australia for an explorer to discover excellent and well-watered regions without coming into deadly conflict with the aboriginal inhabitants,' he reflected. 'The aborigines are always the aggressors, but then the white man is a trespasser in the first instance, which is a cause sufficient for any atrocity to be committed upon him.' He always regretted having to fire on the Aboriginals: 'It always distressed me to have to fire at these savages, and it was only when our lives were in most imminent

Over 200 Aboriginals were frightened by the unfamiliar sight of the explorers' horses; the horses in turn were startled, and only shots fired over the heads of the 'natives' dispersed them. *(From Giles,* Australia Twice Traversed*)*

danger that we did so, for, as Iago says, "Though in the trade of war I have slain men, Yet do I hold it very stuff o' the conscience To do no contrived murder".'[9]

Giles pressed on around the Musgrave Ranges until he arrived on the southern side of what he called Mount Olga, an area now known by its Aboriginal name, Kata Tjuta. The rock formations which now excite tourists also much impressed the first European to see them: their appearance, Giles wrote, 'is truly wonderful; it displayed to our astonished eyes rounded minarets, giant cupolas, and monstrous domes. There they have stood as huge memorials of the ancient times of earth, for ages, countless eons of ages, since its creation first had birth. . . . Time, the old, the dim magician, has ineffectually laboured here, although with all the powers of ocean at his command; Mount Olga has remained as it was born.'[10]

The men paused for a while, enjoying the spectacle as well as refreshing baths in the pools at the foot of the rocks and then pressed on to the south-west and established a camp which Giles called Fort Mueller, at the foot of the Cavanagh Range. It was safe from attack, but the rocks with which it was surrounded gave it a strange air, and Giles came to dislike it intensely: 'I had many strange, almost superstitious feelings with regard to this singular spot, for there was always a strange depression upon my spirits whilst here . . .'.[11]

During October and November he tried repeatedly to make his way westward, but time after time had to turn back in the face of 'terrible, next-to-impassable scrub', 'desolate, waterless desert' and the increasing rarity of waterholes, where the explorers had to compete with Aboriginal tribesmen who were not eager to share the precious commodity with white men. One of the horses failed, and had to be shot. Jimmy and Gibson proved bungling incompetents with guns, and when each had fired a bullet into the poor beast without killing it, Giles had to administer the *coup de grâce*.

And so the misery went on, the horses barely surviving on a third of a bucket of water each, a day. On one occasion Giles, on a solo expedition, found a waterhole full of water so putrid that he could not pull up buckets for his horse without retching. The horse died.

Giles decided to retreat to Fort Mueller. On the way, Gibson became seriously ill (the disappearance of his terrier, Toby, also depressed him); he rode, the others walked to save the dehydrated horses. 'My readers', Giles wrote later, 'must not confound a hundred miles' walk in this region with the same distance in any other. The greatest walker that ever stepped would find more than his match here. In the first place, the feet sink in the loose and sandy soil, in the second it is densely covered by the hideous porcupine [the spinifex]; to avoid the constant prickings from this the walker is compelled to raise his feet to an unnatural height. . . . Again, the ground being hot enough to burn the soles off one's boots, with the thermometer at something like 180° in the sun, and the choking from thirst at every movement of the body, is enough to make any one pause.'[12]

They remained at Fort Mueller for the best part of two months, resting, celebrating Christmas Day with a bottle of rum, a dinner of fried wallaby and some kind of pudding made by Jimmy. Tietkens and Gibson sang several ballads, and Jimmy gave them an Irish song or two. Giles was happy to settle down with his books, in particular with his beloved Byron.

But too soon for comfort, on 16 January, they were off again, exploring to the west, south-west and north-east without being able to make real progress in any direction. Doggedly, for the next three months, they attempted to break through to more comfortable and promising terrain, and time and time again were frustrated by the nature of the country, the intense heat and lack of water. The inability to keep themselves clean was almost as distressing to Giles and Jimmy as was their thirst. It did not, however, worry Gibson, who was notoriously indifferent to personal cleanliness. Indeed, one day when the three were camped near a rare creek, Jimmy came racing up to Giles to ask the date, and to implore him to enter in his journal the fact that Gibson was actually bathing – the first time he had washed for eighteen weeks.

A common occurrence was that the horses were from time to time in trouble: the moment their saddles were removed, they would fall to the ground, and when they reached water they would collapse in the act of drinking. Four of them died from the heat. One day Giles's terrier, Monkey, had to be carried, nearly dead from thirst and heat (the men gave him the last drop of water they possessed). Giles had been holding out in hope of rain, which was clearly not going to come, and they were now living on the smoked flesh of Terrible Billy, an old horse they had slaughtered in March. All the sugar was gone, and though they had a little flour left, it was kept to make a sort of gruel should anyone fall sick. In mid-April, having for the past month explored the Petermann Ranges from Fort McKellar, a depot he established in the Rawlinson Range, Giles decided to make one final vigorous attempt to push westward for at least 160km. Alf Gibson volunteered to accompany him, while Tietkens returned to Fort McKellar.

Giles and Gibson set off from their base at Circus Water on 20 April, Giles riding the Fair Maid of Perth and Gibson a heavier horse, Badger. A bay cob carried a pair of water-bags containing 20 gallons of water, and another horse, Darkie, carried two 5-gallon kegs of water and a week's rather meagre supply of smoked horse. The water did not last long: it was appallingly hot, and apart from horses and men needing to drink, evaporation depleted the supply – and then, at night, one of the horses got at a water-bag and bit it so that all its contents were spilt.

Two days into the journey, Badger and Darkie were turned loose. The water they had been carrying was almost all gone, what was left was insufficient to sustain them, and their best chance was to use their instinct and find their way back to Circus Water. Gibson decided to ride the bay cob, and it and Giles's horse were given all the water which remained in the large water-bags. Giles hung the two 5-gallon kegs in the branches of a tree, and the two men set out again.

By 23 April they had made only 144km when Gibson's horse refused to carry him, lay down and died. It was a fatal moment; had he continued to ride the hardier and more experienced Badger, the situation might have been saved. The two men now had less than half a litre of water left for themselves and Giles's horse. Giles decided that the situation was desperate, and instructed Gibson to ride Fair Maid the 48km back to the water kegs, give her a drink, then return to Tietkens and guide him, with fresh horses and more water, back towards Giles, who would himself retrace his steps as far as he could. Gibson was, above all, to be careful to stick to the tracks the men had left behind them. He disappeared into the distance, and Giles began a weary trek back along the tracks.

He went on walking through the cool of the night until the moon went down, then rested – so thirsty that he was unable to sleep. The following day he reached the spot where the water kegs had been hung. Gibson had been there, and had left about 2½ litres (4 pints) for Giles, which would have to last him until Gibson returned with Tietkens after a round journey of 150km, which would take him five days, or perhaps more.

Apart from thirst, Giles was ravenously hungry, but all the food he could find was eleven small pieces of smoked horse; ½kg (1lb) to last him until Tietkens could reach him. He almost resigned himself to death – but valiantly struggled on, carrying one of the kegs of water on his back.

'The next few days,' he later wrote, 'I can only pass over as they seemed to pass with me, for I was quite unconscious half the time, and I only got over about five miles a day . . . by the third or fourth day – I couldn't tell which – my horse meat was all gone. I had to remain in what scanty shade I could find during the day, and I could only travel by night. When I lay down in the shade in the morning I lost all consciousness, and when I recovered my senses I could not tell whether one day or two or three had passed. At one place I am sure I must have remained over forty-eight hours.'[13]

His fortitude is astonishing, for when he had been following the tracks for about 20km he saw to his dismay that the tracks of the two horses they had turned loose diverged from the main, east–west tracks, and turned off to the east-south-east – *and that Gibson had turned off and followed them*. He followed Gibson's tracks for a little way, then wisely turned back, irrationally convincing himself that the man would have recognised his error, and somehow returned to the right course. He staggered on, arms and legs punctured by spinifex spines, burning with thirst, until at last – he had no idea on what day – he reached Circus Water. There was no sign of Gibson having been there but there was some water, and Giles drank, and drank, and drank.

Once he had revived somewhat, it was almost impossible for him to move. From where he lay, he heard a faint squeak, and saw at his hand a small dying wallaby: 'The instant I saw it, like an eagle I pounced upon it, and ate it, living, raw, dying – fur, skin, bones, skull and all. The delicious taste of that creature I shall never forget.'[14] It was not much, but it was something. After a rest, he started out again. Once, he fancied he heard the sound of a galloping horse, but concluded that it was an illusion.

He staggered into the camp at daybreak on 1 May and woke Tietkens, who was astonished to see him alive. He had, he said, not long returned from riding out to see if there was any sign of Giles; somehow they had missed each other – it explained the sound of hooves. There had been no sign of Gibson, nor for that matter of Badger or Darkie. Giles was, as he said, 'the only one of six living creatures that had returned, or were now ever likely to return, from that desert'.[15] Next day, though suffering from stomach cramps and violent headaches – the result of too freely eating and drinking after so long a fast – he was lifted on to a horse, and he and Tietkens set out to look for Gibson or, as they were now convinced, for his body.

They rode to the point at which Gibson's horse's tracks deviated from the others, and followed them as well as they could; but rain, wind and the activities of animals had almost obscured them, and in the end they had to give up; Fair Maid had still had the strength to carry Gibson further than Giles and Tietkens could afford, with less vigorous animals, to follow. The lost man had simply vanished, presumably having ridden his horse to death in what Giles now called the Gibson Desert.

Back at Fort McKellar, they were altogether out of food. They built a smoke-house, killed another horse, Tommy, and were able to eat some fresh meat, though it was intolerably tough, and Giles wished he had a sausage machine. They smoked the rest of the meat, which they reckoned would last them a month, and on 21 May began their return to civilisation.

They had been away for a year, and Giles could only regard his expedition as unsuccessful. However, he and Tietkens received a warm welcome in Adelaide, riding through the streets in their tattered clothing, cheered on by some twenty thousand onlookers to a reception on the steps of the Town Hall. One elderly citizen, however, patted him on the back with the words 'Ernest, my boy, you should never have come back. You should have sent your journal home by Tietkens and died out there yourself.'[16]

One thing, he thought, was obvious – only an expedition equipped with camels would stand a chance of success in the country through which they had travelled. When camels were promised him, he readily set out for Beltana, a cattle and sheep station 480km north of Adelaide, collected two of the beasts, and on 13 March 1875 set out to look for promising pastoral land beyond Fowler's Bay, on the Great Australian Bight, 480km west of Port Augusta. From there he meant to force his way further westward until he reached Perth, in Western Australia, looking en route for any decent pastoral land.

The journey from Beltana to Fowler's Bay was one of almost 1,000km. From the first, the heat was almost insupportable, rendering the sand so hot that when they paused, neither camels nor horses could bear to stand still. There was not so much as a blade of grass for the horses to eat, though the camels munched happily on the leaves of any bush under which they were sheltering from the sun. Jimmy the Aboriginal guide, led the party from waterhole to waterhole, but often the water was undrinkable, with dead, decaying birds and lizards and rotting vegetation floating in it.

The original party had been quite a large one: four white men, Jimmy, the Aboriginal guide, and three young Aboriginals, with two camels and a calf and a number of horses. On 24 March, at Youldeh, 215km north of Fowler's Bay, Giles dismissed all the men save two – Peter Nicholls and Jimmy – and continued his journey with three horses and the camels. The camels behaved as camels will – often as intransigent and unpredictable as mules. Nicholls rode one of them, or tried to; she was reluctant to move at all, and if he beat her would simply lie down and attempt to roll on top of him. The other was extremely fond of human company and when approached by any one of the party would slaver affectionately all over him. But at least they were excellent beasts of burden.

Jimmy proved an excellent guide, at least as far as Wynbring, a large rock pool to which he led the party. Giles was full of admiration for anyone who could find his way to such a place, a mere pin-prick in a desert, solely by remembering passing that way forty years previously. 'Sometimes he would notice a tree or a sand-hill, or something else that he remembered, and would turn suddenly from that point in an entirely different direction, towards some high and severe sandhill; here he would climb a tree. After a few minutes gazing about, he would descend, mount his horse, and go off on some new line, and in course of a mile or so he would stop at a tree, and tell us that when a little boy he got a possum out of a hole which existed in it.'[17]

Within sight of Wynbring was Mount Finke, and Giles decided to make for it; no white man had been there since Stuart, who had discovered it in 1858. Every Aboriginal he encountered warned him that there was no water either at Mount Finke or on the way there, but for some inexplicable reason he ignored them. He found their statements to be all too true. On the third day of the journey, in intolerable heat and with water rationed, a horse died. Three days later, another collapsed and had to be shot. Next morning, a third horse died. Their supply of water was gone. They could not possibly retreat as far as Wynbring, 320km away; if they stayed where they were they would die. They beat their way onward, through dense scrub. At least the camels were still on their feet.

On the eighth day out from Wynbring, they came across a small clay channel containing some yellow water. They, and the camels, drank until they could drink no more. This, and cooler weather with some rain, was a tonic to them and they marched on more resolutely, eventually reaching Finniss Springs, where they were able to pick up fresh horses and make their way easily on to Beltana, where Tietkens was waiting to take up the position of second in command for the journey on to Perth. There too were 17-year-old Alec Ross and 27-year-old Jesse Young. Ross, though still a boy, had enormous experience of the bush, where he had been born. Young had only recently arrived in Australia and was an ex-naval officer whose training would enable him to take observations and calculate their position. To complete the party, there was an Afghan camel-driver, Saleh Mahomet, and Tommy Oldham, a cheerful and likeable 18-year-old Aboriginal whom Giles had known for some years.

Giles's fourth expedition left Beltana on 17 July 1875 with twenty-two camels – he had been understandably impressed by the beasts' hardihood during the terrible tramp from Wynbring to Finniss Springs. The journey to the border with Western Australia was hard but not perilous. A couple of the camels fell ill from eating poisonous plants, but their driver gave them hot butter as an emetic and they recovered. They were never short of water; indeed at one point it rained so heavily that all the beasts had to do was lower their heads and drink from puddles at their feet.

The landscape that greeted them as they entered Western Australia was not promising. There was nothing but dense, dark, dreary scrub as far as the eye could see; even a bare desert, Giles thought, would be preferable. He felt they were very probably on 'the worst desert upon the face of the earth; but that fact should give us all the more pleasure in conquering it'.[18] This was the Great Victoria Desert, as Giles was later to name it. Knowing absolutely nothing about what lay ahead, he led the party on in the general direction of Perth, the camels carrying as much water as they could bear.

On the sixth day of their march they emerged from the scrubland on to the Nullarbor Plain which made the going easier; but by the eighth day they were almost completely out of water, and there was no sign of any. On the eleventh day they hit scrub again. Saleh, the camel-driver, kept asking Giles when he would get water, and at last Giles answered, 'I didn't come here to find water, I came here to die.' The old man thought for a while, and then said, 'I think some camel he die tomorrow, Mr Gile.'

'Oh, no,' Giles replied, 'they can't possibly live until tomorrow, I think they will all die tonight.'

'Oh, Mr Gile, I think we all die soon now.'

'Oh, yes, Saleh, we'll all be dead in a day or two.'

At which Saleh went away and prayed.[19] The dark humour was scarcely a comfort.

There were five more days of almost waterless travel before they came to Queen Victoria Spring (Giles's name, again) and were able, men and camels, to drink their fill. They paused for all too short a time. The luck of finding the spring – and that is what it was, luck – convinced Giles that such serendipity would persist; they would not die of thirst. They marched on, and indeed after eight days and 280km came to a large and generous well. When they had watered the camels, and themselves, some Aboriginals arrived. The men seemed friendly and, mysteriously, had one or two words of English – 'white fellow', 'what name?', 'boy'. Jesse Young cut up a red handkerchief and they happily tied the strips around their brows, and seemed pleased with the present. The explorers gathered that they called the well 'Ularring'.

A few women and children put in an inquisitive appearance and 'a very pretty little girl came by herself. She was about nine or ten years old, and immediately became the pet of the camp. . . . She had splendid eyes and beautiful teeth, and we soon dressed her up and gave her a good breakfast. In an hour after her arrival she was as much at home in my camp as though I were her father.' The Aboriginal camp was delightful, too, and Giles was inspired to verse:

> Each in his place allotted
> Had silent sat or squatted,
> While round their children trotted
> In pretty youthful play.
>
> One can't but smile who traces
> The lines on their dark faces
> To the pretty prattling graces
> Of these small heathens gay.[20]

It was a delightful interlude. Then, on 16 October, when the explorers had finished their supper and Young had gone for a stroll, he suddenly saw coming towards him a small army of what he reckoned was over a hundred men, painted and feathered and armed with spears and clubs. He turned and called out to the others, who just had time to pick up their firearms before the first spears were thrown. One or two Aboriginals had remained in the camp, and one of them jumped on Giles, preventing him from using his gun, but he cried out 'Fire! Fire for your lives!' and while he struggled the others did as he ordered. By the time he had freed himself, the native army had retreated, carrying some wounded men. He realised later that that afternoon the small girl had attempted to warn him, in mime, of the coming attack, but he had been engrossed in writing his journal and had ignored her.

They remained at the camp until 18 October, then left, fighting their way through scrub for eleven days, now suffering considerably from scurvy, and on 3 November were pleased to arrive at a sheep station where a shepherd gave them a good meal of mutton. They were now back in settled country and as they approached Perth they were met by the carriage and pair sent to greet them by the Governor, Sir William Robinson. At Newcastle they were greeted by a triumphal arch and a dinner had been organised, at which the chairman of the local council expressed surprise that Giles and his men had come, for West Australia had plenty of explorers of their own. Tommy, however, proved a great success; urged to give a speech, he said he didn't know what to say; whereupon a man sitting next to him said, 'Never mind, Tommy; say anything'. Thus encouraged Tommy rose in his seat and said 'Anything', at which there was much applause.

The triumphant progress went on into Perth, where the camels caused a sensation since no one there had seen such animals before. The mayor, local worthies and a brass band greeted them; there was a reception at the town hall and a banquet and ball at Government House. But such a generous reception failed to comfort Giles for what he felt had been his failure: he had discovered no good pastoral land; on the other hand, he consoled himself with the thought that 'the explorer does not make the country, he must take it as he finds it'.[21] Moreover, now he had reached Perth, he had the

Giles and his team ride into Perth. *(From Giles*, Australia Twice Traversed*)*

opportunity to break through the Gibson Desert from the west – and who knew what might result from that?

So on 13 January 1876, the camel train set out again on the journey back to Adelaide, in effect Giles's fifth expedition. In four months the party plodded almost 500km westward; at the end of May they reached what Giles took to be the Gibson Desert, complete with jagged spinifex and endless rolling sandhills. It must be crossed and, carrying as much water as possible, the expedition entered it on 2 June and was soon passing through a region 'so desolate that it is horrifying even to describe'.[22] It seemed that nothing could live there, but when an old camel died, within minutes a swarm of eagles, crows, hawks and vultures were pecking at her carcass, and at night wild dogs attacked the bones.

On 25 June they reached the area where Gibson had been lost, and Giles spent some time searching for his remains, but without success. Happily, the waterholes and other watering places he had visited before were brimming and the remainder of the journey home was without trouble. On 24 August they entered Adelaide.

Giles's welcome there was muted, and if he had hoped for some financial recognition he was sadly disappointed. There was an immediate dispute between the South Australian and West Australian governments as to who should reward him. The West Australians grudgingly awarded him some land, which he had to sell immediately to pay his debts. South Australia did not do even that much. Had he found good pastoral land he might have been more generously treated but the country he had discovered and crossed was almost completely barren. He came to feel he had wasted the best five years of his life, and the gold medal of the Royal Geographical Society hardly seemed sufficient reward. He took part in the gold rush to Coolgardie in 1892, but had no luck, and died five years later.

Giles was probably not far from the truth: at the close of his published journals he called himself 'the last of the Australian explorers'.

Envoi

Giles was not actually 'the last of the Australian explorers'; he was, however, the last to hope, with any kind of justification, to discover large tracts of rich grazing land somewhere towards the centre of the continent. Those who came after him either explored in order to open out new routes, or simply for the adventure. Perhaps the most remarkable of the former were Frank and Alexander Jardine, who in 1864 drove cattle from Bowen, in north Queensland, 1,450km further north, to Somerset, at the very tip of Cape York – an epic journey which took four months. Of those bound for adventure, in 1873 William Christie Gosse, riding out from Alice Springs, saw in the distance a hill which, when he approached it, turned out to be one enormous rock which the Aboriginals called Uluru. He named it Ayers Rock after a former prime minister of South Australia, and it became, with Utzon's Sydney Opera House and the Sydney Harbour Bridge, one of the three Australian icons which every tourist must visit.

But somehow the impetus had gone out of the idea of exploration, with the realisation that there was no more reason to hope that somewhere in the centre of the continent there was, perhaps, an inland sea around which fine pastoral land offered new riches to settlers and stockmen. The four vast deserts of the west – the Great Sandy Desert, the Great Victoria Desert, the Gibson and Tanami Deserts – together with Sturt's Stony Desert and the Simpson further east, were only the most arid areas of Australia; the land which surrounded them, in the interior, had been found to be no more promising. Gradually the truth became obvious: only about one-fifth of the land, along parts of the coast, could support more than frugal development.

Occasional expeditions still set out, with the same hollow hopes, and to suffer the same fate, as previous ones. Sir Thomas Elder's Scientific Exploring Expedition of 1891, sponsored by the Royal Geographical Society, meandered over the south-east of the country, producing excellent maps of about 20 million hectares of land, none of which was suitable for cultivation or capable of sustaining life. Lawrence Wells set out in 1896 to try to open up a route from the goldfields of the north-west to the Northern Territory, keeping a look-out at the same time for the remains of the Leichhardt expedition. He and a companion died after staggering through almost 2,000km of waterless desert.

Simpson Newland, the President of the South Australian branch of the Royal Geographical Society, drew a line under the story of the great explorers of Australia when he wrote:

The chapter of Australian exploration closed as it began, with deeds of splendid endurance and courage, with deeds of awful suffering, and with the loss of heroic lives. I say 'closed' for it can not be supposed that any other expedition will ever be fitted out, for there is nothing more to discover.[1]

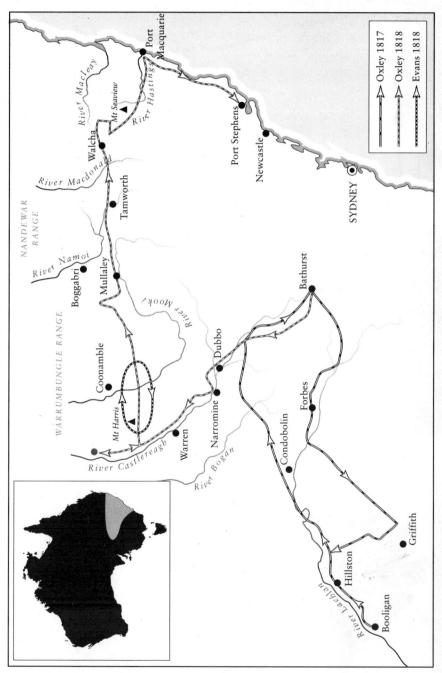

Oxley's and Evans's expeditions.

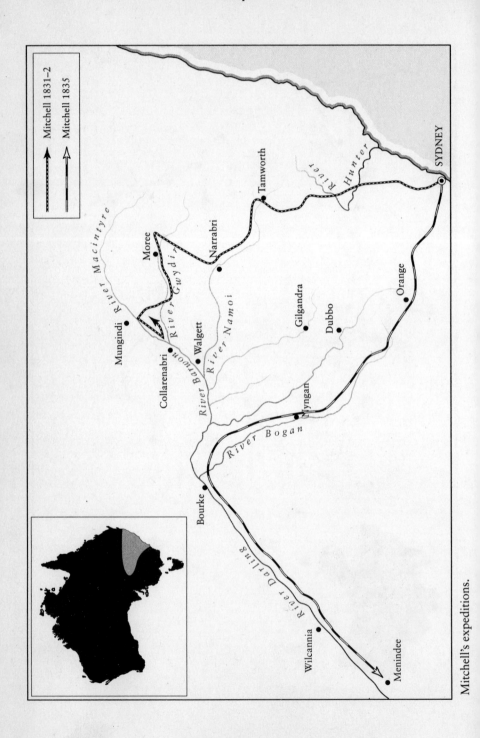

Mitchell's expeditions.

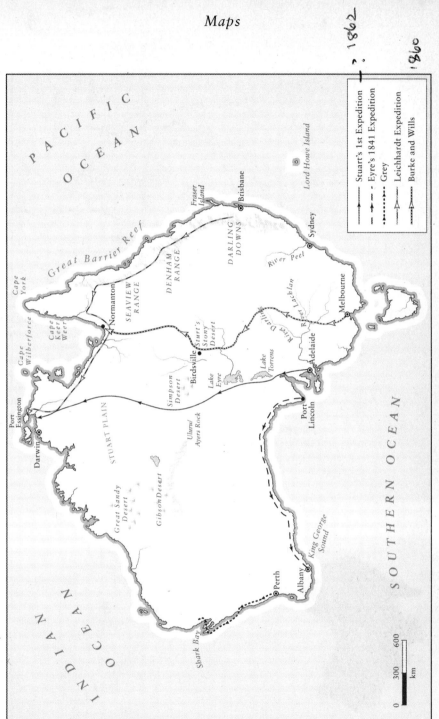

Expeditions of Stuart, Eyre, Grey, Leichhardt and Burke and Wills.

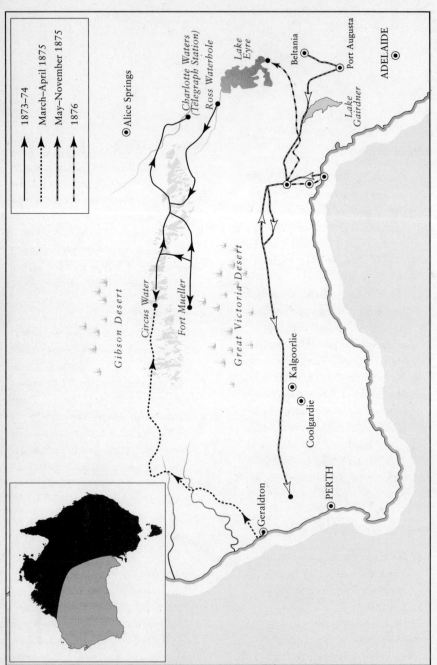

Giles's expeditions.

Notes

Introduction

1. *New York Times*, 18 March 1923.
2. George Grey, *Journals of Two Expeditions of Discovery in North-west and Western Australia, during the Years 1837, 38 and 39*, London: T. & W. Boone, 1841; LBSA, 1964, Vol. 2, p. 264.
3. I have used the form *Aboriginals* throughout; it is preferred now to *Aborigines*, though that was originally the plural of *aboriginal* (derived from *ab origine*, i.e. 'from the beginning' – the first inhabitants of a country). The term *aborigine* seems to have originated in the middle of the seventeenth century.
4. See p. 202ff.
5. Tim Flannery, *The Explorers*, Melbourne: Text Publishers, 1998. p. 4.

One: In the Beginning

1. William Dampier, *Buccaneer Explorer*, ed. Gerald Norris, London: Folio Society, 1994, pp. 120–1.
2. *Ibid.*, pp. 217–18.
3. 'Port Jackson' is actually the harbour of Sydney; 'Sydney' is the settlement which grew up in the bay, and now describes the city. There is some muddle about how and when the terms were differentiated; Port Jackson is now rarely if ever used as a place-name.
4. Watkin Tench, *Complete Account of the Settlement at Port Jackson*, London, 1793; reprinted Sydney: Library of Australian History, 1962, p. 112.
5. *Ibid.*, p. 53.
6. *Cassell's Picturesque Australia*, ed. E.E. Morris, London: Cassell, 1889, p. 272.
7. Hacking did, however, bring back a specimen of the lyre-bird.
8. Letter to Sir Joseph Banks, May 1803; quoted in Ernest Favenc, *The History of Australian Exploration*, Sydney: Turner & Henderson, 1888, at p. 52; no further provenance supplied.

Two: The Great Inland Sea

1. John Oxley, *Journals of Two Expeditions into the Interior of New South Wales, Undertaken by Order of the British Government in the Years 1817–18*, London: John Murray, 1820; replica, LBSA, 1964, pp. 357–8.

217

2. *Ibid.*, pp. 4–5.
3. *Ibid.*, pp. 20–1; 'rubus and bromus' – bushes and high rough grass.
4. Oxley, *Ibid*, p. 47.
5. *Ibid.*, p. 58.
6. *Ibid.*, p. 74.
7. Colonial Secretary's Papers (1788–1825), New South Wales, Sydney (State Records, New South Wales, 1989), SZ7, p. 317a, quoted in Richard Johnson, *The Search for the Inland Sea*, Melbourne: Melbourne University Press, 2001, p. 76.
8. Oxley, *Journals*, p. 240.
9. *Ibid.*, p. 248.
10. *Ibid.*, p. 284. The explorers were almost at the site of the present town of Tamworth.
11. Oxley, *Ibid.*, p. 299.
12. *Ibid.*, p. 312.
13. He recovered, but only after some time.

Three: Mapping the Rivers

1. Charles Sturt, *Two Expeditions into the Interior of Southern Australia, during the Years 1828, 1829, 1830 and 1831, with Observations on the Soil, Climate, and General Resources of the Colony of New South Wales*, London: Smith, Elder, 1833; facsimile edn, Adelaide: LBSA, 1963, Vol. 1, pp. xiv–xv.
2. Edgar Beale, *Sturt: the Chipped Idol*, Sydney: Sydney University Press, 1979, p. 43.
3. Michael Langley, *Sturt of the Murray*, London: Hale, 1969, p. 64; no provenance given.
4. Sturt, *Two Expeditions*, Vol. 1, pp. 187–8.
5. Of James Fraser, one of the two soldiers who accompanied Sturt, nothing more is known; and of Hopkinson, not even his forename.
6. Sturt, *Two Expeditions*, Vol. 1, pp. 13–14.
7. *Ibid.*, p. 26.
8. *Ibid.*, p. 44.
9. *Ibid.*, p. 54.
10. *Ibid.*, pp. 64–5.
11. See Langley, *Sturt*, pp. 73–4.
12. Sturt, *Two Expeditions*, Vol. 1, p. 71.
13. Eight years later the Aboriginals would not be so fortunate, many being slaughtered at the hands of Thomas Mitchell's expedition (see p. 48).
14. Sturt, *Two Expeditions*, Vol. 1, p. 179.
15. *Ibid.*, p. 110.
16. *Ibid.*, p. 143.
17. *Ibid.*, Vol. 2, pp. 9–10.
18. Mulholland had been transported for housebreaking, and had only recently received fifty lashes for procuring spirits for fellow convicts. See Beale, *Sturt*, p. 86.
19. Sturt, *Two Expeditions*, Vol. 2, p. 53.
20. Clayton, 30, had been transported for life for rioting at Manchester.
21. Sturt, *Two Expeditions*, Vol. 2, pp. 83–4.
22. *Ibid.*, p. 103.
23. *Ibid.*, p. 105.
24. *Ibid.*, pp. 110–11.
25. *Ibid.*, p. 126.
26. *Ibid.*, p. 166.
27. *Ibid.*, p. 203.
28. *Ibid.*, p. 170.
29. *Ibid.*, p. 194.

30. *Ibid.*, pp. 211–12.
31. *Ibid.*, p. 220.

Four: Australian Morning

1. At this time New South Wales comprised not only the territory which still bears that name, but also Victoria, South Australia, Queensland and the Northern Territory.
2. National Archives, C.O. 201/198, 483 N.S.W.
3. J.H.L. Cumpston, *Thomas Mitchell: Surveyor General and Explorer*, London: Oxford University Press, 1954, p. 66; no provenance supplied.
4. National Archive, C.O. 201/224, 799 N.S.W. Col Patrick Lindesay was acting governor until Sir Richard Bourke arrived at the end of the year.
5. T.L. Mitchell, *Three Expeditions into the Interior of Eastern Australia, &c,* 2 vols, London: Boone, 1839, Vol. 1, p. 1.
6. Visitors to the farm, now a Historic Houses property, can still see this olive tree.
7. Cumpston, *Thomas Mitchell*, p. 94; no provenance supplied.
8. Mitchell, *Three Expeditions*, Vol. 1, p. 274.
9. Short rifles, originally for cavalry use.
10. Mitchell, *Three Expeditions*, Vol. 2, p. 75.
11. *Ibid.*, p. 93.
12. *Ibid.*, pp. 102–3.
13. The bottle was found, only two years later, by two stockmen driving cattle to South Australia.
14. Swan Hill, located 335km north-west of Melbourne, was settled by sheep-herders in 1846, became a busy river port and is now the market centre of an area of rich fruit, grape, dairy and vegetable farming.
15. Mitchell, *Three Expeditions*, Vol. 2, pp. 143–4.
16. *Ibid.*, p. 145.
17. *Ibid.*, p. 138. *Callitris* is the white cypress pine.
18. Mitchell, *Ibid.*, Vol. 2, p. 159.
19. *Ibid.*, p. 171.
20. T.L. Mitchell, *Journal of an Expedition into the Interior of Tropical Australia in Search of a Route from Sydney to the Gulf of Carpentaria*, London: Longman, Brown, Green & Longman, 1848, p. 146: May 1846.
21. A.E. Andrews, *Stapylton*, Hobart: Blubber Head Press, 1986, p. 140; no further provenance given.
22. Mitchell, *Three Expeditions*, Vol. 2, p. 241.
23. Cumpston, *Thomas Mitchell*, pp. 137–8; no provenance supplied.
24. Mitchell finally achieved his ambition and was knighted in 1846.
25. *Cassell's Picturesque Australasia*, ed. E.E. Morris, 4 vols, London: Cassell, 1889, Vol. 3, p. 285.
26. Port Essington, an inlet of the Arafura Sea situated at the very tip of the Australian Northern Territory, was first surveyed in 1818 by Captain Philip Parker and had been the site of an early, unsuccessful attempt at a settlement; it

remained a highly promising location for development.

27. For Leichhardt's expedition see Chapter Seven. Mitchell was generous in his praise of Leichhardt's achievement: 'The journal of Leichhardt's journey . . . shows what difficulties may be surmounted by energy and perseverance' (W.C. Foster, *Sir Thomas Livingstone Mitchell and His World, 1792–1855*, Sydney: Institute of Surveyors, 1985, p. 32; for Sturt's journey see pp. 16–35 and 132–9.

28. 'Chaining' was a method of measuring distance by which surveyors laid a carefully marked chain as they went.

29. Mitchell, *Journal*, p. 144.

30. *Ibid.*, p. 304.

31. Francesco de Ulloa (d. 1540) who in 1539 explored the west coast of Mexico.

32. Mitchell, *Journal*, p. 309.

33. A Colonial Office minute, quoted in Cumpston, *Thomas Mitchell*, p. 221 (without provenance).

Five: The Heroic Heart

1. See p. 96.

2. *Hobart Town Gazette*, 20 February 1830.

3. The artificial horizon was a device used by mariners, which measured latitude by the observation of celestial bodies in relation to the horizon. Various devices were used, some employing mercury to indicate a level plain. The land over which the explorers travelled was often so featureless that determining one's position was almost like doing so in the middle of an ocean.

4. They managed to find their way there, where they reported that Eyre had 'perished'.

5. *South Australian Gazette and Colonial Register*, 21 July 1838.

6. *South Australian Gazette*, 25 March 1839.

7. Malcolm Uren and Robert Stephens, *Waterless Horizons*, Melbourne: Robertson & Mullens, 1945, p. 75.

8. Named after Eyre by a later governor, Sir George Gawler.

9. *Clianthus formosus*.

10. E.J. Eyre, *Journals of Expeditions of Discovery into Central Australia*, London: T. & W. Boone, 1845, Vol. 1, p. 202.

11. *Perth Gazette*, 20 May 1840.

12. Coles was also a wheelwright, which might make him especially useful.

13. *South Australian Gazette*, 20 June 1840.

14. Eyre, *Journals*, Vol. 1, p. 21.

15. *Ibid.*, p. 58.

16. He does not tell us which boy accompanied him on which occasion.

17. Eyre, *Journals*, Vol. 1, p. 75.

18. *Ibid.*, p. 92.

19. Named by Matthew Flinders for the long bands of seaweed that can still be seen when the wind blows onshore.

20. He was to a degree mistaken: good quantities of wheat, oats and barley are grown in the Eyre Peninsula; sheep are also bred there, and on the coast the fishing is good.

21. Eyre, *Journals*, Vol. 1, pp. 166–75.
22. *Ibid.*, p. 213.
23. *Ibid.*, p. 113.
24. *Ibid.*, p. 292.
25. The *Waterwitch* was out of commission, having sprung a leak.
26. Eyre, *Journals*, Vol. 1, p. 300.
27. *Ibid.*, p. 321.
28. *Ibid.*, p. 353.
29. A cairn now marks the site, just beyond the present Twilight Cove, at the head of what are now called Baxter Cliffs and surely one of the most isolated memorials in the world.
30. Eyre, *Journals*, Vol. 2, p. 11.
31. They were never seen again and either perished or perhaps joined one of the local Aboriginal tribes.
32. Eyre, *Journals*, Vol. 2, p. 16.
33. *Ibid.*, p. 24.
34. *Ibid.*, p. 109.
35. *Ibid.*, p. 113.

Six: 'What for do you walk?'

1. George Grey, *Journals of Two Expeditions of Discovery in North-West and Western Australia during the Years 1837, 38 and 39, under the Authority of Her Majesty's Government, Describing Many Newly Discovered, Important and Fertile Districts, with Observations on the Moral and Physical Condition of the Aboriginal Inhabitants, &c. &c.*, 2 vols, London: T. & W. Boone, 1841, Vol. 1, p. 4.
2. *Ibid.*, p. 76.
3. *Ibid.*, pp. 129–30.
4. *Ibid.*, p. 139.
5. *Ibid.*, p. 152.

6. *Ibid.*, pp. 154–5.
7. *Ibid.*, p. 159.
8. *Ibid.*, p. 179.
9. *Ibid.*, p. 236.
10. *Ibid.*, p. 359.
11. *Ibid.*, p. 389.
12. *Ibid.*, p. 392.
13. *Ibid.*, p. 412.
14. *Ibid.*, Vol. 2, p. 3.
15. *Ibid.*, pp. 61–2.
16. *Ibid.*, p. 75.
17. Ernest Favenc, *The History of Australian Exploration from 1788 to 1888*, Sydney: Turner & Henderson, 1888, p. 411; no further provenance given.
18. Grey, *Journals*, Vol. 2, p. 93.

Seven: 'The Heart of the Dark Continent'

1. F.W. Ludwig Leichhardt, *Letters*, collected and tr. M. Aurousseau, 3 vols, Cambridge: Hakluyt Society, 1968, Vol. 1, p. 392.
2. *Ibid.*, p. 384.
3. There is some suggestion that he never actually posted it.
4. Leichhardt, *Letters*, Vol. 3, p. 827.
5. He nevertheless succeeded in providing enough information for a relatively detailed map to be made of the whole area over which he travelled.
6. Ludwig Leichhardt, *Journal of an Overland Expedition in Australia, from Moreton Bay to Port Essington, a Distance of upwards of 3000 Miles, during the Years 1844–1845*, London: T. & W. Boone, 1847; facsimile edn, Adelaide: Corkwood Press, 1996.

7. The production of emu oil as a cure-all is now, over 160 years later, big business.
8. Leichhardt, *Journal*, p. 65.
9. *Ibid.*, p. 118.
10. *Ibid.*, pp. 266–8.
11. *Ibid.*, p. 311.
12. *Ibid.*, pp. 318–19.
13. *Ibid.*, p. 398.
14. *Ibid.*, p. 414.
15. Leichhardt, *Letters*, Vol. 3, p. 844.
16. Leichhardt, *Journal*, p. 445.
17. Leichhardt, *Letters*, Vol. 3, p. 902.
18. *Ibid.*, p. 892. The letter was to Daniel Bunce, a botanist, who despite it agreed to join the expedition.
19. John Frederick Mann, 'Peak Range', p. 178; MS in Dixon Library, Sydney.
20. Leichhardt, *Letters*, Vol. 3, p. 953.
21. Favenc, *History of Australian Exploration*, p. 173; no other provenance given.

Eight: Seven Months Underground

1. *Proceedings of the South Australia branch of the Royal Geographical Society of Australasia*, Vol. 19.
2. Charles Sturt, *Narrative of an Expedition into Central Australia . . . during the Years 1844, 5 and 6*, 2 vols, London: T. & W. Boone, 1849; LBSA, 1964, p. 13. What is loosely called Sturt's journal was really a long series of letters written, in journal form, for his wife.
3. Sturt's pleas were successful, although attempts were made on the men's virtue; on one occasion (14 March 1845) 'six ladies [came]

on a visit to us; on their arrival they placed each their fire stick on our fire, one remaining at it, the other five sitting down one at the foot of each of our blankets. At once seeing their motive, they were told to be off to their squalling children. When they knew we would not let them stop, they abused us as roundly as so many Billingsgate Fish Fags'; quoted in Brock, *To the Desert*, p. 137.
4. Daniel George Brock, *To the Desert with Sturt*, Adelaide: Royal Geographical Society of Australasia, 1975, pp. 8–9.
5. Sturt, *Narrative*, Vol. 1, p. 27 (all subsequent references are to the 1984 edition).
6. *Ibid.*, p. 45.
7. *Ibid.*, p. 46.
8. *Ibid.*, Vol. 2, p. 48.
9. *Ibid.*, p. 52.
10. *Ibid.*, p. 71.
11. *Ibid.*, p. 78.
12. *Ibid.*, p. 79.
13. Michael Langley, *Sturt of the Murray*, London: Hale, 1969, p. 229.
14. Daniel George Brock, *To the Desert*.

Nine: To the Very Centre

1. See pp. 133–8.
2. Charles Sturt, *Narrative of an Expedition into Central Australia . . . duringthe Years 1844, 5 and 6*, 2 vols, London: T. & W. Boone, 1849; LBSA, 1964, Vol. 2, p. 173.
3. *The Journals of John McDouall Stuart during the Years 1858, 1859, 1860, 1861 and 1862, when He

Fixed the Centre of the Continent and Successfully Crossed It from Sea to Sea, ed. William Hardman, London: Saunders, Otley, 1865, p. 35.

4. Stuart, *Journals*, ed. Hardman, p. 37.

5. Sometimes recorded as Wingelbunna or Tirrewah, rumour kept the place alive for a generation; it was rumoured that Leichhardt and his men had died on its banks.

6. Crown Lands and Immigration Office, South Australia, 1220/1860.

7. Stuart, *Journals*, p. 146.

8. *Ibid.*, p. 169.

9. *Ibid.*, p. 331.

10. *Ibid.*, p. 164.

11. *Ibid.*, pp. 165–6.

12. The MS of Stuart's journal is in the Mitchell Library, Sydney. It is not known who took the decision to rename Central Mount Stuart.

13. Stuart, *Journals*, p. 212.

14. *Ibid.*, p. 180.

15. *Ibid.*, pp. 216–17.

16. *Ibid.*, p. 234.

17. *Adelaide Observer*, 23 October 1860.

18. Stuart, *Journals*, p. 321.

19. *Ibid.*, pp. 389–90.

20. *Ibid.*, p. 407. He also named the place Chambers Bay, after a Miss Chambers of Adelaide, who had presented him with the silk Union Jack, his name proudly embroidered at its centre.

21. Auld quoted in Ian Mudie, *The Heroic Journey of John McDouall Stuart*, Sydney: Angus & Robertson, 1968, at p. 209; no other reference given.

22. Stuart, *Journals*, pp. 460–1.

23. Health prevented him from doing this adequately, and the text finally published was incomplete and badly edited by someone who knew nothing of Australia, and perpetrated many errors.

24. *South Australian Chronicle*, 22 January 1863.

Ten: 'Unburied as I lie'

1. In fact, Mueller had been a great nuisance on this expedition, continually going off alone in search of botanical specimens, and getting lost.

2. Andrew Jackson, *Robert O'Hara Burke and the Australian Exploring Expedition*, London: Smith Elder, 1862, p. 15.

3. Hermann Beckler, *A Journey to Cooper's Creek*, tr. Stephen Jeffries and Michael Kertesz, Melbourne: Melbourne University Press, 1993; Introduction, p. xxvi.

4. Quoted in Tim Bonyhady, *Burke and Wills*, Balmain: David Ell, 1991; letter, William Wills to his mother, in Wills, *A Successful Exploration through the Interior of Australia, from Melbourne to the Gulf of Carpentaria*, London: Bentley, 1860, pp. 29–30.

5. This is perhaps rather a comment on the suitability of the other applicants than an aspersion on Wills's knowledge and aptitude. His desultory medical knowledge was only of minimal use to the expedition.

6. Beckler, *A Journey*, p. 16.

7. Quoted in Tim Flannery, *The Explorers*, Melbourne: Text Publishing, 1998, at p. 71; no further provenance given.
8. Beckler, *A Journey*, p. 11.
9. Charles D. Ferguson, *The Experiences of a Forty-Niner during Thirty-Four Years' Residence in California and Australia*, Cleveland, Ohio: Williams, 1888, p. 392; quoted in Bonyhady, *Burke and Wills*, at pp. 84–5.
10. Beckler, *A Journey*, p. 21.
11. *Ibid.*, p. 22.
12. Situated 335km north of Melbourne, Swan Hill is now a major holiday destination, with water sports and recreation on its river, and an equable climate.
13. Beckler, *A Journey*, p. 35.
14. Not far from what is now the town of Bedourie, about 175km inside the border between South Australia and Queensland.
15. Wills was able to undertake far less proper observation than he had planned, for, intent on reducing the weight the horses and camels had to carry, Burke had insisted on abandoning much of Wills's scientific equipment.
16. W.J. Wills, *The Burke and Wills Exploring Expedition*, Melbourne 1861; facsimile edn, LBSA, 1963, p. 27.
17. Burke and Wills Commission, *Report of the Commissioners Appointed to Enquire into and Report upon the Circumstances Connected with the Sufferings and Deaths of Robert O'Hara Burke and William John Wills, the Victorian Explorers*, Victorian Public Papers; *Burke and Wills Exploring Expedition*, at p. 26.
18. Wills 'planted' or buried his remaining surveying and astronomical instruments.
19. W.J. Wills, 'Notebook', La Trobe MS Collection, State Library of Victoria, Box 2083/1d; entry for 13 March.
20. *Ibid.*; entry for 17 April.
21. *Ibid.*; entry for 21 April.
22. Wills, *The Burke and Wills Exploring Expedition*, p. 2.
23. Wills, 'Notebook'; entry for 28 April 1861. As his strength was sapped, not surprisingly Wills's punctuation and grammar suffered; I have not corrected them.
24. Wills, 'Notebook'; entry for 6 May.
25. *Ibid.*; entry for 11 May.
26. *Ibid.*; entry for 3 June.
27. *Ibid.*; entry for 23 June.
28. *Ibid.*
29. Wills, *The Burke and Wills Exploring Expedition*, p. 5.
30. *Ibid.*
31. Burke and Wills Commission, *Report of the Commissioners*, p. 83.
32. Almost all the party's deaths were the result of beri-beri, a disease caused by a severe deficiency of vitamin B1 (thiamine) in the diet.
33. Ernest Favenc, *The History of Australian Exploration from 1788 to 1888*, Sydney: Turner & Henderson, 1888, p. 421; no further provenance supplied.

Notes

Eleven: The Last Australian Explorer

1. Ray Erickson, *Ernest Giles*, Melbourne: Heinemann, 1978, p. 7.
2. Palm Valley is now one of the major tourist attractions of the Finke Gorge National Park, west of Alice Springs.
3. Ernest Giles, *Australia Twice Traversed: the Romance of Exploration*, 2 vols, London: Sampson Low, Marston, Searle & Rivington, 1889, Vol. 1, pp. 25–6.
4. *Ibid.*, p. 67.
5. *Ibid.*, p. 98.
6. *Ibid.*, p. 115.
7. *Ibid.*, pp. 121–2.
8. *Ibid.*, p. 178.
9. *Ibid.*, p. 180. The quotation is from *Othello*, Act I, sc. ii, l. 1.
10. Giles, *Australia Twice Traversed*, Vol. 1, p. 191.
11. *Ibid.*, p. 263.
12. *Ibid.*, p. 245.
13. *Ibid.*, Vol. 2, p. 40.
14. *Ibid.*, p. 42.
15. *Ibid.*, p. 43.
16. *Ibid.*, p. 71.
17. *Ibid.*, p. 101.
18. *Ibid.*, p. 185.
19. *Ibid.*, pp. 191–2.
20. *Ibid.*, p. 221.
21. *Ibid.*, p. 246.
22. *Ibid.*, p. 317.

Envoi

1. Royal Geographical Society, South Australia branch, *Proceedings 1920–21*, Vol. 22, p. 165.

Bibliography

Abbreviations

LBSA   Libraries Board of South Australia
FSLSA   Friends of the State Library of South Australia
PLSA   Public Libraries of South Australia

Alexander, C.L., *John McKinley, Explorer, 1819–1872*, Royal Geographical Society of Australasia, Proceedings, Vol. 63, 1961
Andrews, A.E.J., *Stapylton*, Hobart: Blubber Head Press, 1970
——, *Major Mitchell's Map 1834*, Hobart: Blubber Head Press, 1986
Auld, W.P., *Recollections of McDouall Stuart*, Adelaide: Sullivan's Cove, 1984
Austin, K.A., *Matthew Flinders on the Victorian Coast*, Melbourne: Cypress Books, 1974
Badger, G.M., *Robert O'Hara Burke and the Australian Exploring Expedition of 1860*, London, 1862
Badger, Geoffrey, *Explorers of Australia*, East Roseville: Kangaroo Press, 2001
Banks, Joseph, *The Journal of Joseph Banks in the* Endeavour, facsimile edn, Adelaide: Rigby, 1980
Barwick, John, *The Search for Farmland*, Melbourne: Echidna, 2000
Bassett, J.G., *Great Exploration: an Australian Anthology*, Melbourne: Oxford University Press, 1996
Beale, E., *Sturt: the Chipped Idol*, Sydney: Sydney University Press, 1979
Beckler, Hermann, *A Journey to Cooper's Creek*, tr. S. Jeffries and M. Kertesz, ed. S. Jeffries, Melbourne: Melbourne University Press, 1993
Bergin, T.J., *In the Steps of Burke and Wills*, Sydney: Australian Broadcasting Commission, 1981
Bladin, F.M. (ed.), *Historical Records of New South Wales, 1892–1901*, Sydney: Government Printer; facsimile edn, 7 vols, Mona Vale, 1978
Boden, K.M. (ed.), *Matthew Flinders' Narrative of Tom Thumb's Cruise to Canoe Rivulet*, Melbourne: South Eastern Historical Association, 1985
Bonyhady, T., *Burke and Wills: from Melbourne to Myth*, Balmain: David Ell, 1991

Bibliography

Branagan, D.F., 'Ludwig Leichhardt: Geologist in Australia' in *Australia: Studies on the History of Discoveries and Exploration*, Frankfurt am Main: Johann Wolfgang Goethe-Universität Verlag, 1994

Brock, Daniel George, *To the Desert with Sturt: A Diary of the 1844 Expedition*, Adelaide: Royal Geographical Society of Australasia, 1975

Browne, J.H., *Journal of the Sturt Expedition 1844–1845*, ed. H.J. Finniss, *South Australiana*, Vol. 5, 1872

Bunce, D., *Travels with Dr Leichhardt in Australia*, Melbourne: Oxford University Press, 1979

Burke and Wills Commission, *Report of the Commissioners Appointed to Enquire into and Report upon the Circumstances Connected with the Sufferings and Deaths of Robert O'Hara Burke and William John Wills, the Victorian Explorers*, John Ferres, Govt Printer, Melbourne: Victorian Public Papers, 1861

Cannon, Michael, *The Exploration of Australia*, Surrey Hills: Reader's Digest, 1998

Cassell's Picturesque Australiasia, ed. E.E. Morris, London: Cassell, 1889

Chisholm, Alec H., *Strange Journey*, Adelaide: Rigby, 1941

Connell, Gordon, *The Mystery of Ludwig Leichhardt*, Melbourne: Melbourne University Press, 1980

Cumpston, J.H.L., *Charles Sturt: his Life and Journeys of Exploration*, Melbourne: Georgian House, 1951

Dampier, William, *Buccaneer Explorer*, ed. Gerald Norris, London: Folio Society, 1994

Eldershaw, M. Barnard, *Philip of Australia: An Account of the Settlement at Sydney Cove, 1788–92*, London: Harrap, 1938

Ericksen, Ray, *Ernest Giles, Explorer and Traveller*, Melbourne: Heinemann, 1978

Eyre, Edward John, *Journals of Expeditions of Discovery into Central Australia and Overland from Adelaide to King George's Sound in the Years 1840–1*, 2 vols, London: T. & W. Boone, 1845; LBSA, 1966

Favenc, Ernest, *The History of Australian Exploration from 1788 to 1888*, Sydney: Turner & Henderson, 1888

Ferguson, Charles D., *The Experiences of a Forty-Niner during Thirty-Four Years' Residence in California and Australia*, Cleveland, Ohio: Williams, 1888

Fitzpatrick, Kathleen, *Australian Explorers: A Selection from their Writings*, London: Oxford University Press, 1958

Flannery, Tim, *The Explorers*, Melbourne: Text Publishers, 1998

Flinders, Matthew, *A Voyage to Terra Australis*, 2 vols, London, 1814; LBSA, 1966

——, *Observations on the Coasts of Van Diemen's Land*, London, 1801; LBSA, 1969

Foster, W.C., *Sir Thomas Livingstone Mitchell and his World 1792–1855*, Sydney: Institution of Surveyors NSW, 1985

Bibliography

Giles, Ernest, *The Journal of a Forgotten Expedition*, Adelaide, 1880; Adelaide: Sullivan's Cove, 1979

——, *Australia Twice Traversed*, 2 vols, London: Sampson Low, Marston, Searle & Rivington, 1889; LBSA, 1964

Grey, George, *Journals of Two Expeditions of Discovery in North-west and Western Australia, during the Years 1837, 38 and 39*, 2 vols, London: T. & W. Boone, 1841; LBSA, 1964

Johnson, Richard, *The Search for the Inland Sea: John Oxley, Explorer, 1783–1828*, Melbourne: Melbourne University Press, 2001

King, John, *A Successful Exploration through the Interior of Australia*, ed. W. Wills, London: Bentley, 1863; facsimile edn, FSLSA, 1996

King, Philip Parker, *Narrative of a Survey of the Intertropical and Western Coasts of Australia*, 2 vols, London, 1826; LBSA, 1969

Langley, Michael, *Sturt of the Murray: Father of Australian Exploration*, London: Hale, 1969

Leichhardt, F.W. Ludwig, *Journal of an Overland Expedition in Australia from Moreton Bay to Port Essington*, London: T. & W. Boone, 1847; LBSA, 1964; Sydney: Doubleday, 1980

——, *The Letters of F.W.L. Leichhardt*, coll. and tr. Marcel Aurousseau, 3 vols, Cambridge: Hakluyt Society, 1968

——, *Letters*, ed. M. Aurousseau, 3 vols, London: Hakluyt Society, Cambridge University Press, 1968

Mitchell, Thomas, *Journal of an Expedition into the Interior of Tropical Australia; Three Expeditions into the Interior of Eastern Australia in Search of a Route from Sydney to the Gulf of Carpentaria*, London, 1848; LBSA, 1965

——, *Three Expeditions into the Interior of Eastern Australia; with Descriptions of the recently Explored Region of Australia Felix, and of the Present Colony of New South Wales*, 2 vols, London: Boone, 1839

Mudie, Ian, *The Heroic Journey of John McDouall Stuart*, London: Angus & Robertson, 1968

Oxley, John, *Journals of Two Expeditions into the Interior of New South Wales*, Adelaide: LBSA, 1964

Roderick, Colin, *Leichhardt, the Dauntless Explorer*, London: Angus & Robertson, 1988

Rutherford, J., *Sir George Grey, K.C.B., 1812–1898*, London: Cassell, 1961

Stokes, Edward, *To the Inland Sea: Charles Sturt's Expedition, 1844–45*, Victoria, NSW: Hawthorne, 1986

Stuart, John McDouall, *Narrative of an Expedition into Central Australia Performed under the Authority of Her Majesty's Government, during the Years 1844, 5 and 6, together with a Notice of the Province of South Australia in 1847*, 2 vols, London: T. & W. Boone, 1849

——, *A Diary of Mr John Stuart's Exploration to the North of Murchison Range, in 20° Lat., 1860–1, Journal of the Royal Geographical Society*, Vol. 32, London, 1864

——, *The Journals of John McDouall Stuart . . .*, ed. W. Hardman, London: Saunders, Otley, 1865

——, *Fourth Exploration Journal March to September 1860*, Adelaide: Sullivan's Cove, 1983

Sturt, Beatrix, *Life of Charles Sturt*, London: Smith, Elder, 1899

Sturt, Charles, *Two Expeditions into the Interior of Southern Australia*, 2 vols, London: Smith, Elder, 1833; facsimile edn, Sydney: Doubleday, 1982

——, *Narrative of an Expedition into Central Australia*, 2 vols, London: T. & W. Boone, 1849; ed. Jill Waterhouse, London: Caliban, 1984

——, *Narrative of an Expedition into Central Australia . . . during the Years 1844, 5 and 6*, 2 vols, London, 1849; LBSA, 1964

Swan, Keith, *In Step with Sturt*, Armadale: Graphic Books, 1979

Tench, Watkin, *Complete Account of the Settlement at Port Jackson*, London, 1793; repr. Sydney: Library of Australian History, 1962

Tipping, M., *Ludwig Becker: Artist and Naturalist with the Burke and Wills Expedition*, Melbourne: Melbourne University Press, 1979

Turnbull, Henry (ed.), *Leichhardt's Second Journey*, Sydney: Ferguson, 1985

Uren, Malcolm and Stephens, Robert, *Waterless Horizons*, Melbourne: Robertson & Mullens, 1945

Vancouver, G., *A Voyage of Discovery 1757–98*, ed. W. Kaye Lamb, 4 vols, London: Hakluyt Society, 1984

Walker, J.B., *Early Tasmania*, Hobart: Government Printer, 1914

Webster, M.S., *John McDouall Stuart*, Melbourne: Melbourne University Press, 1958

Whyte, D., *Sketch of Explorations of the Late John McKinlay in the Interior of Australia 1861–2*, Glasgow: Aird & Coghill; facsimile edn, PLSA, 1962

Wills, W.J., *A Successful Exploration through the Interior of Australia, from Melbourne to the Gulf of Carpentaria*, ed. W. Wills, London: Bentley, 1860

——, *The Burke and Wills Exploring Expedition*, Melbourne 1861; facsimile edn, LBSA, 1963

Winnecke, C.G., *A Last Exploration in the Northern Territory*, London, 1884

Index

Page numbers in **bold** type refer to illustrations within the text

Index